Caesar and the Crisis of the Roman Aristocracy

Oklahoma Series in Classical Culture

OKLAHOMA SERIES IN CLASSICAL CULTURE

Series Editor

Susan Ford Wiltshire, *Vanderbilt University*

Advisory Board

Ward W. Briggs, Jr., *University of South Carolina*

Susan Guettel Cole, *State University of New York, Buffalo*

Carolyn Dewald, *University of Southern California*

Thomas M. Falkner, *College of Wooster*

Elaine Fantham, *Princeton University*

Nancy Felson-Rubin, *University of Georgia*

Arther Ferrill, *University of Washington*

Helene P. Foley, *Barnard College*

Ronald J. Leprohon, *University of Toronto*

Thomas R. Martin, *College of the Holy Cross*

John P. Sullivan, *University of California, Santa Barbara*

A. Geoffrey Woodhead, *Corpus Christi College,*
   Cambridge/Ohio State University

Caesar and the Crisis of the Roman Aristocracy

A Civil War Reader

By James S. Ruebel

University of Oklahoma Press : Norman and London

All maps were drawn by James S. Ruebel.

Caesar and the crisis of the Roman aristocracy : a civil war reader /
[selected and edited] by James S. Ruebel.
  p. cm. — (Oklahoma series in classical culture : v. 18)
  English and Latin.
  Selections chiefly from the writings of Julius Caesar, Cicero, and
Pompey.
  For students of college Latin.
  Includes bibliographical references and index.
  ISBN 0-8061-2590-X
  1. Latin language—Readers—Rome—History. 2. Rome—History-
-Civil War, 49–48 B.C. I. Ruebel, James S., 1945- . II. Caesar,
Julius. III. Cicero, Marcus Tullius. IV. Pompey, the Great,
106–48 B.C. V. Series.
PA2095.C24 1994
808'.04717—dc20   93-21007
                                                              CIP

Caesar and the Crisis of the Roman Aristocracy: A Civil War Reader is
Volume 18 of the Oklahoma Series in Classical Culture.

The paper in this book meets the guidelines for permanence and
durability of the Committee on Production Guidelines for Book
Longevity of the Council on Library Resources, Inc. ∞

1 2 3 4 5 6 7 8 9 10

UXORI

FILIISQUE

Contents

Maps

Acknowledgments

I first became seriously interested in Caesar while auditing a graduate course in Caesar at the University of Cincinnati in 1971–72 with my doctoral adviser Archie Christopherson, to whom I owe innumerable debts, and who has now for a quarter century been *vir optime de me meritus*. Thanks are also due to several of my own former undergraduate students: to my Latin class of 1983, especially Richard C. White (now Ph.D., Virginia), where this version of the course was first perpetrated on living subjects; to an extraordinary trio that read the *Civil War* with me in summer 1986, all of whom went on to graduate work elsewhere: Jay Korf (M.A., Virginia), Randall Saunders (Ph.D., Cincinnati), and Andrea Fritz (M.A. in German from Michigan); and finally to Shana Grey (B.A., Iowa State), now a Latin teacher in North Dakota, who served as willing foil during summer 1990 on some of what is included here. I am also grateful to Professor Mark Clark of the University of Southern Mississippi, and to my colleague Professor Madeleine Henry, who provided early, consistent, and helpful criticism of the project, and whose customary acute critiques sharpened the work substantially.

I should also like to thank Iowa State University for significant help both direct and indirect in the completion of this project: first, for a leave from administrative duties during the summer of 1988; second, for providing various levels of technology that immeasurably assisted carrying out this work. I am also grateful to the editors and readers of the University of Oklahoma Press for their splendid work in bringing this book to completion. The learning, diligence, and acuity of the readers saved me from many infelicities and errors, some of them egregious: those that remain are of course to be attributed entirely to my own stubborn persistence.

Although I have had the project in mind for some time, and much of the preliminary planning, research, and selection of the pieces to be assembled was carried out over a period of some years, this book was composed primarily in the interstices of teaching during 1991, and somewhat revised during the fall of 1992. The entire text and typescript of this book was created with WordPerfect 5.1, and all the maps were drawn with DrawPerfect 1.1.

Preface

The readings provided in this book are envisioned as a course in Latin for advanced undergraduate or graduate students. The aim of the course is to present a view of Julius Caesar through his own words and the words of his contemporaries. The assumption behind the arrangement and selection of these materials is that the period just before and just after the outbreak of the Civil War between Caesar and Pompey is of independent interest, apart from Caesar's future career. These events and persons require our evaluation in their historical moment in a way that will not permit detachment or neutrality. By conducting such a reading, our understanding of the wider issues involved will be substantially enhanced. Thus, the study of Caesar provides not only a feeling of participation in exciting and momentous events but also the opportunity for rigorous humanistic inquiry into questions of value, morality, and political action and expediency.

The study and evaluation of Caesar is a useful enterprise in itself. As one of the greatest military and political geniuses in Western history, Caesar invites commentary and arouses immediate interest; in view of the course of his career, his successful civil war, his dictatorship, and his assassination, he compels any reader to consider the issues of tyranny and civil war. In addition, the events of the Civil War, in which Caesar is both a principal actor and an interpreter, call into question the values and political system of the classical Roman Republic. In Caesar's case, we are doubly fortunate: not only is his career richly documented by secondary ancient sources, but we have two complete works written by Caesar himself, which provide us with direct access to his mind. While he may seek to disguise from us his thoughts and intentions, we have open to us the full array of modern methods of analysis and inquiry, as well as the hindsight of history, to allow us to judge his sincerity and (from actions) his motives.

By examining Caesar's own words, through passages from his *De bello civili*, the reader will be compelled to confront him as a politician, statesman, and propagandist; these selections will be interrupted at intervals to present material from the "opposition," especially extracts from letters written to and by Cicero within the circle of Caesar's opponents. We should understand from the outset that all participants in such a violent conflict will portray events in a way that is most favorable to themselves and least favorable to their opponents. Pompey's supporters—or Caesar's opponents, who may or may not be the same people—will seek to undermine the constitutional position held by Caesar and will characterize his actions and motives from that perspective; Caesar, in turn, will be at pains to defend the legality of his actions, especially his early actions, and to portray his proposals for peace in the best light. (Caesar's military virtuosity will not be emphasized here. Actual maneuvers and battles will not be treated, except insofar as they portray Caesar as a leader of men rather than a military strategist.) The intent of this course is to provide a view of Caesar that can be attacked or defended by the reader. The assumption will be that neutrality to Caesar is neither desirable nor possible; the reader, in other words, must confront the same choices that Cicero and others had to make in this period of civil upheaval.

These are not new questions. Nor is the evidence itself new. The same sources have been used by scholars for centuries to portray Caesar either as a warmongering opportunist or as a defender of the ideals of the Republic, as a sincere apologist or as a liar, as an aggressor or as a defender of his rank and status against unjust personal assaults from jealous political enemies. Our purpose will be to highlight Caesar's actions, first by concentrating our attention on his own presentation, and second by referring to other contemporary points of view whenever possible.

The selections from *De bello civili* will be presented in Latin. At appropriate moments, letters—especially by Cicero, by Pompey, and by Caesar himself—will be included. We shall also read some additional "connecting" material, or anecdotes, from these or other ancient authors. Except for a few letters from Pompey and Caesar, all of these additional documents will be given in English. Our closest analysis will be of the first half year of the Civil War, from January through April of 49. During this period Caesar's course was not yet fixed; he still affects to speak and to act like a general of the Roman Republic, seeking the approval of his Republican aristocratic peers, whose reactions are of crucial interest. But we shall also read his account through the end of the war, to let the narrative reach its conclusion and to allow Caesar to finish his story. In this period he was surer of victory and, practically speaking, already in control. In these later passages we shall examine the shift in Caesar's tone, and the premises that he expresses or implies for his actions at that time.

We shall not, however, treat the questions of Caesar's dictatorship after the Civil War, of his ultimate plans, or of the degree to which his actions and plans as dictator were consonant with those of his previous career. These latter questions have in fact been endlessly debated and studied, and have tended to obscure the moment of choice in 49 that forms the focus of our study.

NOTES TO INSTRUCTORS

This book is intended for advanced undergraduate or graduate students in Latin, whose reading will focus on content and style rather than on small points of vocabulary or grammar. I have assumed that such students will want to read as quickly as possible. This book therefore omits some of the usual kind of annotation that is commonly found in texts, and the notes are designed to foster critical reading with speed and (if possible) pleasure. For example, there is no Latin-English glossary, since students should already have or can acquire a good dictionary, such as *Langenscheidt's Shorter Latin Dictionary*, (ed.) S. A. Handford, or an equivalent. Further, I have tried to gloss words or idioms that will be difficult to find or that are used in ways that are not immediately transparent, to save the student time in thumbing through dictionaries wherever possible. The grammatical explanations have also been kept short. I assume that students know Latin grammar but may need an occasional reminder to speed their reading; I have not tried to explain constructions in full, and I have not cross-referenced one of the standard grammars. Once again, students will presumably have access to a grammar if they need or want to examine the details of grammar or syntax, such as indirect statement or sequence of tenses. I have tried to provide students with some abbreviated morphological aids; for example, many readers forget that *sublatus* derives from *tollere*, and I have indicated such derivations in the form, *sublatus* < *tollere*, without elaborate commentary. The point in every case is to direct the student quickly to the right meaning, not to review morphology or conduct small seminars on syntax.

Cross-referencing has also been kept to a minimum. I have usually preferred to repeat a gloss rather than send the student to another page that provides no additional information. Where cross-references do occur, students are urged to check them, particularly in the case of proper names, for which I have given short biographical accounts either at the first mention of the individual or at the first place in the narrative where that individual assumes a significant role. I have not used the standard appendix with biographies of proper names, because in my experience students do not sufficiently refer to them, while they will refer to a note at the bottom of the page.

Finally, I offer the standard *apologia* for the scantiness of references to secondary sources in the notes, and especially to scholarship in languages other than English. Where controversy is omitted, or the originator of a discovery unnamed, I intend to imply neither ignorance of nor contempt for modern debate, but rather to provide an uncluttered and accessible guide to reading for students. I take for granted that scholarly readers will recognize where I have silently adopted or rejected a particular view and evaluate accordingly. My principle has been that Caesar's words are of paramount importance, and that the attention of students should be drawn in the first instance to them, not what is said about them.

A NOTE ON THE LATIN TEXT

The text of *De bello civili* used was R. du Pontet's Oxford Classical Text. I have made no attempt to construct a new text (though I have suggested one small addition at 1.5.3, and found other small alterations unavoidable). While I feel strongly that not even undergraduates are damaged by being made aware of the difficult state of our texts, in the absence of a reliable *apparatus criticus* it would not be productive to dwell on textual difficulties. I have therefore printed what I consider a readable text, with minimal variation from du Pontet and a minimum of textual comment. Where the OCT is comprehensible, I have usually reproduced it, except where I have been thoroughly persuaded that another reading both is necessary and simplifies the sense. In general, such changes as I have made tend toward omission of bracketed material or omission of brackets or cruces where the text is readable. I have also freely and silently changed or adjusted punctuation whenever different punctuation seemed clearer. All variations from the OCT other than those in punctuation are listed below.

Reference	OCT Reading	Change
Book 1:		
1.1	[a Fabio]	deleted
5.2	†consuerat†	cruces removed
5.3	latorum audacia	*latorumque audacia*
6.6	[quod ... acciderat]	brackets removed
6.7	†quod ... exemplat	cruces removed
7.6	[nulla lex ... facta]	brackets removed
14.4	[omnibus]	deleted
30.2	II	*III*
35.4	[Cn. Pompeium et C. Caesarem]	deleted
67.2	[a]	brackets removed
Book 3:		
10.11	†turbiumque†	deleted
13.5	†ut ... civitatis ... essent praesidio†	*ut ... civitates ... essent.*
16.4	componerentur	*componeretur*
	se[d]	*se*
18.3	†reversus est†	cruces deleted
19.2	†duos†	deleted
41.1	[Macedoniam]	deleted
44.4	†videbant†	*habebant*
	[timebant]	deleted
44.6	multique	*[7] multique*
48.1	†a valeribus†	*in alaribus*

The Latin of all Ciceronian correspondence is quoted from Shackleton Bailey's editions in the Cambridge Classical Texts Series, again with silent changes in punctuation as it seemed best. Translations are my own except where otherwise indicated.

Caesar and the Crisis of the Roman Aristocracy

Introduction

POLITICAL POWER IN THE ROMAN REPUBLIC

Roman politics in the Republic involved a complicated interplay between the demands of law and tradition and the demands of status (*dignitas et auctoritas*, see below). Roman politicians vied with one another and with the standards set by their ancestors in the acquisition of status and the exercise of influence, both official and unofficial. It is important, therefore, to be aware of the various terms for status and power in Rome. Roman magistrates held power of a sort that was specific to their office, and often specific to a particular place or period of time. Latin words for power, therefore, are revealing in their specificity.

The political words for power include:

imperium: the power once held by a King—absolute right of life and death over citizens, formally bestowed by the Centuriate Assembly. It includes the right to wage war and to command Roman armies. In the Republic, unlimited *imperium* was not held exclusively by one individual but rather was divided between the two consuls, or shared among consuls and praetors (see below). A dictator, who can be thought of as an official magistrate with unshared *imperium*, was usually not appointed except in an emergency, for a specific purpose (usually to preside over elections) and for a strictly limited period of time (usually less than six months).

potestas: in general, is the "power to act," almost always requiring further definition. In constitutional terms, *potestas* could also be conferred by an assembly, either the Tribal Assembly or the Concilium Plebis. *Potestas* is inferior to *imperium* except in specific areas of authority.

dignitas: closely associated with *auctoritas* (below). *Dignitas* is the expression of an individual's public value or self-worth; this sense of "status," "honor," or "respect" cannot be precisely measured, but it is manifested in the degree to which an individual is accorded respect by his peers and to which his claims to distinction and eminence are recognized, even by his opponents. It arises from the nobility of one's birth, from the glory of one's deeds, and from the continued exercise of political influence through magistracies or in the Senate. As we shall see, Caesar interpreted the attacks on his special privileges as attacks on his *dignitas*, which he could not allow to go unanswered.

auctoritas: unofficial, informal power held by individuals or groups as a result of previous distinguished actions. Syme defines the term as the ability to bring about one's wishes without resorting either to violence or to legislation. In modern terms, the word approximates the colloquial clout:

some modern American senators have clout (other important people listen to
them and do what they say) and some do not. *Auctoritas*, then, is *dignitas* in
action, or the ability to transform *dignitas* into concrete results.

The "higher" magistrates are those elected with *imperium*: the
two annually elected consuls (who were the highest official
magistrates) and the eight to ten annually elected praetors. The
chief function of the praetors in Caesar's time was the
administration of the various Roman criminal courts. Both consuls
and praetors could propose legislation.

The "minor" magistrates are those without *imperium*, whose
power is therefore only their own *potestas*. The aediles were city
magistrates in charge of festivals and such duties as the sewer system
and maintenance of order. The duties of Roman magistrates rarely
overlapped, so that a hierarchy of power is somewhat misleading;
but politically speaking, the aediles were regarded as next in line in
authority to the praetors and above the quaestors. Quaestors were
usually attached to a higher magistrate, like a consul, as a kind of
quartermaster, in charge of supplies and paying the troops. Their
functions were bureaucratic rather than active. These offices were
both regarded as stepping stones to the higher magistracies and had
to be held in sequence with a space of two years in between, a
system of advancement known as the *cursus honorum*.

For a plebeian, an alternative to the quaestorship was to be
elected tribune (technically, *tribunus plebis*). The tribune was a
special magistrate, whose power (*tribunicia potestas*) was valid only
within the sacred city limits of Rome (the *pomerium*). A tribune had
the right to veto any public business and could intercede within the
city on behalf of citizens, even against a consul; his person was
sacrosanct, so that he could not be harmed or even touched by
another person while in the exercise of his duties. A tribune could
also propose legislation, to the Tribal Assembly or the Concilium
Plebis. Moreover, the tribune held a special symbolic position in
the political propaganda of the Late Republic: originally created as
a protector of the People against arbitrary action by a consul within
the city, the tribune had now become symbolic of the voice of the
People in aristocratic politics. Hence, the "rights" of the tribunes
could become a volatile political issue.

Patricians, like Caesar, were not eligible to be tribune. The *cursus honorum* for a patrician began with the quaestorship or aedileship (the quaestorship could be omitted). The political advantages of some of the tribune's powers were well understood, however, and many higher magistrates, both those who were patrician and those who were plebeian by birth, supported the early careers of plebeians by assisting them in their efforts to become tribune; and they, in turn, would employ the powers of that office to defend the interests of their political "patron." In the case of Caesar, for example, Mark Antony had just begun his active political career as a tribune-elect and was in Rome during the summer of 50 defending Caesar's interests.

After the time of Sulla, the Senate was composed of a maximum of six hundred men, consisting of all former elected magistrates; these men held their rank as senator for life, or until they suffered some severe loss of civil status (*capitis deminutio*)—such as by being convicted of a capital crime—or were expelled from the senatorial order by a censor. Seniority was very important within the Senate, since the highest ranking magistrates or exmagistrates spoke according to rank on any given issue. Senators were heavily influenced by the opinions (*sententiae*) of those who had spoken before them. Senators who were not currently magistrates nevertheless possessed enormous influence (*auctoritas*), which they achieved largely through the exercise of previous magistracies and military commands. Indeed, the phrase that indicates receipt of senatorial approval, *patrum auctoritas*, is revealing of the nature of senatorial power. Very infrequently, a junior senator, or "backbencher," could acquire an unusual degree of *auctoritas* because of his abilities and personal reputation (for example, Cato the Younger).

The Senate as a whole had limited official powers, for its official function was theoretically to advise the magistrates. But it did hold vast collective *auctoritas*, by virtue of which it could as a group oppose almost any individual. Moreover, the range of issues on which the Senate might deliberate was virtually unlimited, encompassing domestic and foreign policy; religion; and proposed, or even already enacted, legislation (which the Senate could try to invalidate by citing technical flaws in procedure). Among the most important of the Senate's traditional prerogatives was the right to allocate funds for various purposes from the public treasury, so that the Senate was normally in control of public expenditures. Finally, the Senate was the only permanent governing body in Rome: elected magistrates went out of office after a year, and even promagistrates (see below) had limited terms. The Senate, therefore, was a unique source of continuity in the tradition and interpretation of the constitution.

The Senate could render a judgment or "pass" a "decree" (*senatus consultum*) on any given issue. These decrees or judgments had overwhelming force because of the combined *auctoritas* of the individual senators and the strength of tradition, in accordance with which individuals and the People complied with these decrees. It is, however, a little misleading to speak of "the Senate," especially in the context of the debate over Caesar, as if it were a monolithic and unified body of official state opinion; individual senators were often strongly divided, with first loyalties to other individuals and smaller groups than the Senate as a whole. Nonetheless, the Senate, insofar as it represented the will of most senators and (by implication) of the People, remains an approximate guide to the sentiment of Roman politicians on a given issue.

Finally, there was also a group of promagistrates (proconsuls, propraetors, proquaestors) who were appointed either by the Senate or by special legislation; their power was designated in the terms of their appointment. Proconsuls and propraetors were virtually indistinguishable: both held the *imperium*, usually for several years at a time, and usually for military reasons associated with a specific campaign. Caesar, for example, was proconsul in Gaul but had no special powers outside his province. This was a major sticking point for him in his struggle with the Senate over demands that he give up his command and return to Rome.

Although Roman magistracies, especially the important ones, tended to be associated with the military, these offices were as much political as military. A consul or proconsul was a "general" insofar as he led troops, but his position as political leader was paramount. A *legatus* was an appointed deputy of a magistrate (or nation), not a military "lieutenant" comparable to an officer with that title in a modern army.

CAESAR AND ROMAN ARISTOCRATIC VALUES

It is often assumed that Roman history consists of the study of *leges et bella*, laws and wars; from one perspective, this is true enough: the study of the Civil War between Pompey and Caesar defines and organizes our present study. But this is a superificial perspective, one that would be inadequate for understanding the issues we are about to confront. We will be concerned in this book not only with what happened but with why it happened and how the characters in the drama understood their own actions and roles. Proper understanding of the situation from which the Civil War arose, and of Caesar's and Pompey's reactions during its course, depends not only on knowledge about the political situation of the late 50s (as outlined below) but also on an appreciation of the moral suppositions, the "values," of Roman aristocrats at this time.[1] A discussion of these values will help us understand what Caesar and Pompey thought were fundamental to decisive or persuasive arguments, and what constraints upon their actions they regarded or should have regarded as irresistible—what, in short, a Roman would have understood within his own culture by our notion of "moral."

This is not a topic that is easy to isolate, nor is it one that typically appears in studies of the events before us, or in studies of political events in general. But the opposition to Caesar was highly personalized. The charges against him have to do with his

---

1. To be clear at the outset: what follows is of necessity limited to the Roman elite, to the wealthiest and noblest. It is also limited, for simplicity, to Roman men, for only men were officeholders, and only men were generals. There is no reason to think that lower class Romans did not understand or accept these values in some form, but our information is severely limited, and any discussion would be highly speculative. Nor is it my intention to exclude Roman women from *virtus* (despite the apparent oxymoron: see the Sallustian definition discussed below) or *pietas*, and so on; but that discussion would take us far afield from our present study.

character, his leadership, and his patriotism, and those charges were contemporary with the events, not discovered by modern historians. Further, we shall see that Caesar was aware of the essence of these charges: in his portrayal of himself and his enemies the thematic principle is to show that he excels his enemies in these three areas—character, leadership, and patriotism. Of course, his subject is military, and military virtuosity is part of all three of these elements; it is unsurprising, then, that Caesar displays his military virtuosity. That aspect of his character is visible without much scrutiny, however, and it will be de-emphasized here in order to highlight other, moral qualities.

What will be striking is the degree to which the whole political crisis became heavily and explicitly personal and individual. Where modern politicians, at any rate in the United States, emphasize issues or ideologies, Romans emphasized themselves or their families, friends, or enemies, and the obligations that attended those relationships. The whole system, if we may call it that, was individualistic and highly competitive; modern historians, however, tend to speak as if these constraints did not really apply or were unimportant, or in terms of "factions" and groups. Although group action certainly occurred, individual action was the first avenue of approach. For example, it is stunning to us, but evidently perfectly reasonable to the Romans, that during the Hannibalic War a Roman general, whose presence in Spain might fairly be regarded as vital to the war effort, asked to be relieved in mid-command to return to Rome and settle his daughter's dowry (Valerius Maximus 4.4.10). Or consider the tenor of this letter to Cicero written in March of 49 by two of Caesar's supporters, as Cicero is debating what course of action he should take after Caesar has invaded Italy:

> Balbus and Oppius to M. Cicero, Greetings:
> . . . If we knew from Caesar himself that he will do what we think he should do, in our judgment—take action for restoration of good will [*gratia*] between himself and Pompey as soon as he arrives in Rome—we would not cease to urge you to take part in these matters willingly, so that the whole problem might be settled more easily and with greater respect [*maiore cum dignitate*] through you, who are tied to both. Or on the other hand if we thought that

Caesar will not do this and we knew that he wanted a war with Pompey, we would never exhort you to bear arms against a man who has treated you well [*hominem optime de te meritum*], just as we have always pleaded that you not fight against Caesar. But since even now what Caesar will do is more a matter of opinion than of knowledge, we can say nothing except that it does not suit your own honor [*dignitatem*] or your good faith [*fidem*], which is well known to everyone, to bear arms against either one, since you are so closely bound [*necessarius*] to both. And we have no doubt that Caesar would thoroughly approve, in accordance with his own human feelings [*humanitate*]. (*Att.* 9.7A.1–2)

We note the absence of argument about what we might consider crucial issues, like "right" and "wrong" in our terms, and the emphasis on Cicero's personal connections to both Pompey and Caesar. But Balbus and Oppius obviously expected these arguments to be telling, and the phrases highlighted bear more weight than a mere translation can offer. Surely, if we can understand what lies unarticulated here, we will have come a long way toward understanding Caesar and Pompey as particular examples of how Romans functioned in the Late Republic.

Our topic therefore must be approached by indirect means, and it will be necessary to keep in mind that our goal is to understand the moral presuppositions of the actors in the drama.

As in all cultures, Roman values find expression in a cluster of ideas that presuppose them, and that are often expressed in specific words or groups of words associated with specific customs. First, then, we must speak of some fundamental Roman ideas, some of which may fairly be described as "values" themselves. As L. R. Lind notes,

The Roman national character as the essential component of the Roman tradition can be summed up in such words as *gravitas, pietas, dignitas, virtus, constantia, libertas, fides, res publica*. They serve as a guide to Roman thinking on moral and political behavior down to the age of Tacitus.[2]

To this I would add the important words for power outlined above, and the concepts and behaviors associated with them, as

---

2. Lind, 174. Overall, see also Wirszubski; Earl, *Moral and Political Tradition.* Also very useful are Adcock, *Roman Political Ideas and Practice,* and Wiseman.

well as some additional concepts to be discussed below. But the important point made by Lind is that ideals of Roman character can be usefully delineated by the study of important Latin words, not just or even mainly by the events of Roman history. Inasmuch as our study is politically oriented, let us begin with the patron-client relationship, which is at the heart of Roman society, and is the key to understanding Romans of the Republic.

In a hierarchical society such as Rome's, everyone knew his place within the hierarchy. At the lowest end of the social scale were uneducated slaves of burden; at the highest end were those senators with the most *dignitas* and *auctoritas* (in the next generation, first place would be located clearly in the person of the emperor, the *princeps*). In the considerable intermediate positions were young nobles, plebeian non-nobles, freedmen, and so on.[3]

Indeed, an individual's choices of response to such a system are ultimately limited. One can refuse to participate or to reciprocate as expected; in which case, the individual either forfeits a claim to his society and its values or departs from it. A form of refusal to participate might be to try to redefine those values, or to argue for a new way to interpret them. Or, on the contrary, one can "submit"—that is, participate unwillingly—which is essentially the behavior and thinking of a slave or a captive. Finally, one can actively accept, adopt, or embrace the system and conform in one's behavior to its presuppositions and injunctions.[4] While many approaches are possible, the stereotypical Roman response was for the weaker party to seek a patron (*patronus*). The person in need would petition the stronger citizen for assistance. The *patronus*, then, would perform a favor (or benefaction, *beneficium*) on behalf

---

3. The following discussion attempts to simplify (even oversimplify) an extraordinarily complex issue. There has indeed been much recent work on the Roman system of status and various manifestations of entitlement, including such difficult issues as multiple clientship and the process of entering into *clientela*. The student may be referred above all to Wallace-Hadrill, a series of essays that mainly address Rome and have full bibliography; and Saller. See also Brunt's essays "Clientela," 382–442, and "Factions," 443–502, in his *Fall of the Roman Republic*.

4. Of interest here is the discussion ("The Ideology of Status") by Thompson, 142–56.

of the weaker party. The performance of this _beneficium_ would create in its recipient a sense of obligation to repay the favor, _officium_, often translated as "duty." The system of patronage, in short, consisted of a complex web of _beneficia_ and _officia_, benefactions and obligations, from which no Roman could be entirely free. If the two individuals were far apart on the social scale, the hierarchy of the relationship would be clearly defined: the stronger protects the weaker, the weaker is loyal to the stronger in return. For example, a freed slave, or freedman, would become a client to his former master, who is now his patron. The freedman by virtue of this relationship would owe his patron certain duties.

The Romans viewed the patron-client relationship as essentially moral rather than legal.[5] A patron performed benefactions on behalf of his clients of his own free will, from a sense of obligation to the weaker. A client repaid those favors with whatever actions his patron demanded in return, because he felt obligated to do so and therefore wished to do so; necessity and will were the same. The bond that cements this relationship is called _fides_. From the point of view of the patron, _fides_ is the obligation to protect and succor his clients; from the point of view of the client, _fides_ is the obligation to be loyal to his patron. Hence, dictionaries provide both meanings, "protection" and "loyalty" or "trust," and associated words, like _fidus_, "loyal," have to do with return of obligation or the sense that an obligation will be returned. Further, such a clear-cut relationship was heavily overlaid with specific duties, summarized in such notions as the _salutatio_ (attendance upon and greeting of the patron in the morning) and _obsequium_ (deferential behavior). Its details are not our concern here; rather, we note that words like _patronus_ and _cliens_—and more particularly the words that attach value to that relationship, like _fides_—imply a dynamic process rather than a static condition. _Fides_ is reciprocal and concrete: it is manifested in action.

---

5. The bibliographical references provided will indicate that this "system" of patronage had deteriorated by the Late Republic. Nevertheless, its presuppositions and assumptions remained central to Roman views of moral action.

If the two individuals involved were close together within the hierarchy, on the other hand—both nobles, for example—there was little question of a patron-client relationship in the strict sense. The party in need of a favor would not, by virtue of receiving it, incur unambiguous obligations of *obsequium*, but the sense of obligation (*officium*) was nevertheless strong. At this level, the relationship became *amicitia*, "friendship," which clearly need not entail affection (though surprisingly often it did so), or *gratia*, "influence."[6] The coalition among Caesar, Pompey, and Crassus which became known as the First Triumvirate was such an *amicitia*, entered into for mutual advantage and mutual obligation. The bond was strong and, as we shall see, broken by Caesar at any rate with reluctance. It is a bond to which Caesar appeals directly in his opening chapters. But we should not mistake the essence of these bonds: they were at root the same sort of mutual obligations, perceived as moral and bonded by *fides*, as were found in patron-client relationships. In fact, in everyday interaction, Romans often used terminology from the patron-client relationship to describe these "friendships," and they often spoke of expectations that were quite similar. We find idioms like *esse in gratia*, "to be friends with," or *redire in gratiam*, "to be reconciled with." The use of the vocabulary of patrons and clients to describe the relationship with a social peer or near peer clearly signaled a difference in status, and an expectation of deference from one party. At the national level, we find such idioms as *deditio in fidem populi Romani*, "surrender," or *rex et amicus populi Romani*, and it explains why the Romans so easily adopted the concept of the "client king."

A Roman politician's obligations, of course, were complex. He had obligations by birth to his family and his family's long-standing supporters. He had obligations to those with whom he had exchanged or not yet exchanged favors. The degree to which any one obligation would prove decisive on any given issue was difficult

---

6. Considerable work on *amicitia* has been done by P. A. Brunt, whose earlier studies have now been incorporated into and superseded by his essay, "Amicitia in the Roman Republic," in *Fall of the Roman Republic*, 351–81, with an analysis of the outbreak of the Civil War, 490–99.

to assess in the face of so many conflicting claims.

Within this context of moral constraint upon an individual's action, and within a society that was self-consciously hierarchical and socially static, the concept of *pietas* and its range becomes more understandable. On the mundane level of daily activity, it was at all times obvious to every Roman that factors outside his control had powerful influences on his life. A patron, client, or *amicus* might call upon you to perform some action that could be annoying and might well disrupt your plans for the day or the month.[7] Or your own desires might conflict with those of the extended family (your parents or siblings, for example). This sense of dependency, then, was inculcated in every Roman, and in both trivial and profound ways.

It was equally clear that forces beyond the individual level could dramatically affect your life. To cooperate with these forces, to acknowledge your dependency at any given moment upon your family, your state, or your gods, is the basic meaning of *pietas*. This concept was by no means confined to the sphere of religion, and dictionaries include meanings like "loyalty" that quite properly recall the notion of *fides*. An *impius* was one who through his actions would deny the validity of these recognized claims from family, state, and gods; a *perfidus*, one who broke bonds like those of friendship or clientship. *Pietas*, to differentiate it (a bit artificially) from *fides*, requires or assumes no reciprocity in the relationship: one is *pius* toward one's father or to Jupiter or to the state because their benefactions on your behalf can never be repaid, and because their power to affect your life is unlimited; one is *fidus* to a friend because the friend would do the same for you. *Pietas*, therefore, is noncompetitive, a selfless kind of duty, and implies or can imply love, devotion, and affection.

As a final restraint to individualism stands the ideal of *libertas*. It is only in very recent times, indeed from the Enlightenment, that this concept became in a sense distorted, away from the

---

7. The inconveniences of patronage are evidenced in a comic way from as early as the late third or early second century B.C. (Plautus, *Menaechmi* 571–600).

dependence upon the common enterprise, the *res publica*, toward
the rights of the individual against the state. In Rome, *libertas*
certainly described individual rights, but these were rights within
and constrained by the *res publica*. In a society where individual
achievement counted for so much, there was always to be a tension
between the desire for independent action and the need for social
conformity. To some extent, it is fair to characterize *popularis*
politicians like Caesar as testing and extending the limits of self-
assertion. Thus was *libertas*, freedom within social restraints,
distinguished from *licentia*, unbridled assertion of individuality.
Briefly, then, the political meaning and value of *libertas* was to
assert the right of all aristocratic Romans to participate in public
life, within the bounds of the immutable importance of the
common enterprise (*salus rei publicae suprema lex*). It therefore
includes the need to subordinate personal desires to the good of all,
in addition to the right of the individual to participate. *Libertas*
summarizes the rights to independent political action of all Roman
citizens.[8] For any one citizen to exercise his right to act so
thoroughly that others would be deprived of it would not be
libertas at all, but tyranny (*regnum*).

Such then are the constraints. What about self-interest, which
is of course amply attested? What was the "moral" approach to
self-interest for a Roman? Inevitably, there was a conflict, or a
potential conflict, between the recognition of the right and
desirability of every noble Roman to seek personal distinction, and
the desire of the group to restrain any specific individuals who seem
to be approaching preeminence. Livy, writing in the next
generation after Caesar, called this conflict *contentio libertatis
dignitatisque* (4.6.11).[9] We have already seen that the Romans
valued *dignitas*, the worthiness of an individual that was manifested
by public reflections of "honor," or "respect."

---

8. Still fundamental on this concept is Wirszubski. For a very full
supplementary discussion, see Brunt's essay "*Libertas* in the Republic," in *Fall of
the Roman Republic*, 281–350.

9. Wirszubski, 15–30.

> Dignitas, in a political sense . . . contains the notion of worthiness on the part of the person who possesses [it], and the respect inspired by merit on the part of the people. But unlike . . . gloria, which is transient, dignitas attaches to a man permanently, and devolves upon his descendants. And it is dignitas above all other things that endows a Roman with auctoritas.[10]

This formulation, which is certainly valid, raises two important questions. If *dignitas* is "inspired by merit," what constitutes merit? And if *dignitas* can be inherited, in what ways is it definable in strictly individual terms?

Both questions can be answered together. Merit, or excellence, is most directly expressed in Latin by the abstract sense of the word *virtus*, a word whose meaning in the public domain is best illustrated by Sallust, writing shortly after Caesar's assassination. The word was of course not originally or always an abstraction: its basic and original meaning is "courage," or "manli-ness" (*vir-tus*). But the abstract use of the word in Sallust crystallizes and gives coherence to a concept of aristocratic excellence that had previously been somewhat hazy; further, he is writing as a near contemporary of the Civil War, so that his use of the word has particular relevance for our discussion. Sallust's conception of *virtus* has been neatly defined as "the functioning of *ingenium* to achieve *egregia facinora*, and thus to win *gloria*, by the exercise of *bonae artes*."[11] While this definition of the word *virtus* pertains specifically to Sallust, there is little doubt that it would be held as essentially valid as a definition of excellence or merit by Romans from the third century B.C. to at least the end of the Republic: epitaphs and tombstones from the time of the Hannibalic War confirm the nobility's pursuit of individual glory through action, and this is confirmed by Cato the Elder's dictum "Iure, lege, libertate, re publica communiter uti oportet; gloria atque honore quomodo sibi quisque struxit" ("Rights, laws, freedom, and civic life should all

---

10. Wirszubski, 36.

11. Earl, *Sallust*, 28; his chapter "*Virtus* as an Aristocratic Ideal" is also pertinent (18–27). Our discussion is not intended to confine the meaning of *virtus* to Sallust's special usage but to provide a focus for our discussion of competitive excellence.

be held in common; but glory and respect to the extent that each individual has earned them").[12]

If anything in Sallust's concept is surprising, it is perhaps the prominence given to *ingenium*, or the emphasis on *bonae artes*, but we must remember that *egregia facinora* could include "intellectual" excellence, in oratory for example; the important criterion is its active public manifestation. In fact, the centrality of *ingenium* to distinction in political life is confirmed by the only slightly earlier witness of Lucretius (2.10, *certare ingenio*, *contendere nobilitate*, written no later than 52)—though Lucretius (who here is satirizing) meant this scornfully and insisted that the real basis for the struggle was wealth. For *bonae artes* we need cite only the Elder Cato's famous definition of the good orator, *vir bonus dicendi peritus*.[13] But Cato, Lucretius, and Livy highlight the essential fact that this pursuit was a competition, and in any competition there will be losers and (relatively speaking) winners. "This preoccupation with personal achievement and competition for the greatest glory . . . can be traced right through the history of the middle and late republic and into the early Empire.[14] Thus, the definition of merit, from a Roman point of view, entails individual effort; while a Roman could be born with a high level of *dignitas*, his own actions could either reduce it or enhance it and thus produce *auctoritas*.

Significantly, Sallust explicitly admits *virtus* in his special sense for only two men from his day, Cato the Younger and Caesar himself. Throughout the *Gallic War* Caesar portrays his own pursuit of *gloria* through *egregia facinora*; he is decidedly more restrained about his victory in the *Civil War*, but he makes no effort to diminish the credit due him for defeating Pompey. In his opening chapters, he defends his position and his decision to march; after that, he takes for granted that he should make every

---

12. Cato, frg. 252 *ORF*³, quoted from Festus, p. 408L. See also frg. 17 *ORF*³, "si quid vos per laborem recte feceritis, labor ille a vobis cito recedet, bene factum a vobis dum vivitis non abscedet" (quoted by Aulus Gellius 16.1.1).
13. Quintilian, *Inst.* 12.1.1.
14. Wiseman, 4.

effort, within the constraints of Roman morality, to win. We witness these events principally through Caesar's own words, so that his *ingenium* both describes and is displayed by his writing. It is important to recall, as we confront the genuine issues of civil strife, that Caesar's pursuit of his self-interest and his defense of his *dignitas* were entirely within the code of the Roman aristocracy, and that while his enemies may deplore and condemn his actions, these actions were altogether comprehensible to them.

In our assessment of Caesar, it is of considerable importance to note that he appeals to traditional values in order to defend his actions. He criticizes his enemies in general for their unfairness to his position, but he especially criticizes Pompey, his former son-in-law and long-standing *amicus*, for violating the bonds of kinship and friendship. This argument is a fundamentally Republican argument; it is the argument of one whose hopes are for preeminence within the traditional system of competition among equals, not one who hopes for sole power (*dominatio* or *regnum*). That Caesar in fact aspired to *regnum*, the serious charge laid against him by his enemies, seemed in the end to be verified by his eventual position as dictator. But in the *Civil War*, especially in Book 1, when the outcome is still in the balance, his posture is quite different. Caesar is at pains to prove himself no second Sulla, to illustrate by his words and deeds that there will be no purges and that the restoration of public order, the *res publica* itself, is possible.

Because this argument is so central to his presentation of the events in the *Civil War*, it is probable that the book was written virtually contemporaneously with the events it describes and published (if at all) soon after it was written, even though the ending is quite abrupt and even though there are inconsistencies in the cross-references in the narrative. The arguments about the date and manner of composition, and about the literary antecedents of the *Civil War*, are ultimately unresolvable. As a literary work it has no clear or direct antecedents, and the objective evidence will support almost any rational dating scheme. While the work is certainly not unedited, for it is plain that considerable thought has gone into large sections of the writing, the argument Caesar was contriving would not have carried the sense of urgency, which is clearly perceptible, once he had successfully completed the Alexandrian and Spanish wars.

It is worth quoting in full the extracts made by Suetonius from the comments of other ancient writers about Caesar's narratives:

> Cicero speaks in his *Brutus* [262] as follows: "He wrote *Commentaries* that are greatly to be admired. They are bare, straightforward, and graceful, for he has removed all trappings of rhetoric as if taking off a cloak. But while he intended for others to have ready-made material from which those who want to write history might draw, he has perhaps created a work congenial to the artless, who will want to cook it with curling irons;[15] but he has frightened off sensible people from writing at all." On these same *Commentaries* Hirtius holds forth in this way: "They are so well thought of in the judgment of everyone that opportunity for other writers seems to have been snatched away rather than provided. But my own admiration for his achievement is greater than that of others; for everyone else knows how well and how carefully he wrote them, but I know how easily and quickly." Asinius Pollio considers them written quite carelessly and with insufficient regard for the truth, since Caesar in general trusted uncritically accounts that were provided by others and he published his own full of faults either from design or from forgetfulness. And he thinks that Caesar was planning to revise and correct them. (*Jul.* 56)

Pollio's comments, if interpreted literally, are the strongest evidence we have that Caesar's narratives were not published during his lifetime but were allowed to circulate essentially unchanged after his death, and presumably after his assassins had fled from Rome. If so, the book remains a document of 49 and 48, not of Caesar's dictatorship in 45 or a bit earlier. For our purposes, this is a crucial point, which allows us to treat Caesar's presentation from the perspective of events contemporary with the Civil War, not with his dictatorship. "The *Bellum Civile* forms a complete narrative, vindicating Caesar's claims to Republican *honos* and *dignitas*."[16]

It is also important to remember that Caesar was not writing

---

15. *calamista*, evidently a pun on *calamus*, "pen."

16. Boatwright, 38. Boatwright concludes that the *De bello civili* could not have been written later than the last quarter of 47. See also Adcock, *Caesar as Man of Letters*, for a clear discussion of the issues of composition and genre.

"history," in either the modern or the ancient sense. The *commentarius* form, in which he imitates the dispatches or reports from a general in the field to the Senate, gave him considerable latitude within ancient assumptions about historical narrative—assumptions that themselves differed radically from modern ones. Hence he writes of himself in the third person with a surface of simplicity and objectivity that are largely absent from ancient histories, which were avowedly moralistic or propaedeutic. As Cicero notes in the passage from the *Brutus* quoted above, Caesar was not writing history but the raw material for history. Most of what is said by these ancient writers about Caesar, on the other hand, seems to apply most conspicuously to his *De bello Gallico*. In *De bello civili* his technique is markedly different (he does not, for example, divide his books into annual reports, nor is his "dispatch" written as if it were a report to the Senate from its subordinate magistrate), and clear guidelines according to genre are difficult to circumscribe.

Ironically, it was the threat of the naked exercise of his own *dignitas et auctoritas*, defended so successfully that his former peers could see an end to the very competition that gave meaning to their public lives—the threat in short against the *dignitas* of all other Roman politicians—that would eventually lead to Caesar's assassination in 44. Caesar tried vigorously to counteract the reaction against him: he rewarded, promoted, and encouraged *amicitia*, all of which in normal times would perhaps have led to bonds of *fides* and *pietas* toward him. Instead, his actions were seen as autocratic and demeaning, and it was left for his posthumously adopted son, who became Augustus, to blend successfully monarchic power and traditional values.

CAESAR AND ROMAN INTERNAL POLITICS, 63–50

In a sense, Caesar's career may be said to begin during the Catilinarian conspiracy. In the period before 63, his political reputation was languishing, particularly among the powerful aristocrats whose favor would be vital to a successful, independent political position in the long term. While it would be unfair to say that Caesar was inactive before 63, it remains the case that he was not a front-runner in the race for prominence in Roman politics.

To be sure, he had begun with advantages. Born a patrician in 100, he could expect, and his peers would expect, the usual advancement through the *cursus honorum*, up to and including an eventual consulship. He had pursued, more or less with consistency, a "popular" brand of political action, proposing legislation on behalf of the urban poor and prosecuting Roman nobles. And yet, it is generally thought that his early career was financed by the relatively conservative financier Marcus Licinius Crassus, to whom Caesar would remain deeply in debt for a long time. Moreover, his sexual inconstancies were well known and, while laughed at, were not approved by stauncher Romans.

In 63 Caesar's reputation was in fact in serious disrepair. It appears that he was regarded as something of a political lightweight, a man not lacking in wit and ability but not to be taken too seriously. He was heavily in debt, a problem that he hoped would be solved by a successful military campaign after his praetorship, but he was also regarded as a womanizer and as one who courted the mob. He had been active in the early months of 63, prosecuting Rabirius for the forty-year-old crime of violence in the affair of Saturninus and backing popular agrarian legislation, throughout all of which he was successfully and energetically opposed by the consul Marcus Tullius Cicero. He was elected praetor for the year 62, but between the elections and his assumption of office, affairs of state took a nasty turn when Cicero uncovered the Catilinarian conspiracy. Both Caesar and Crassus were slandered as secret conspirators, but there was no convincing evidence linking either man to the plot. And yet, during these tense moments, Caesar rose in the Senate to speak for leniency against the conspirators captured in the city. His proposal was resisted by Cicero, but it was the speech of Cato the Younger, then tribune-elect, that carried the day for the death penalty, which Cicero rapidly (though, it seems, legally) enforced. Caesar's courageous stand in this affair may have given notice that he was not to be taken lightly, though it did little to answer questions about his loyalty to the Republic.

Caesar somehow avoided serious entanglement in the Bona Dea scandal of 62, a puzzling and embarrassing affair in which Publius Clodius was caught spying on sacred rites to which only women were allowed. The rites were held that year in Caesar's house (because he was urban praetor) and were hosted by his wife, Pompeia. Clodius was unsuccessfully but spectacularly prosecuted for *incestum*. The scandal was actually fortuitous for Caesar, allowing him to divorce Pompeia on suspicion of adultery and then marry Calpurnia, the daughter of L. Calpurnius Piso, in the nick of time for his consular campaign. An unfortunate side effect of Clodius' trial, however, was to pit him and Cicero irretrievably against one another: Cicero had testified against Clodius in the trial, and Clodius was determined to get revenge. The career of Clodius, indeed, would repay close scrutiny. The Bona Dea scandal throws him into the spotlight of the ancient sources for the first time. After that, he achieves little of final importance but remains a constant catalyst for the actions of others, an independent political force who was something of an enigma both to the traditionalists in the Senate and to their opponents. In a sense, his presence kept the coalition of Caesar and Pompey together, and it was after his death in 52 that Pompey was able to achieve a rapprochement with the Senate and distance himself from Caesar.

When Caesar was setting out on the way to his propraetorian province in Spain in 61, however, he was still in dire straits: he was detained at the city gates by his creditors, who refused to allow him to leave until his debt was underwritten by Crassus to the tune of eighty talents. But he returned from his province a rich man, paid off Crassus in full, and began earnest preparations for the consulship, which he planned to hold in 59 after a vigorous candidacy in 60. But difficulties with senatorial conservatives, especially the Younger Cato, were already becoming an obstacle. Caesar's return from Spain in 60 presented him with a difficult choice. He had hoped to campaign for the consulship in absentia, so that he could retain his *imperium* long enough to hold a triumph for his exploits in Spain. He could not enter the city while holding *imperium*, and he could not run for consul from outside the *pomerium*. Cato successfully blocked any effort to secure special permission for Caesar to run in absentia; finally, in some frustration, Caesar abandoned his chance at a triumph, laid down his *imperium*, and entered the city to campaign for office. Pompey had also been frustrated by these conservatives for over a year. He had returned from the East in 62 and had been thwarted by Cato the Younger and others in the ratification of his *acta* and in acquisition of land for his veterans. For his part, Crassus, ever on the lookout for financial advantage, needed concessions for his constituency among the Equites, and wanted the principal role in settling the wealthy province of Egypt.

By 60, as is well known, the alliance between Caesar, Crassus, and Pompey was formed, the unofficial First Triumvirate. Cicero was invited to join but declined, partly from sincere disgust, partly from mistrust of Caesar and dislike of Crassus, and partly from a rather too generous estimate of his own power. Caesar's daughter Julia married Pompey, a lucky match in that the two found a genuine affection for one another that firmly cemented the alliance and greatly smoothed the relationship between the two generals.

Caesar's actions as consul, by which he obtained for Pompey and Crassus much-needed legislation, ran close to the edge of legality, such that he was in grave danger of a subsequent prosecution that could have brought his career to a sudden halt. He was therefore determined to hold proconsular *imperium* for the full ten-year interval before he could legally run again in 49 for the consulship (for 48), not only to win greater glory in the field but to retain immunity from prosecution. For this purpose he needed a significant province outside Italy, where his military virtuosity could win *gloria* for him from afar. Pompey was instrumental in having him appointed to Northern Italy (Cisalpine Gaul) for five years (ensuring continuous *imperium*) and to Transalpine Gaul for a year at a time as need continued. To be on the safe side, Caesar also obtained Illyricum, where police action against one Burabista could have been invoked if needed. His Gallic campaign, in the event, was a brilliant success for eight years, to the dismay of his enemies.

Politically, there were a few rough spots. The enmity between Clodius and Cicero came to a head in 58 when Cicero was exiled as a result of Clodian legislation. Cicero had expected Pompey to intervene on his behalf, but Pompey was never able to deal with Clodius and Caesar refused to act. Within eighteen months, however, Cicero was to be recalled, as Clodius, pursuing an agenda that did not necessarily correspond to that of the Triumvirs, proved to be uncontrollable. His violent and unpredictable course also exacerbated the pressure on the alliance already being applied by conservative senators, who hoped to split Pompey or Crassus away from Caesar. But the unraveling edges of the Triumvirate were stitched back together at the conference at Luca in April of 56, and Pompey and Crassus held the consulship together in 55.

During that year a law of Pompey's allowed Caesar the privilege of standing in absentia for the consulship, a vital point for Caesar. Even more, having won it he could not lightly allow it to be taken away, for the affront to his stature would be considerable, and the danger to his person greatly increased.

In 54 the first serious blow to the Triumvirate came when Julia died in childbirth. Though nothing indicates any breach between Caesar and Pompey until the eve of the Civil War itself, the loss of this bond was irremediable. Caesar went to some effort to try to arrange another marriage bond between himself and Pompey, but Pompey declined and the matter was dropped (Suet. *Jul.* 27). Meanwhile, that same winter, Caesar found himself in desperate need of manpower, and Pompey agreed to supply him with one of his own legions, for the good of the State and for their friendship (Caes. *BG* 6.1).

But in 53, a year marked by gang violence in Rome so severe that proper elections could not be held, Crassus and his son were both killed in Parthia at the battle of Carrhae, a severe loss for the domestic political plans of Caesar and Pompey. Electoral violence continued throughout the latter part of 53. In January of 52 Clodius, one of the principal perpetrators of this tumult, was murdered in a chance encounter with a rival gang leader—and a friend of Cicero's—T. Annius Milo. In the chaotic aftermath of Clodius's death, Pompey became sole consul in a senatorial effort to restore stability, though he later took Metellus Scipio, whose daughter he married in mid-52, as a colleague (see chapter 2, n. 6).

In Gaul, Caesar was faced with a massive uprising led by Vercingetorix, and he had to trust to Pompey to maintain order and protect his interests, in which hope he was apparently satisfied (see *BG* 7.6: "cum iam ille urbanas res virtute Cn. Pompei commodiorem in statum pervenisse intellegeret"). A crucial ingredient in the coalition between Caesar and Pompey remained Caesar's special right to stand for the consulship in absentia. The enemies of Caesar or of the coalition never ceased to attack or to try to undermine this right. In March of 52, in the thick of the turmoil surrounding the fate of Milo, Cicero promised Caesar that he would use his influence with the tribune M. Caelius to elicit his support; and, with Pompey's strong urging, the college of tribunes sponsored a bill specifically affirming Caesar's privilege, referred to as the *ratio absentis*. Certainly, this provision of the Law of the Ten Tribunes was designed precisely to prevent Caesar's having to make the same choice after his return from Gaul in 49 that he had had to make in 60 after his return from Spain, a choice between *gloria* and *honor*. Rather than allow debate on this special dispensation later, at a time when he could not have afforded to wait for a decision, Pompey helped Caesar secure this privilege well in advance.

The *ratio absentis* would be a cornerstone of Caesar's sense of security in returning from his province. Pompey's later legislation to require all those who wished to run for office to appear in person was not an abrogation of his commitment to Caesar but rather an affirmation of it, for Caesar was explicitly and uniquely exempted from that provision. The Gallic campaign, and its general, were accorded special status and consideration. Finally, Pompey also enacted a bill in the year 52 that required a five-year hiatus between holding a magistracy and obtaining a senatorial province; but both Pompey himself (Spain) and Caesar (Gaul) held special commands that had been granted by popular legislation in 55, and these would not (it was assumed) fall under the provisions of Pompey's new law.

During the year 51 Caesar's position came under heavy fire, but he appears to have emerged unscathed. One of the consuls, M. Marcellus, directed his efforts squarely at the two pillars of Caesar's position, the continuation of his command in Gaul and the *ratio absentis*. He had made his plans well known as early as spring of 51, but he began his campaign against Caesar in earnest in June, when he had made a point of flogging a citizen of Novum Comum, a colony established by Caesar, thus displaying his contempt for Caesar's putative grant of Roman citizenship to the colony. In addition, he reacted to the news of the defeat of Vercingetorix by arguing that since Gaul was now pacified, Caesar had no further reason to retain his Gallic command, and in addition that he had no reason not to return to Rome to stand for election in person. Marcellus proposed that a vote be taken on these issues, but the vote was postponed time after time: first to 13 August, then to 1 September. Throughout this period, Cicero's friend M. Caelius reported to him that Marcellus was trying to muster votes but was unable to get a quorum in the Senate. Finally, it appears that a vote on the issue was taken in September. But before that could happen, Pompey had taken a trip to Ariminum, where, it has been plausibly argued, he met with Caesar's agents and came to an agreement with Caesar about the position he should adopt on these matters. When the debate eventually took place in the Senate, Pompey stated that no senatorial action should be taken at this time, and that no discussion of Caesar's recall could be conducted before 1 March 50 without injustice to Caesar. This stance appears to have settled the issue, and there is no sign that Caesar found that decision distasteful at the time. Thus it appears that through the latter months of 51 Pompey was still working diligently on Caesar's behalf, especially in support of the *ratio absentis*, with a view to Caesar's securing a second consulship.

The meaning of the "terminal date" of 1 March 50 has been endlessly debated. According to a long-prevailing view, the debate in March 50 would appoint a successor to Caesar for 49, and Caesar planned to run for the consulship of 49 in the summer of 50. These two conjectures should be treated separately. The phrase "terminal date" is itself misleading, since it implies that it was known that Caesar's command would expire on this date, or that some specific date of expiration for his command was generally known. In fact, neither of these propositions can be proven from

any ancient evidence, as Seager (193–95) shows; he believes that
the terminal date of Caesar's command was left deliberately
unspecified, and that both Caesar and Pompey would have
preferred to keep it so, for thus they would have the greatest
flexibility in action when the time came. What, then, was the
original point of the 1 March 50 date, and what was to be decided
then?

Neither of the most recent treatments of this issue accepts the
once standard view that 1 March 50 was either the terminal date of
Caesar's command or the date on which he would be "replaced."
According to both J. M. Carter (10–11) and T. N. Mitchell
(238–39), following the general lines argued in 1958 by P. J. Cuff,
the 1 March date was the day on which Caesar's province could
(legally and normally) be reassigned in accordance with the *Lex
Sempronia de provinciis*, which was still operative when his right to
stand in absentia was granted in 55 by the *Lex Licinia Pompeia* and
reaffirmed by the Law of the Ten Tribunes in March 52.[17]
According to the procedure specified in the *Lex Sempronia*,
provinces would be assigned in 50 for the year 48, in advance of
the election of the consuls for the year 49 to whom these provinces
would be assigned. Since the elections were normally held in July,
it is likely that 1 March was the usual date after which provinces
were assigned: that is why Pompey found that date congenial and
in full accordance with his obligations of past friendship to Caesar.
Hence, the purpose of specifying 1 March 50 was in fact to
guarantee Caesar his full five additional years (53, 52, 51, 50, 49)
after 54, when his initial five-year appointment (58, 57, 56, 55, 54)
expired in Cisalpine Gaul (Carter). In addition, Caesar raised no
objection to that date, presumably because he expected to run in
absentia in (July) 49 for the consulship of 48 while still in

---

17. For a bibliography of this issue, see Mitchell, 238 n. 22. Mitchell's analysis
and mine are close, except that Mitchell emphasizes the evidence for hostility
against Caesar by Pompey as early as 51. Carter evidently still believes that Caesar
had intended to run for the consulship of 49, with even 50 not excluded, but
changed his mind before the elections in 50. In my view, Caesar always intended
to run in 49 for the consulship of 48 (discussed below).

possession of his province; he could then return to Rome after the election, and give up his province to his successor.

But Pompey had passed another law in 52 while he was sole consul that revamped the procedures for assigning provinces: according to that *Lex Pompeia*, there had to be a five-year interval between holding a magistracy and a promagistracy; this would prevent lobbying for provinces in the year before a consular campaign. To fill in the gap between available exmagistrates beginning in 51, Pompey's law specified that former consuls and praetors who had not held promagistracies must assume responsibility for the provinces of 51, 50, 49, and 48. None of these men would actually be in office, so there was no reason why they could not depart from the city whenever it was convenient to assume those duties (thus was a very reluctant Cicero compelled to take on the governorship of Cilicia in 51). Technically, this law should have no particular effect on Caesar's Gallic province, but his opponents now argued that these "new rules" (Carter) applied to reassignments of old provinces. Hence, Caesar's enemies considered that there was no reason why he could not be replaced immediately after 1 March 50, when discussion was "permitted."

Thus, in Caesar's view, what was to be determined on 1 March 50 was not a replacement for him in 49 (still less in 50), but the allocation of the province for the year 48, according to his previous understandings; for Caesar's enemies, however, the province would be up for grabs on 1 March 50 under the new provisions of the *Lex Pompeia* of 52. In the event, attempts to replace Caesar in 50, or to have the province reassigned for 49, came to naught during the year 50, since Caesar found tribunes willing to veto any attempt to reassign Gaul.

Modern debate on this issue has been obscured by accepting as valid the propositions of Caesar's enemies. The actual debate was precisely about whether a case for replacing Caesar could be manufactured, and there were well-founded arguments (citing one law or the other) in support of either side. But tribunician vetoes and Pompey's illness in mid-50 forestalled a conclusion to the debate, and so the matter remained unresolved that year.

Even so, some scholars still hold that Caesar originally intended to run during 50 for the consulship of 49, and therefore accept that his opponents were right about the constitutional issue to be debated after 1 March 50. On that view, it could be argued that Pompey had staked his own prestige on persuading Caesar of that position, and had allowed debate after 1 March because he took for granted that Caesar would be elected consul that summer and could thus leave his province and return to Rome in 49 as a magistrate with *imperium*. Caesar's inexplicable and presumably (to Pompey) surprising decision not to run in 50, then, could be read as a blow to Pompey's public image and perhaps as the final provocation that drove him from Caesar and into the fold of the senatorial conservatives.

While there is a certain tidiness to this explanation, particularly in finding a clear-cut motive for Pompey's split from Caesar, I remain unconvinced, for it rests upon a combination of two weak conjectures. The first, as we have seen, is that Caesar's position after 1 March would be constitutionally untenable; but events do not sustain that view, which was debated vigorously in Rome at the time without resolution. The second conjecture is that Caesar planned at any time to seek the consulship of 49, for which there is no evidence whatever. If Caesar had believed that his command was in genuine danger of expiring in 50, and had planned (perhaps with Pompey's agreement) to run for consul during that year, why did he not simply do so? No satisfactory explanation of such a reversal has been provided. While the situation in Gaul was certainly serious, no one doubts that Caesar would have been elected if he had chosen to run. His *ratio absentis* was still intact and (on this view) should have been strongly upheld by Pompey as the final justification of his allowing the debate on 1 March. But the evidence will not sustain all this conjecture: neither Caesar nor any other ancient source ever indicates that the consulship of 49 was considered an issue. As far as we can tell, Caesar always thought in terms of the consulship of 48, not 49: his ten years in the province will have run from 58 through 49, inclusive, and he expected to be a candidate in the last year of his provincial command.

There are four passages where Caesar's consulship is actually discussed by Caesar or his supporters, and in all of these his holding office in 48 is taken for granted. In *De bello Gallico* 8.50, Caesar's friend Hirtius indicates that Caesar came back to Italy in late 50 to set the stage for his consular campaign, which would have to be the campaign of 49 because the elections of 50 were already over. In *De bello civili* 1.9.2, Caesar refers to the "next" elections (*proximis comitiis*) when he planned to run, that is, the campaign in the current year 49 for the consulship of 48: this is Caesar's only direct reference to a consular campaign. In *De bello civili* 1.7.2, Caesar states that by January of 49 his soldiers had now waged successful military campaigns for nine years, and in 1.32.2 he refers to his actual election in 49 to the consulship of 48 as *legitimo intervallo*, a reference to the traditional requirement of a ten-year interval between consulships. Caesar's manner of reckoning his ten years in Gaul, then, seems to be the same as the one I am supporting, for which 49 would be the tenth year, and 48 the year in which he was constitutionally eligible. This reading also reconciles the attitude of his opponents with the evidence: none of them argues that Caesar should not be in Gaul in 49, only that he should not leave it with his army, and Cicero states clearly that the *ratio absentis* gave him the right to retain his command until after he had run for the consulship (*Att.* 7.7.6: "cum id datum est, illud una datum est").

Pompey's position requires some further elaboration, an effort that is complicated by our having no direct testimony from Pompey and because he himself was seldom clear about his thoughts or intentions, even to his closest advisers; he was given to vague generalizations about the good of the state or the authority of the Senate or People when asked a specific question about troublesome matters. As things stood in late 51, Pompey was evidently still working with Caesar, or at any rate was not working against him, and was of course trying to arrange his own position more satisfactorily within the senatorial hierarchy. Pompey had suffered in the Senate since his return from the East in 62; that was of course one of his principal motives for joining the coalition with Caesar and Crassus in the first place. In the 50s the coalition had had prosperous results for Pompey despite the inevitable envy and resistance aroused by his power. While the relations between Caesar and Pompey have been debated, Pompey's continuing support through 51 is made clear by Cicero's litany of "old grievances" against Pompey for not abandoning Caesar, which echoes the analysis above.

> Our friend Pompey has done nothing prudently, nothing bravely, and nothing that was not opposed to my advice and influence [*auctoritatem*]. I pass over those old grievances—that he nourished, promoted, and armed that man against the Republic; that he supported the passing of laws by violence and against the auspices;[18] that he added Transalpine Gaul to Caesar's provinces; that he became his son-in-law; that he was present as augur for the adoption of Clodius; that he was more energetic in my recall than in keeping me in Rome; that he prolonged Caesar's command in Gaul; that he aided him in his absence in every way; that even in his third consulship, after he had begun to act as a guardian of the Republic,[19] he strove to have the tribunes pass the law that allowed Caesar to run in absentia, which he then sanctioned by some law of his own; that he opposed the consul M. Marcellus, who was trying to put a limit on Caesar's tenure—but to pass over these, what could be more hideous or more disruptive than his present withdrawal from the city, or rather this utterly disgraceful flight in which we are now participants? (*Att.* 8.3.3, written in 49)

Pompey's opposition to Marcellus continued throughout 51. While Caesar's position had become more powerful, on the other hand, senatorial reaction against him was also much stronger; and those who were Caesar's enemies were relentless and powerful, while those who opposed Pompey seem to have been less numerous and less resolute. By the end of 51, especially in view of his new acceptability to the Senate, Pompey may have felt that his support of Caesar was more of a disadvantage than an advantage, and indeed he may have felt that independence of Caesar would be an intrinsically good thing. If that was in his mind, he would have needed an alternative set of supporters, for clearly the hard-line senators were not to be trusted any more at this point than they were in the late 60s.

---

18. During Caesar's consulship in 59.

19. In 52, following the murder of Clodius, when Pompey became sole Consul and restored order to the city.

Pompey aimed perhaps at a coalition encompassing not only supporters of the triumvirate but also prestigious clans of the *nobilitas*. The resultant combination would erode the power of the Catonians and other foes of the dynasts, leaving the field clear for political ascendancy. It was a perfectly conventional goal in the tradition of Roman politics.[20]

Gruen is arguing here that Pompey was cultivating support in this way for both Caesar and himself, but it is an equally good explanation of his acting in his own individual interests (as would of course be the first consideration for any Roman politician), not intending to force a civil war, but trying to play both ends against the middle in traditional fashion. Pompey's individual status had been significantly, rapidly, and somewhat unexpectedly enhanced by his role in the events following the murder of Clodius in 52, by which it became clear both that he wished to be seen as the most important defender of oligarchic tradition and that the key oligarchs were now willing to cast him in that role. Pompey's thinking along these lines was manifested in words and deeds that were variously interpreted as hesitancy or secret hostility to Caesar; of course, he may have been harboring thoughts about separation from Caesar from early on, whether or not he chose to manifest those thoughts in action. Any number of ancient sources suggest that Pompey was jealous of Caesar because he could not bear to have an equal. In any case, the opponents of the coalition were encouraged to step up their attempts to separate Pompey from Caesar, and some of these attempts will have taken the form of overtures to Pompey that led him to see that his political position would be concretely enhanced by distance from Caesar. While some of his actions were sufficiently ambivalent that Caesar's enemies could have taken heart for some months, the moment was right, and the situation was now more unstable than ever before. If it is true that Pompey finally broke from Caesar in 50, not in 52 or 51, then we should look for something in the year 50 that could finally and decisively have turned his mind from his old ally.

Early in 50, at the same time as the debate on the fast-

---

20. Gruen, 465.

approaching date of 1 March, another factor had come into play—the possibility of a war in Parthia, which had been under consideration for some months. Pompey was interested in receiving this command, but many senators felt that he should remain close to home to ensure that events in the city did not get out of hand. The other leading candidate was Caesar. Many were unwilling to send either general to Parthia for fear of the other, or else for fear that whoever went would be too successful. In the end, although troops were raised, no war was commissioned, for it appears that no acceptable solution could be found to the dilemma of not wanting to give Caesar further opportunity for glory, not wanting Pompey to leave Italy, and not having a convincing third option.

In the midst of this frustrating discussion, an unexpected factor appeared: the turnabout of C. Scribonius Curio, who had been elected tribune for 50. He had been a staunch opponent of both Caesar and Pompey, and it was fully expected that he would maintain this posture as tribune. Curio had entered his tribunate with an ambitious program of legislation, which he tried vigorously to push through in January and February; but he became impatient when he encountered resistance, especially to his proposals on land redistribution. Evidently in order to give himself more time for promulgation and debate of his laws, he proposed the addition of an intercalary month, which would by tradition have been added between February and March. But this proposed delay ran headlong into the squabble over debate on Caesar's return, which was scheduled to begin after 1 March, and no postponement of that debate was going to be allowed. Curio, in fact, was expected to support the proposal that Caesar lay down his command; but when the debate actually took place, he added without apparent warning the additional stipulation that Pompey should also resign his commands and dismiss his armies. This clause was widely interpreted as support of Caesar, a dramatic change of sides, which Cicero's friend Caelius attributed to Curio's being miffed over not having been given his intercalary month, and later sources attributed to bribery. In any case, Curio now became the most stubborn adherent of this plan, which appealed to many senators because it seemed to offer hopes for peace on the one hand and diminution of the danger from both generals on the other.

Perhaps it was the volte-face of Curio and his subsequent popularity that decided Pompey against Caesar. Before Curio's move, Pompey had had a clear majority of support in the Senate, and he perhaps felt either that a final decision on his part about Caesar was not needed or that any determination made independently by the Senate in the current climate would significantly favor his own position. Perhaps, too, Pompey believed that Caesar had suborned Curio to speak against him and was offended by what he could construe as an open split. As time went on, Curio became located more and more securely in Caesar's camp, but it is entirely possible that Curio himself originally devised this stratagem, initially in order to assume a stance independent of both Caesar and Pompey, perhaps overestimating his own popularity or ability (he would be far from the first Roman politician to err in this way).

Caesar clearly hoped to remain in his province for another year, perhaps maneuvering for the appointment to Parthia after all, perhaps intending to secure Roman administration of Gaul before leaving the province. In any case, he was now vulnerable to revision of the terms of his command, for Pompey felt free to allow negotiations on these issues.

While ancient writers, with a propensity to clear distinctions, attribute the hostility against Caesar to the dark plottings of Pompey, some modern scholars (following the lines of Cicero's letter quoted above) have instead argued that Pompey and Caesar remained on good terms up to the very eve of the conflict, and that Caesar truly hoped to dissuade Pompey from leaving Italy after it erupted, at which point all hope of reconciliation would be lost. But by summer of 50, as we shall see, at least some Romans believed that Pompey was behind, or solidly in support of, the maneuvering to force Caesar to give up his army (see letter from M. Caelius to Cicero in August of 50, quoted in chapter 1). For example, Pompey had accepted the commission to conduct a levy of fresh troops in Campania, even though he was aware that this would reduce the chances of Caesar's giving up his provinces; and he provoked Caesar further by taking two of his legions, about which Caesar complains repeatedly. The complexity of these matters is not helped by the deliberate attempts of both sides to blur the issues. Whatever may have been the understanding or intent of the Triumvirs in 55, or even of Pompey in 53 and 52, by late 50 Pompey had clearly cast his lot against Caesar and was fostering by innuendo, by provocative action, and by silence interpretations of Caesar's position that left Caesar virtually without legal recourse.

My own view, for which I have no direct evidence, is that Pompey's difficulty in the winter of 51/50 was not legal but personal. He had promised Caesar that he would support him in his claims through the end of his tenure in Gaul. Although he had since decided that he wanted to support the conservative senators, he felt bound to Caesar by past ties. While Pompey could, without technically violating the bonds of friendship, on the one hand support Caesar's *ratio absentis* in accordance with understandings that he and Caesar had apparently reached, and on the other hand demand that Caesar give up his army, the latter demand was obviously perceived by Caesar as increasingly threatening both politically and personally. This is the context in which the debate around the discussion of Caesar's province after 1 March 50 begins to make sense, for Pompey evidently felt that he could allow Caesar to be replaced after that date *sine iniuria* (Cic. *Fam.* 8.9.5, 8.8.9). His agreement with Caesar would by then have technically expired, and he was free to act or not act without perfidy.

It is also possible, as various episodes indicate, that Caesar was for a long time unwilling to believe that Pompey had abandoned him. His return of Labienus and the two legions that Pompey had "loaned" to him, for example, imply that he did not expect them to be used against him, and perhaps we can take as at least superficially sincere his appeals in early 49 for Pompey to meet with him to iron out their problems. After all, he had successfully negotiated difficulties in their alliance before (at Luca), and his confidence in his own persuasiveness was immense.

1

Prelude to Civil War

By the summer of 50, the course of political events in Rome had produced an impasse of dangerous intensity. Most senators clearly wanted Caesar to return to Rome, but many of the most noble and most conservative of this group also wanted him deprived of a substantial part of his prestige. They hoped to bring that about by forcing him to choose between returning as a private citizen (in theory, either to run as such for consul or not) placing himself outside the constitution, in which case they could legitimately send armies against him and destroy him. The intensity of this feeling is remarkable, for Caesar's activity in Roman politics was by no means more provocative than that of many other "popular" politicians. But this group of senators believed that they now had Pompey on their side and could afford to force the issue.

Perspective on the events of the summer of 50 is provided by two documents: first, the letter quoted below from Caelius to Cicero, written in August; second, by the account of that summer written at an unknown time during the early months of the Civil War by Aulus Hirtius, a loyal Caesarian general.

Caelius had been tribune in 52 and was now curule aedile; long a protege of Cicero's, this Caelius is the famous object of the trial that produced Cicero's speech *Pro Caelio* in 56. Until now, Caelius has been an outspoken opponent of Caesar. This letter forecasts his switch at the outbreak of the war and illustrates the dilemma faced by all Romans, and their entirely human reaction: not so much war or peace, but Caesar or Pompey; not good or evil, but survival.

M. CAELIUS RUFUS TO CICERO, ABOUT 8 AUGUST 50 (*Fam.* 8.14.2–4)

As to the general state of the Republic, I have often written to you that I do not see peace into next year. And the closer the dispute [*contentio*] that must happen approaches, the more distinct this danger appears. The issue on which the rulers are about to fight it out has been offered as this: Cn. Pompey has decided that he will not allow C. Caesar to be elected consul unless Caesar hands over his army and his provinces; but Caesar has been convinced that he cannot be safe if he gives up his army, although he submits this proposal: that they should both hand over their armies. Thus their love affair and jealous union has not retreated to private vituperation but has broken out into war. Nor have I found any plan to adopt for my own situation; and I am sure that resolving this question will trouble you as well. For I have obligations and close relationships with the one group, whereas I love the other cause but hate the men.

I think it has not escaped you that men ought to follow the more honorable side in a domestic squabble, as long as the fighting is chivalrous and without weapons. But when it has come to war and the camp, we must follow the stronger side and the better choice is what is safer. In this dispute I see that Pompey has the Senate and the decision makers with him, whereas those who live in fear or but little expectation will go to Caesar. The army is not to be compared. All in all, there is enough time to evaluate each of their forces and to choose one's side.

. . . In short, you want to know what I think is going to happen. If neither of the two goes to the Parthian war, I see that great conflicts are imminent that will be settled with the force of the sword. They are both ready, in spirit and in resources. If it could be put on without the danger, Fortune would be arranging a great and interesting show for you.

AULUS HIRTIUS' ACCOUNT OF THE END OF THE GALLIC CAMPAIGN (*BG* 8.50–55)

The final book of *De bello Gallico* (for the year 51) was written by Caesar's loyal general Aulus Hirtius. The final surviving chapters of that book provide the context for and transition into Caesar's account of the Civil War. Hirtius goes on to report the crucial events of the next year (50), in recognition of their importance to the outbreak of the war. Caesar had made a point over the winter of placating the Belgian tribes and spreading good will among the tribal chiefs throughout Gaul, so as not to risk a rebellion at his back after he returned to Italy. The events take place in the summer and autumn months of the year 50, and the point of view is Caesarian.

50 Ipse hibernis peractis contra consuetudinem in Italiam quam maximis itineribus est profectus, ut municipia et colonias appellaret, quibus M. Antonii,[1] quaestoris sui, commendaverat sacerdotii petitionem.[2] Contendebat enim gratia cum[3] libenter pro homine sibi coniunctissimo, quem paulo ante praemiserat ad petitionem, *[2]* tum acriter contra factionem et potentiam paucorum, qui M. Antonii repulsa[4] Caesaris decedentis gratiam convellere cupiebant. *[3]* Hunc etsi augurem prius factum quam Italiam attingeret,[5] in itinere audierat, tamen non minus iustam[6] sibi causam municipia et colonias adeundi existimavit, ut iis gratias ageret, quod frequentiam[7] atque officium suum Antonio

---

1. *M. Antonii, quaestoris sui* is subjective genitive qualifying *petitionem*; *sacerdotii* is objective genitive qualifying the same word: "Antony's campaign for a priesthood."

2. Mark Antony was a candidate for a place in the College of Augurs, and Caesar had planned to campaign on his behalf. Antony would also become tribune on 10 December. Born in January of 83, Antony had just begun his political career in the late 50s. He had served with some distinction as a cavalry commander in Palestine and Egypt from 57 to 54, then came to Gaul to join Caesar, who was quickly impressed by his ability. He became quaestor in 51 and tribune in 49; he will be one of the tribunes defending Caesar's interests forced to flee the city in January of that year (see *BC* 1.2.7, below).

3. *cum*, "not only" (correlative with *tum*, "but also," in section 2).

4. *M. Antonii repulsa*, "by the defeat of Antony."

5. After *factum*, *esse* should be supplied as the verb in indirect statement depending on *audierat*. The subject of *attingeret* is Caesar: "he had heard en route that Antony had been elected augur before he (Caesar) got to Italy." The election took place in late September, in the context of the debate led by the consul M. Marcellus over Caesar's Gallic command and whether he should still be allowed to run in absentia.

6. Again, supply *esse* for indirect statement.

7. *frequentiam*, "great numbers."

praestitissent, simulque se et honorem suum in[8] sequentis anni
commendaret[9] petitionem, propterea quod insolenter adversarii sui
gloriarentur L. Lentulum et C. Marcellum consules creatos[10] qui
omnem honorem et dignitatem Caesaris spoliarent,[11] ereptum Ser.
Galbae[12] consulatum, cum is multo plus gratia suffragii
valuisset,[13] quod sibi coniunctus et familiaritate et necessitudine
legationis[14] esset.

51 Exceptus est Caesaris adventus ab omnibus municipiis et
coloniis incredibili honore atque amore. Tum primum enim
veniebat ab illo universae Galliae bello. *[2]* Nihil relinquebatur,
quod ad ornatum portarum, itinerum, locorum omnium, qua
Caesar iturus erat, excogitari poterat.[15] *[3]* Cum liberis omnis
multitudo obviam procedebat, hostiae omnibus locis
immolabantur, tricliniis stratis[16] fora templaque occupabantur, ut
vel spectatissimi triumphi laetitia praecipi posset.[17] Tanta erat
magnificentia apud opulentiores, cupiditas apud humiliores.

---

8. *in . . . petitionem*, "for his campaign for the next year." Caesar hoped to
run for the consulship of 48 during the next year (49), and he was already busily
rounding up voters.

9. *commendaret*, "that he might commend," continues the purpose clause *ut
ageret*, above.

10. *creatos (esse)*, "had been elected"; *creari* is the technical term.

11. *qui . . . spoliarent*, relative clause of purpose or characteristic, "to (or,
"who would") strip away," rather than merely subjunctive in subordinate clause
in indirect statement.

12. Servius Sulpicius Galba, who had been *legatus* to Caesar in Gaul, was
defeated in the consular elections for 49, a blow to Caesar's hopes of keeping loyal
partisans in positions of power until he himself could be reelected.

13. *cum . . . valuisset*, "although he (Galba) had had more strength." *Gratiā*
is ablative.

14. *et familiaritate et necessitudine legationis*, "both by friendship and by the
obligations imposed by his office as *legatus*."

15. *quod . . . excogitari poterat*, "which could be imagined."

16. *tricliniis stratis*, ablative absolute. The *triclinia* were dining couches,
arranged on three sides of a rectangle with a table on the open side. They were
here set out in the ritual known as the *lectisternium*, banquets laid out for the
gods. Images of the gods were placed on the *triclinia*. See Livy 22.10.

17. *vel* is used, as often, as an intensive adverb, "even." *spectatissimi*, "eagerly
anticipated." *praecipi posset*, "could be enjoyed in advance."

52 Cum omnes regiones Galliae togatae[18] Caesar percu-
currisset, summa celeritate ad exercitum Nemetocennam rediit
legionibusque ex omnibus hibernis ad fines Treverorum[19] evocatis
eo profectus est ibique exercitum lustravit.[20] *[2]* T. Labienum[21]
Galliae praefecit togatae, quo maiore commendatione conciliaretur
ad consulatus petitionem.[22] *[3]* Ipse tantum itinerum faciebat
quantum[23] satis esse ad mutationem locorum propter salubritatem
existimabat. Ibi quamquam crebro audiebat Labienum ab inimicis
suis sollicitari, certiorque fiebat id[24] agi paucorum consiliis, ut
interposita senatus auctoritate aliqua parte[25] exercitus spoliaretur,
tamen neque de Labieno credidit quicquam[26] neque contra senatus
auctoritatem ut aliquid faceret adduci potuit. Iudicabat enim liberis

---

18. *Gallia togata* refers to the enfranchised towns and colonies of Italy north
of the Po and south of the Alps.

19. The Treveri were a people of Belgic Gaul whose territory was between the
Meuse and the Rhine. The town of Nemetocenna, mentioned above, was also in
Belgic Gaul on the left bank of the Rhine.

20. *lustrare* is here the technical word for conducting a review of the troops,
which was a religious ceremony.

21. Titus Labienus (tribune in 63 and praetor in or around 59) had been
Caesar's most effective general in Gaul, serving him there as *legatus pro praetore*. He
was from the area of Picenum in northeastern Italy where Pompey's family had
powerful connections, deeply entrenched. Very soon, Labienus will accede to the
temptations described here and defect to the camp of Pompey, whereupon he
became one of Caesar's bitterest enemies, as we shall see.

22. *quo maiore commendatione conciliaretur ad consulatus petitionem*, "so that
(*quo*) he (Labienus) could be brought over to his (Caesar's) campaign for the
consulship by this more important sign of support." Hirtius may be implying that
Caesar wanted Labienus to be his consular colleague (Gelzer, 186 n. 3), but the
Latin does not make this inevitable. In any case, Caesar is working hard to keep
Labienus' good will.

23. *tantum itinerum faciebat quantum*, "he marched only so far as."

24. *id agi paucorum consiliis ut*, "that the schemes of a few men were causing."
Id anticipates the whole *ut* clause that follows as grammatical subject of the
impersonal infinitive *agi. Consiliis* is ablative of means. The construction is difficult
to reproduce gracefully in the English passive.

25. *aliquā parte*, ablative of separation after a verb of depriving.

26. Caesar shows remarkable trust in Labienus, or else remarkable naïveté.
Hirtius' account of Caesar's motives in the next sentences reads like the report of
a close confidant: can we detect a hint of exasperation at what sounds like limitless
patience and tolerance?

sententiis[27] patrum conscriptorum[28] causam suam facile obtineri. *[4]* Nam C. Curio[29] tribunus plebis, cum Caesaris causam dignitatemque defendendam suscepisset, saepe erat senatui pollicitus,[30] si[31] quem timor amicorum Caesaris laederet et quoniam Pompei dominatio atque arma non minorem terrorem foro inferrent, discederet[32] uterque ab armis exercitusque dimitteret; fore[33] eo facto liberam et sui iuris[34] civitatem. *[5]* Neque hoc tantum pollicitus est, sed etiam per se discessionem[35] facere coepit; quod ne fieret[36] consules amicique Pompei evicerunt

---

27. *liberis sententiis*, an ablative phrase with conditional force = *si liberae essent sententiae.*

28. *patres conscripti* was an ancient and formal designation for senators. *Sententia* was used for the formal declaration of a senator's views; hence, it could in the right context mean "proposal," "opinion," or "vote." Here, "vote" seems indicated.

29. C. Scribonius Curio, a tribune in 50 who had been thought to be a supporter of the optimates, exchanged numerous letters with Cicero. In 49, after having supported Caesar throughout 50, as we have seen in the Introduction, he served with him and was killed on campaign in Africa. Caesar devotes a lengthy section of Book 2 of *De bello civili* to the exploits and death of Curio.

30. *erat . . . pollicitus*, "he had proposed." The dependent verbs are *discederet* and *dimitteret*, below; the conditional and causal clauses that follow *pollicitus* are parenthetical.

31. *si*, "in case."

32. *discederet* and *dimitteret* are jussive: "each should give up arms and disband his army." This proposal had now become Curio's hallmark: he had introduced it in March, and had held on to it for over six months.

33. *fore* = *futuram esse.*

34. *sui iuris* is a technical expression borrowed from private law, meaning "legally independent (lit., subject to his own law)." Persons were either *sui iuris* or *alieni iuris.*

35. *discessio* is the technical word for a "division" of the House. Voting in the Senate was done literally by walking apart (*discedere*), to one side of the hall or the other.

36. *quod ne fieret* = *sed ne hoc fieret*, "but that this might not happen," depending on *evicerunt*, "they prevailed." A smoother translation might go, "But they prevented this from happening." The consuls did not want this vote to take place because Caesar's proposal would have been approved. In fact, when a vote was permitted, the measure passed 370 to 22, but the consuls voided the meeting. This does not mean that the Senate supported Caesar; rather, a vast majority wanted to avoid civil war. If in accomplishing that goal both Caesar and Pompey could be deprived of their armies, so much the better.

atque ita rem morando discusserunt.

53 Magnum hoc testimonium[37] senatus erat universi[38] conveniensque[39] superiori facto. Nam M. Marcellus[40] proximo anno
cum impugnaret Caesaris dignitatem, contra legem Pompei et
Crassi[41] rettulerat[42] ante tempus[43] ad senatum de Caesaris provinciis, sententiisque dictis discessionem faciente Marcello qui sibi
omnem dignitatem ex Caesaris invidia quaerebat, senatus frequens
in alia omnia transiit.[44] *[2]* Quibus non frangebantur animi
inimicorum Caesaris, sed admonebantur quo maiores pararent
necessitates,[45] quibus cogi posset senatus id probare quod ipsi
constituissent.

54 Fit deinde[46] senatus consultum, ut ad bellum Parthicum
legio una a Cn. Pompeio, altera a C. Caesare mitteretur; neque
obscure hae duae legiones uni[47] detrahuntur. *[2]* Nam Pompeius
legionem primam quam ad Caesarem miserat, confectam ex dilectu

---

37. Take *hoc* as subject and *testimonium* as predicate.

38. *universi*, "(the Senate) as a whole."

39. *conveniensque*, "and consistent with."

40. Marcus Claudius Marcellus, consul in 51 and a cousin of the C. Marcellus
who is consul in 50, has been a steadfast opponent of Caesar. In the coming war,
he fights for Pompey.

41. The *Lex Pompeia Licinia* was passed in 55 by the consuls, Cn. Pompey and
M. Licinius Crassus, part of the cooperation of the Triumvirs. The law guaranteed
Caesar an additional five years in Gaul and established some kind of commitment
for that command that would have been favorable for his plans to be reelected in
49 for the consulship of 48. In addition, Pompey's own law of that same year *De
iure magistratuum* made explicit Caesar's right to campaign in absentia. Following
efforts by Marcellus to undermine these privileges, the Senate resolved to put the
issue of the Gallic command to a vote after 1 March 50. See Introduction.

42. *rettulerat* < *referre ad senatum*, "to put a motion to the Senate."

43. I.e., earlier than allowed in the law. Marcellus had tried (see Introduction)
to introduce this question as early as June of 51 but had found little support and
(in particular) no backing from Pompey.

44. *in alia omnia transiit*, "rejected the motion." Again, this is the technical
phraseology (*discessit* sometimes replaces *transiit*). This vote was taken sometime in
late September of 51, after which the date of 1 March 50 was agreed to.

45. *necessitates*, "sources of pressure."

46. April (Gelzer, 181) or perhaps May of 50. By the end of the year (Dio
40.66), these two legions had been specifically entrusted to Pompey.

47. *uni*, dative of separation, "from only one (of them)."

provinciae Caesaris, eam tamquam ex suo numero dedit.[48] *[3]*
Caesar tamen, cum de voluntate minime dubium esset
adversariorum suorum, Pompeio legionem remisit et suo nomine
quintam decimam, quam in Gallia citeriore habuerat, ex senatus
consulto iubet tradi; in eius locum tertiam decimam legionem in
Italiam mittit, quae praesidia tueretur,[49] ex quibus praesidiis
quinta decima deducebatur. *[4]* Ipse exercitui distribuit hiberna: C.
Trebonium cum legionibus IIII in Belgio conlocat, C. Fabium cum
totidem in Haeduos deducit. *[5]* Sic enim existimabat tutissimam
fore Galliam, si Belgae, quorum maxima virtus, et Haedui, quorum
auctoritas summa esset, exercitibus continerentur.[50] Ipse in Italiam
profectus est.

    55 Quo cum venisset, cognoscit[51] per C. Marcellum consulem
legiones duas ab se missas, quae ex senatus consulto deberent ad
Parthicum bellum duci, Cn. Pompeio traditas[52] atque in Italia
retentas esse. *[2]* Hoc facto quamquam nulli erat dubium quidnam
contra Caesarem pararetur, tamen Caesar omnia patienda esse

---

    48. In 55 a levy of troops had provided both Caesar and Pompey with
additional forces. Pompey "loaned" one of these newly enrolled legions to Caesar
in 53, and now claims this legion as his contribution to the Parthian war,
supposedly in retaliation for the defeat of Crassus in 53. The Parthian campaign
never took place. Thus Caesar was in effect deprived of two legions. Under
Pompey's command this legion was called the First (*legionem primam*), but was
renamed the Sixth under Caesar.

    49. *quae praesidia tueretur* = *ut ea (legio) praesidia tueretur*, "to look after the
garrisons." It is possible that Caesar in fact sent the Thirteenth to Ravenna
directly, since it is already there when he decides to march in January.

    50. It is standard in Caesar that the Belgae are the fiercest fighters among the
Gauls, but that the Haedui (or Aedui), who had a long-standing alliance with
Rome and at whose invitation Caesar had come to Transalpine Gaul in the first
place, had the greatest influence among the other tribes.

    51. From Hirtius himself, in fact, who was Caesar's liaison in Rome, working
toward a peaceful settlement.

    52. *per Marcellum consulem . . . legiones . . . Pompeio traditas.* Marcellus had
taken this action on his own authority in early December, as he was getting the
worst of his confrontation with Curio. Cicero found out about these events from
Marcellus himself on 10 December: Cicero was returning to Rome from Cilicia,
and Marcellus was on his way to Capua to hand over the legions (Cic. *Att.*
7.4.2–3).

statuit, quoad sibi spes aliqua relinqueretur iure potius disceptandi quam belligerandi.

2

Events at Rome
and Caesar's Response

Thus did the year 49 begin, amid great tension. Increasingly, hope for a peaceful resolution was lost, as moderate senators lost ground to the extremists who wanted the issue decided by force.

In the passages that follow, Caesar portrays himself in moderate terms. He claims to want only a resolution that will be fair both to himself and to Pompey—a solution that will allow him to maintain his *dignitas*—and for respect to be shown for tradition and the constitution. His opponents, by contrast, are depicted as unwilling to negotiate for fair terms, resorting to unconstitutional and untraditional methods, and violating the sanctity of the tribunes. From the Romans' point of view, the lineup of supporters and opponents told strongly against Caesar: his supporters tended to have questionable reputations and doubtful loyalties, his opponents tended to be from the oldest and most honorable families. Although Caesar's power was feared, the anti-Caesarians clearly believed that, with Pompey's support, they would win.

The beginning of the work, which would have contained Caesar's own introduction, has been lost; we begin in the midst of a senatorial debate on 1 January 49.

CAESAR, *DE BELLO CIVILI* 1.1–5

1 Litteris C. Caesaris consulibus redditis[1] aegre ab his

---

1. *litteris . . . redditis*, ablative absolute (*consulibus* is dative, and refers to L. Lentulus and C. Marcellus, both opponents of Caesar). This letter repeats Caesar's offer, previously conveyed through Curio, that both generals should give up their commands (Suet. *Iul.* 29.2; Gelzer 190 n. 5).

impetratum est[2] summa tribunorum[3] plebis contentione ut in senatu recitarentur; ut vero ex litteris ad senatum referretur, impetrari non potuit. *[2]* Referunt consules de re publica infinite.[4] L. Lentulus[5] consul senatui rei publicae se non defuturum pollicetur, si audacter ac fortiter sententias dicere velint; *[3]* sin Caesarem respiciant atque eius gratiam sequantur, ut superioribus fecerint temporibus, se sibi consilium capturum neque senatus auctoritati obtemperaturum; habere se quoque ad Caesaris gratiam atque amicitiam receptum. *[4]* In eandem sententiam loquitur Scipio:[6] Pompeio esse in animo rei publicae non deesse, si senatus sequatur; si cunctetur atque agat lenius, nequiquam eius auxilium, si postea velit, senatum imploraturum.

2 Haec Scipionis oratio, quod senatus in urbe habebatur Pompeiusque aderat, ex ipsius ore Pompei mitti[7] videbatur.[8] *[2]*

---

2. *aegre ab his impetratum est*, "they were barely persuaded."

3. The two tribunes are Mark Antony and Q. Cassius Longinus.

4. *infinite*, "in general," rather than *ex litteris*, "as proposed by Caesar's letter" (above). The consuls did not want this proposal voted on because there was a very good chance that it would pass; principles aside, most senators still wanted peace rather than civil war.

5. L. Cornelius Lentulus Crus.

6. Q. Caecilius Metellus Pius Scipio. A Cornelius Scipio Nasica by birth, he had been adopted by the Caecilii Metelli. He had been tribune in 59, during Caesar's consulship, and had run for the consulship in 53, a year when electoral violence was so great that in the end no magistrates could be elected; in 52, after the murder of P. Clodius, Pompey was appointed sole consul. Pompey married Cornelia, Scipio's daughter, during these months and chose Scipio as his colleague for half the year. Scipio's virulent opposition is the clearest evidence of Pompey's intentions. Caesar had little respect for Scipio, who appears often in the *Civil War*.

7. *mitti*, "to be launched" (so Carter, who explains the metaphor: in Caesar, *mittere* is used for throwing weapons, and the verb is not found with *orationem* in the standard prose authors).

8. Lentulus (who is consul for this year) and Scipio, whose ties to Pompey are exceedingly close, are threatening, in effect, to go their own way if the Senate refuses to pursue a confrontation with Caesar. Wavering senators are torn by the double-sided fear that a successful Caesar will carry out a purge of his enemies, and indeed that Pompey will do the same if he should defeat Caesar on his own. Nothing would be helped if Pompey simply backed off and allowed Caesar to have his way. The violent statements of Scipio, especially, raise doubts about Pompey's

Dixerat aliquis leniorem sententiam, ut primo M. Marcellus,⁹ ingressus in eam orationem, non oportere ante de ea re ad senatum referri quam dilectus tota Italia habiti et exercitus conscripti essent, quo praesidio tuto et libere senatus quae vellet decernere auderet; *[3]* ut M. Calidius,¹⁰ qui censebat ut Pompeius in suas provincias¹¹ proficisceretur, ne qua esset armorum causa: timere¹² Caesarem ereptis ab eo duabus legionibus, ne ad eius periculum reservare et retinere eas ad urbem Pompeius videretur; ut M. Rufus,¹³ qui sententiam Calidi paucis fere mutatis rebus sequebatur. *[4]* Hi omnes convicio L. Lentuli consulis correpti exagitabantur. *[5]* Lentulus sententiam Calidi pronuntiaturum¹⁴ se omnino negavit, Marcellus perterritus conviciis a sua sententia discessit. *[6]* Sic vocibus consulis, terrore praesentis exercitus, minis amicorum Pompei plerique compulsi inviti et coacti Scipionis sententiam sequuntur: uti ante certam diem Caesar exercitum dimmitat; si non

---

intentions and desires. "It was a classic example of a small minority stampeding the House through half-truths, slogans, and threats" (Gruen, 489).

9. M. Claudius Marcellus (consul in 51) was the brother of the C. Marcellus who was now consul with Lentulus Crus (see chapter 1, n. 40). Both were cousins of the consul of 50, also named C. Marcellus.

10. M. Calidius had been praetor in 57 and had run unsuccessfully for the consulship in 51. Calidius had sided with Cicero in the defense of Milo in 52; during the war, he fights for Caesar.

11. That is, Nearer and Farther Spain, over both of which Pompey held proconsular *imperium*. Pompey was also in charge of the city grain supply and on that pretext remained close to Rome throughout his tenure over the Spanish provinces; the actual administration in Spain was handled through *legati*.

12. *timere*, infinitive in indirect statement, of which the subject is *Caesarem*. The verb of fearing, in turn, introduces *ne . . . Pompeius videretur*. The phrase *ereptis . . . legionibus* following *Caesarem* is ablative absolute.

13. M. Caelius Rufus, Cicero's friend, who had been tribune in 52 and among the supporters of Milo after the murder of Clodius. We have read his letter about the perils of choice in this war in chapter 1. By this time, he has clearly decided for Caesar.

14. *pronuntiaturum (esse)* < *pronuntiare (sententiam)*, "to announce a motion for discussion" in the Senate. This differs from *referre* in that *pronuntiare* indicates a formal motion has been put; *referre* is used for introducing a subject for discussion.

faciat, eum adversus rem publicam facturum videri.[15] *[7]*
Intercedit[16] M. Antonius, Q. Cassius, tribuni plebis. Refertur
confestim de intercessione tribunorum.[17] *[8]* Dicuntur sententiae
graves; ut quisque acerbissime crudelissimeque dixit, ita quam
maxime ab inimicis Caesaris collaudatur.

3 Misso ad vesperum[18] senatu omnes qui sunt eius ordinis a
Pompeio evocantur. Laudat promptos atque in posterum
confirmat, segniores castigat atque incitat. *[2]* Multi undique ex
veteribus Pompei exercitibus spe praemiorum atque ordinum
evocantur,[19] multi ex duabus legionibus quae sunt traditae a
Caesare arcessuntur. *[3]* Completur urbs, clivus, comitium
tribunis,[20] centurionibus, evocatis. *[4]* Omnes amici consulum,
necessarii Pompei atque eorum qui veteres inimicitias cum Caesare
gerebant in senatum coguntur;[21] *[5]* quorum vocibus et concursu

---

15. This formal and stylized wording (*contra* could replace *adversus*) served
notice to recalcitrant politicians (usually generals) that the state was now
authorized to take drastic measures if necessary. It stops short of declaring the
victim a public enemy (*hostis*) and establishes no penalty. But it was nonetheless
a very severe action that placed its target, short of total capitulation, in an
untenable political position.

16. *intercedit*, "interposed his veto."

17. One of Caesar's principal complaints was the eventual senatorial disregard
of the rights of the tribunes. But this possibility had been anticipated more than
a year previously by Caesar's opponents. In September 51, during the debate on
the date of 1 March 50 for discussion of Caesar's provinces, Pompey was asked
specifically how he would react to a veto of that discussion; his reply was that a
veto would be the equivalent of failing to obey the order.

18. On 2 January. Voting could not take place after dark.

19. *ordinum*, "promotions." Ordinary soldiers could hope for promotion as
high as centurion through valorous service. *Evocati* were former soldiers who had
served out their military obligation; although exempt from further required duty,
they could be voluntarily reenlisted under inducement of exemption from menial
duties and the prospects of a lucrative campaign. No doubt personal loyalty to
certain commanders also played a role.

20. *tribunis* (sc. *militum*), "military tribunes."   Caesar juxtaposes three
manifestations of war (*tribuni, centuriones, evocati*) and three emblems of peace
(*urbs, comitium, clivus*).

21. The date is 5 January. Cicero had returned to Rome from Cilicia the
previous day.

terrentur infirmiores, dubii confirmantur, plerisque vero libere decernendi potestas eripitur. *[6]* Pollicetur L. Piso[22] censor sese iturum ad Caesarem, item L. Roscius[23] praetor, qui de his rebus eum doceant; sex dies ad eam rem conficiendam spati postulant. *[7]* Dicuntur etiam ab non nullis sententiae, ut legati ad Caesarem mittantur qui voluntatem senatus ei proponant.

4 Omnibus his resistitur omnibusque oratio consulis, Scipionis, Catonis[24] opponitur. Catonem veteres inimicitiae Caesaris incitant et dolor repulsae.[25] *[2]* Lentulus aeris alieni magnitudine et spe exercitus ac provinciarum et regum appellandorum largitionibus[26] movetur seque alterum fore Sullam inter suos gloriatur, ad quem summa imperi redeat. *[3]* Scipionem eadem spes provinciae atque exercituum impellit, quos se pro necessitudine[27] partiturum cum Pompeio arbitratur, simul iudiciorum metus, adulatio atque ostentatio sui et potentium,[28] qui in re publica iudiciisque tum

---

22. L. Calpurnius Piso, consul in 58, censor in 50, a longtime supporter of Caesar. Caesar had married Calpurnia, his daughter.

23. L. Roscius Fabatus, praetor for 49 and a former *legatus* for Caesar in Gaul.

24. M. Porcius Cato the "Younger," later "Uticensis." He entered high politics with a flourish as tribune in 62—following his denunciation of the Catilinarians the year before—with a series of obstructive moves against Pompey that eventually drove Caesar and Pompey together. He consciously modeled himself on the image of his famous ancestor, Cato the Censor (234–149), championing strict moralism to such an extent that even Cicero once complained that he belonged in the Republic of Plato rather than in the sewer of Romulus. During 52 he ran for consul (for the year 51) but was defeated. Cato has often been seen as the driving force against any reconciliation between Pompey and Caesar, and as an intransigent opponent of any compromise that would allow Caesar an honorable retreat without civil war.

25. *repulsae*, "at his defeat" in his campaign during 52 for consul.

26. *regum appellandorum largitionibus*, "by (anticipated) bribes for naming (foreign rulers) kings." The Roman Senate had often honored a foreign ruler with nominal titles, such as *rex et amicus populi Romani*, in order to establish good relations and if possible a sense of obligation to Rome.

27. *pro necessitudine*, "in return for his close relationship" as Pompey's father-in-law.

28. *adulatio et ostentatio sui et potentium*, "the public display of flattery both of himself and of the powerful."

plurimum pollebant.²⁹ *[4]* Ipse Pompeius,³⁰ ab inimicis Caesaris incitatus et quod neminem dignitate secum exaequari volebat, totum³¹ se ab eius amicitia averterat et cum communibus inimicis in gratiam redierat,³² quorum ipse maximam partem illo adfinitatis tempore iniunxerat Caesari; *[5]* simul infamia duarum legionum permotus, quas ab itinere Asiae Syriaeque ad suam potentiam dominatumque converterat, rem ad arma deduci studebat.

5 His de causis aguntur omnia raptim atque turbate. Nec docendi Caesaris propinquis eius spatium datur nec tribunis plebis sui periculi deprecandi neque etiam extremi iuris intercessione retinendi, quod L. Sulla reliquerat, facultas tribuitur, *[2]* sed de sua salute septimo die³³ cogitare coguntur, quod illi turbulentissimi³⁴ superioribus temporibus tribuni plebis post octo denique mensis variarum actionum³⁵ respicere ac timere consuerant. *[3]* Decurritur³⁶ ad illud extremum atque ultimum senatus consultum, quo nisi paene in ipso urbis incendio atque in desperatione omnium salutis latorumque audacia³⁷ numquam ante discessum

---

29. *plurimum pollebant*, "exercised the most power." *Plurimum* is adverbial.

30. Here Caesar lays out his charges against Pompey in full for the only time in the account. Clearly, to Caesar, his offense was personal as well as political.

31. *totum*, "entirely" (i.e., adverbial with *averterat*).

32. *in gratiam redierat* < *cum aliquo in gratiam redire*: often translated "to become reconciled with someone," the idiom in fact usually makes more logical sense as "to go over to the side of someone," for it is often used of associations between those who have never before been friendly.

33. That is, on the seventh day of the debate, 7 January. Caesar is speaking loosely, inasmuch as only five days in early January were available for official business, as he goes on to explain below (1.5.4). His point here is that all these decisions were made with undue and unseemly haste.

34. *turbulentissimi*, "excessively disruptive." Caesar contrasts these notorious tribunes of the past (invoking the legend of the two Gracchi) with the reasonable and moderate actions of Antony and Cassius.

35. *actionum*, "official acts." Take as partitive genitive with *octo mensis*, "eight months of diverse actions."

36. *Decurritur*, "Hasty recourse was had" (Perrin), capturing the flavor of *-currere* in the verb.

37. *latorumque audacia*, "and the insolence of the men proposing laws." The text of the mss., *latorum audacia*, has been doubted but is stoutly defended by Carter (citing Cicero, *Pro Sestio* 77), though if Caesar meant to include the *latorum*

est: dent operam consules, praetores, tribuni plebis, quique pro consulibus sunt ad urbem, ne quid res publica detrimenti capiat.[38] *[4]* Haec senatus consulto perscribuntur a.d. VII Id. Ian.[39] Itaque V primis diebus quibus haberi senatus potuit, qua ex die consulatum iniit Lentulus, biduo excepto comitiali[40] et de imperio Caesaris et de amplissimis viris, tribunis plebis, gravissime acerbissimeque decernitur. *[5]* Profugiunt statim ex urbe tribuni plebis seseque ad Caesarem conferunt. Is eo tempore[41] erat Ravennae exspectabatque suis lenissimis postulatis responsa,[42] si qua hominum aequitate res ad otium deduci posset.

CICERO TO TIRO, 12 JANUARY 49 (*Fam.* 16.11)

Tiro was one of Cicero's freedmen, a loyal secretary who transcribed his speeches for him. This letter was sent just after Caesar crossed the Rubicon, an event that Caesar himself does not describe. After offering good wishes to Tiro's health (he has just been ill), Cicero goes on to news of the city.

I got to the city on 4 January. The turnout for me could not have been more impressive. But I walked into the very flames of

---

audacia in his list of dreadful contexts for the decree, along with *urbis incendium* and *desperatio omnium salutis*, some sort of additional connective seems called for. I have therefore added *-que* but have otherwise made no changes.

38. *dent* . . . *capiat*: the official wording of the "final decree" of the Senate, the so-called *senatus consultum ultimum*, "let the (magistrates) see to it that the state receive no harm." The magistrates are often listed differently. This decree, which was easily recognized by its wording, had no official name in antiquity: in fact, the adjective *ultimum* is found with this *consultum* only in this passage, where Caesar means to pair it with *extremum* to illustrate how drastic it was, not to give the decree's name.

39. 7 January.

40. On "comitial" days the Senate could not (in theory) be formally convened. Thus, only five days were allowed for debate on such weighty matters.

41. 10 January.

42. Presumably contained in the letter referred to at the beginning of the book (1.1), which Caesar must have exposed in detail in the lost original. Cicero's view of this letter is quite different, as we shall see.

civil dissension; or war, rather. Although I want to cure the problem, and I think I could, the ambitions of men whose identities are obvious get in my way (for there are those on both sides who want to fight). After all, not only has Caesar himself, our friend,[43] sent a threatening and harsh letter to the Senate,[44] and is insolent enough to keep his army and his province against the will of the Senate, but my ally Curio keeps spurring him on. Our Antonius, in fact, and Q. Cassius, who have been driven out with no force at all, went to Caesar along with Curio when the Senate gave to the consuls, praetors, tribunes, and us proconsuls the task of ensuring that the state receive no harm.[45] Never has the state been in greater peril, never have the shameless had a better leader. To be sure, careful preparations are being made on our side, too. This is being done with the authority and initiative of our friend Pompey, whose fear of Caesar has begun late.

CAESAR, *DE BELLO CIVILI* 1.6–10

6 Proximis diebus habetur extra urbem[46] senatus. Pompeius eadem illa quae per Scipionem ostenderat agit; senatus virtutem constantiamque collaudat; copias suas exponit: legiones habere sese

---

43. This apposition and the apparently favorable characterization of Curio and Antony below are ironic. The phrase "driven out with no force at all" may also be intended as an ironic oxymoron.

44. According to Gelzer, this is the letter read to the Senate on 1 January by Curio, Caesar's *lenissima postulata* (1.5.5), in which Caesar offers again to disband his army if Pompey will do likewise, and threatens to act swiftly if not (Appian *BC* 2.32). Caesar does not mention the threat.

45. The formula for the *senatus consultum ultimum*, on which see n. 38 above.

46. That is, outside the *pomerium*, which would allow Pompey to attend. This practice, which had gone on for some time whenever Pompey's attendance seemed crucial, did not involve much distance: in 52 the Senate held meetings in the portico attached to Pompey's Theater in the Campus Martius (Asconius 52C).

paratas X;[47] [2] praeterea cognitum compertumque sibi[48] alieno esse animo[49] in Caesarem milites neque eis posse persuaderi[50] uti eum defendant aut sequantur. [3] Statim de reliquis rebus ad senatum refertur: tota Italia dilectus habeatur; Faustus Sulla[51] propere in Mauretaniam mittatur; pecunia uti[52] ex aerario Pompeio detur; refertur etiam de rege Iuba,[53] ut socius sit atque amicus. [4] Marcellus consul passurum in praesentia negat; de Fausto impedit Philippus,[54] tribunus plebis. [5] De reliquis rebus senatus consulta perscribuntur. Provinciae privatis decernuntur,[55] duae consulares, reliquae praetoriae. Scipioni obvenit Syria, L. Domitio Gallia.

---

47. This is at best an exaggerated figure. He was evidently counting the troops in Spain (six legions, readiness uncertain), the two legions he had received from Caesar (which were in fact in good battle condition), and two that he had recently been allowed to raise (also of doubtful strength).

48. *cognitum compertumque sibi*, "that he had discovered and ascertained," an emphatic redundancy. The construction is impersonal passive in indirect statement.

49. *alieno . . . animo*, "hostile." This, of course, as well as the claim in the following clause, turned out to be quite untrue.

50. *neque eis . . . persuaderi uti*, "they could not be persuaded that (they should)." *Eis* is dative; the intransitive verb *persuadere* is used only impersonally in the passive and introduces an indirect command.

51. Faustus Cornelius Sulla, a son of the dictator; he had married Pompey's daughter. His political career was just beginning (he was quaestor in 54) when the normal course of politics was interrupted. He did not survive the Civil War.

52. *uti* is the infinitive of *utor*, so that *pecunia* is ablative (*pecunia uti*, "the use of money," thus becomes the subject of *detur*).

53. Another African king, Juba was friendly to Pompey's cause because his two rivals in Mauretania were protégés of Caesar.

54. The son of L. Marcius Philippus, consul in 56. This family was very closely connected to Caesar: Philippus' father was the second husband of Atia, Caesar's niece and Octavian's mother. The son mentioned here became praetor in 44.

55. Caesar certainly meant *privatis* ("nonmagistrates") as a slur of sorts. Pompey's law of 52 required a five-year interval between a consulship or praetorship and a special command, which then had to be specifically approved. But the key word is *decernuntur*, "were determined (by the Senate)," for all such appointments should have been formally ratified by bills (however pro forma) before the People, not by the Senate. The Senate had traditionally assumed the power to prolong an *imperium* but had no legal authority to institute such a command. Caesar makes this objection explicit below (1.6.6).

Philippus et Cotta privato consilio praetereuntur,[56] neque eorum sortes deiciuntur. In reliquas provincias praetores mittuntur. *[6]* Neque exspectant, quod superioribus annis acciderat, ut de eorum imperio ad populum feratur, paludatique votis nuncupatis exeunt. *[7]* Consules, quod ante id tempus accidit numquam, ex urbe proficiscuntur lictoresque habent in urbe et Capitolio privati contra omnia vetustatis exempla.[57] *[8]* Tota Italia dilectus habentur, arma imperantur, pecuniae a municipiis exiguntur, e fanis tolluntur, omnia divina humanaque iura permiscentur.

In the preceding paragraph, Caesar has compressed the events of the first two weeks of January, leaving the impression that all these events were in his mind when, in the next two chapters, he crosses into Italy with his army. The sequence of his report suggests that he learned what happened at Rome before he met the tribunes Antony and Cassius near Ariminum. Further, he has shifted to Ravenna an address to the soldiers that contains references to events that he could not have known about until he had later met with the tribunes. By our standards of history, this is clear misrepresentation. But Caesar's main goal is not journalistic, to produce an account of precise events; it is rather to interpret those events in a historical narrative. Hence, in the previous paragraph, very much in the ancient historiographic tradition, he follows "events in the city" to their dramatic conclusion before going on to other matters. While the speech

---

56. Because they were partisans of Caesar, presumably.

57. This sentence is a bit odd, since it appears to be either untrue or pointless. There are in fact numerous examples of consuls departing the city during their term of office. Carter rescues Caesar's logic as to what was unexampled by accepting La Penna's emendation, the addition of *ne auspicato quidem* ("without even taking the auspices") before *ex urbe proficiscuntur*. Without emending the text it would still be possible to read *ex urbe proficiscuntur* closely with the next phrase: the consuls left the city while nonmagistrates had lictors. The reference to nonmagistrates (*privati*) has been a puzzle, for nonmagistrates never had lictors; but Caesar here is still using *privati* tendentiously, as above. The Senate doubtless considered Scipio and Domitius (pro)magistrates, but Caesar calls them *privati* to emphasize (or create) the illegality of their position. Thus he contrasts constitutional magistrates (*consules*) going *from* Rome with illegal magistrates ("*privati*,") parading the symbols of their office *in* Rome. La Penna's emendation, however, remains attractive, and would not require a stressed reading of *-que* ("while") in the phrase *lictoresque habent*.

that he goes on to report could not have been delivered in Ravenna, and very possibly was not delivered at all in these terms, consistent with the standards of ancient historiography it illustrates the character of the general and the significance of the events. The chronology is certainly impressionistic, but chronology is not Caesar's main point and his account is not by ancient standards mendacious. To take another example, in *BC* 1.24.1, quoted below, Caesar says that Pompey left for Brundisium only after events at Corfinium were known; but it is clear that Pompey had left well before that issue was resolved. Although it would have been to Caesar's advantage here to narrate the true sequence of events, he evidently does not care to make the point.

So Caesar is not so much rearranging events in his interest as sorting them to show the reader the most important thread of the story. Thus, his presentation justifies his actions to his readers by showing that these events were proceeding inexorably, and that his preparations and anticipations were wholly vindicated. If, strictly speaking, he invaded before the Senate overtly moved against him, he was exonerated in his own mind and in the minds of his soldiers by the fact that the Senate did move against him and would have done so in any case. In fact, the whole thrust of Caesar's account is to make clear that he was marching to Ariminum with his soldiers' consent (1.7.8, below) and that he had felt compelled to ask for it (1.8.1);[58] the chronology of the Senate's decisions is not at issue. In the elaboration of his theme, he is wholly consistent.

7 Quibus rebus cognitis[59] Caesar apud milites contionatur. Omnium temporum iniurias inimicorum in se commemorat; a quibus deductum ac depravatum Pompeium queritur inividia atque obtrectatione laudis suae, cuius ipse honori et dignitati semper faverit adiutoremque fuerit. *[2]* Novum in rem publicam introductum exemplum queritur, ut tribunicia intercessio armis notaretur atque opprimeretur, quae superioribus annis armis esset restituta. *[3]* Sullam nudata omnibus rebus tribunicia potestate

---

58. So Gelzer, 193 n. 3.

59. Chronologically tendentious, as we have just explained. Caesar's crossing of the Rubicon (which he does not mention himself) follows this speech, and is usually dated to 11 or 12 January.

tamen intercessionem liberam reliquisse;[60] *[4]* Pompeium, qui amissa restituisse videatur bona, etiam quae ante habuerint ademisse.[61] *[5]* Quotienscumque sit decretum darent operam magistratus ne quid res publica detrimenti caperet, qua voce et quo senatus consulto populus Romanus ad arma sit vocatus, factum in perniciosis legibus, in vi tribunicia, in secessione populi, templis locisque editioribus occupatis; *[6]* atque haec superioris aetatis exempla expiata[62] Saturnini atque Gracchorum casibus docet; quarum rerum illo tempore nihil factum, ne cogitatum quidem: nulla lex promulgata, non cum populo agi coeptum, nulla secessio facta. *[7]* Hortatur, cuius[63] imperatoris ductu VIIII annis rem publicam felicissime gesserint[64] plurimaque proelia secunda fecerint, omnem Galliam Germaniamque pacaverint, ut eius existimationem dignitatemque ab inimicis defendant. *[8]* Conclamant legionis XIII., quae aderat,[65] milites—hanc enim initio tumultus evocaverat, reliquae nondum convenerant—sese paratos esse imperatoris sui tribunorumque plebis iniurias defendere.

From a constitutional point of view, Caesar's position could never be "legal." He can at best show that he has just grievances and the support of his army. As to his preparations, which were obviously extensive, in

---

60. Sulla had tried to destroy or at least severely limit the office of tribune in various ways, especially by barring a holder of that office from any higher magistracies; but as Caesar notes, he did not try to remove the tribunes' right of intercession, which had been secured according to legend by rebellion of the plebeians. Pompey himself, as consul in 70, had finally restored all the powers of the tribune.

61. *ademisse* < *adimere*.

62. *expiata* (*esse*), "had been atoned for," dependent on *docet* (sc. *Caesar*).

63. *cuius* anticipates *eius*, below. In English, we would say, "of that general whose" rather than "of which general . . . his." In Latin, the antecedent is often attracted into the relative clause.

64. *rem publicam felicissime gesserint*, "had fulfilled their duty to the state most propitiously."

65. The Thirteenth Legion had been in Gaul, but Caesar had sent it into Italy to replace the Fifteenth, which had been turned over to the Senate in the previous year for the ephemeral Parthian campaign (see chapter 1, Hirtius *BG* 8.54.3). If the Thirteenth was already in Ravenna, Caesar must have called for it well before the Senate's actions of which he has complained above.

Roman terms he was doing what he had to do. If the Senate had allowed more time for negotiation, even at Ariminum (where he now marches quickly) Caesar's political position would not have been irretrievable. But if they did not, as in fact happened, Caesar had no intention of adopting a passive stance, which would certainly have been fatal. Hence, he arranged his position in early January with the worst case in mind, and as a result beat the Senate to the march.

Of interest is the character of Caesar's rhetoric: he appeals as much as possible to traditional values and to traditional privileges, the arguments of a man who still thinks as a member of the constitutional government and the old political order; these are, in short, the arguments of a republican, not an invading conqueror whose goal is a dictatorship in the mold of Sulla. These are arguments of the moment, of the year 49, not a program for his long-range goals, but his words are nevertheless revealing. He is appealing to his supporters, on the one hand, and to Romans still undecided, on the other, with arguments that he believed would justify his actions under the circumstances. It is a modern bias to separate Caesar's military actions from his political position. Caesar's enemies took for granted that he would act in such a way as to give himself the best chances for victory (Caesar later makes the same assumptions about Pompey's conduct of the war); where they were mistaken was in their reading of his goals, and it is those goals that provide the theme of his account.

8 Cognita militum voluntate[66] Ariminum cum ea legione proficiscitur ibique tribunos plebis qui ad eum confugerant convenit;[67] reliquas legiones ex hibernis evocat et subsequi iubet. *[2]* Eo L. Caesar[68] adulescens venit, cuius pater Caesaris erat legatus. Is reliquo sermone confecto cuius rei causa venerat habere

---

66. This is the key factor, as mentioned above.

67. By crossing the Rubicon, Caesar leaves Cisalpine Gaul (his province). The move to Ariminum must certainly be illegal, even in Caesar's own mind, for he has now crossed from his province in command of an army. Once Caesar made up his mind, he moved swiftly and decisively.

68. A distant relative who supported Pompey. The date is about 18 January. This Lucius Caesar continues to act as a messenger between Pompey and the Senate and Caesar.

Ravenna

Rubicon Fl.

Ariminum

Pisaurum

Fanum

Cingulum

Ancona

Firmum

Alba

Corfinium

Rome

Luceria

Canusium

Capua

Brundisium

Italy in the Civil War

se a Pompeio ad eum privati offici[69] mandata demonstrat: *[3]* velle
Pompeium se Caesari purgatum,[70] ne ea quae rei publicae causa
egerit in suam contumeliam vertat. Semper se rei publicae
commoda privatis necessitudinibus habuisse potiora.[71] Caesarem[72]
quoque pro sua dignitate debere et studium et iracundiam suam rei
publicae dimittere neque adeo graviter irasci inimicis ut, cum illis
nocere se speret, rei publicae noceat. *[4]* Pauca eiusdem generis
addit[73] cum excusatione Pompei coniuncta. Eadem fere atque
eisdem verbis praetor Roscius[74] agit cum Caesare sibique
Pompeium commemorasse demonstrat.

9 Quae res etsi nihil ad levandas iniurias[75] pertinere
videbantur, tamen idoneos nactus homines per quos ea quae vellet
ad eum perferrentur, petit ab utroque,[76] quoniam Pompei mandata
ad se detulerint, ne graventur sua quoque ad eum postulata deferre,
si parvo labore magnas controversias tollere atque omnem Italiam
metu liberare possint: *[2]* Sibi semper primam fuisse dignitatem

---

69. *privati offici*: the choice of words is telling; Pompey wants to absolve
himself of perfidy with Caesar on a personal level. Caesar quotes the letter to
illustrate precisely the opposite and—as he goes on to say—to show that Pompey
is not addressing the key issues of the *iniuriae* to Caesar's position.

70. *velle Pompeium se Caesari purgatum*, "Pompey wanted to be exculpated
in Caesar's eyes." The imagery in *purgari* reflects the moral relationship between
Caesar and Pompey.

71. A typically oracular pronouncement from Pompey, and certainly not
strictly true from the perspective of many prominent Romans. The diction should
be kept in mind (*commoda . . . necessitudinibus habuisse potiora*) in anticipation of
Caesar's answer, below.

72. This sentence runs as follows: "(Pompeius dixit) Caesarem quoque debere
dimittere et studium et iracundiam suam (= Caesaris) rei publicae pro sua
(= Caesaris) dignitate, neque (debere) adeo graviter irasci inimicis ut, cum speret
se (Caesarem) illis nocere, noceat rei publicae."

73. The subject is the *adulescens* L. Caesar.

74. L. Roscius Fabatus, above, chapter 2, n. 23.

75. Pompey's letter did not address the points of Caesar's grievances, but he
would send back a reply in any case.

76. That is, both L. Caesar and Roscius.

vitaque potiorem.[77] Doluisse se quod populi Romani beneficium sibi per contumeliam ab inimicis extorqueretur ereptoque semestri imperio[78] in urbem retraheretur, cuius[79] absentis rationem haberi[80] proximis comitiis[81] populus iussisset. *[3]* Tamen hanc iacturam honoris sui rei publicae causa aequo animo tulisse; cum litteras ad senatum miserit, ut omnes ab exercitibus discederent, ne id quidem impetravisse. *[4]* Tota Italia dilectus haberi, retineri legiones II, quae ab se simulatione Parthici belli sint abductae, civitatem esse in armis. Quonam[82] haec omnia nisi ad suam perniciem pertinere? *[5]* Sed tamen ad omnia se descendere paratum atque omnia pati rei publicae causa. Proficiscatur[83] Pompeius in suas provincias, ipsi exercitus dimittant, discedant in Italia omnes ab armis, metus e civitate tollatur, libera comitia atque omnis res publica senatui populoque Romano permittatur. *[6]* Haec quo facilius certisque condicionibus fiant et iure iurando sanciantur, aut ipse[84]

---

77. This famous sentence, for which Caesar has often been condemned ("Caesar was able to advance such an intensely personal reason for his treason" [Carter]) is not a position statement; it is the first sentence in Caesar's reply to Pompey. Caesar is answering Pompey's claim that to him the good of the state was *privatis necessitudinibus potiora*, that is, that Pompey was abandoning his private obligation to Caesar for allegedly patriotic reasons. Caesar counters that his own public stature (not any concern for the moral sensibilities of Pompey, see n. 71 above) was of prime importance. He then goes on to detail the attacks on that *dignitas* that he has already endured for the public good, and states that he will overlook them all if Pompey will agree to certain conditions (secs. 5–6).

78. *ereptoque semestri imperio*, "and with six months of his *imperium* stolen away."

79. *cuius = cum* (although) *eius*.

80. *cuius absentis rationem haberi*, "his right (to run for the consulship) in absentia should be considered."

81. *proximis comitiis*, "for the next elections," i.e., in summer of 49 for the consulship of 48.

82. *Quonam . . . pertinere?* "What was the point?"

83. *proficiscatur . . . dimittant . . . discedant . . . tollatur . . . permittatur*, . . . *accedat . . . patiatur*, a series of hortatory subjunctives encapsulating Caesar's terms for peace. *Fiant* and *sanciantur*, on the other hand, are subjunctives of purpose introduced by *quo* (= *ut eo*), as regularly with a comparative word.

84. *ipse . . . se = Pompeius . . . Caesarem*.

propius accedat aut se patiatur accedere; fore uti[85] per colloquia omnes controversiae componantur.[86]

10 Acceptis mandatis Roscius cum Caesare Capuam[87] pervenit ibique consules Pompeiumque invenit; postulata Caesaris renuntiat. *[2]* Illi deliberata re respondent scriptaque ad eum mandata[88] per eosdem remittunt, quorum haec erat summa:[89] *[3]* Caesar in Galliam reverteretur, Arimino excederet, exercitus dimitteret; quae si fecisset, Pompeium in Hispanias iturum. *[4]* Interea, quoad fides esset data Caesarem facturum quae polliceretur, non intermissuros consules Pompeiumque dilectus.

SELECTIONS FROM TWO LETTERS BY CICERO

These two letters represent the result of intensive lobbying by Cicero on behalf of peace, the price of which appears to be conceding to Caesar. It is clear, however, that Cicero's interest is to avert war and not to support Caesar, for he represents these negotiations as a diplomatic defeat for the Senate. It is of interest that Cicero indicates that Caesar has abandoned his insistence on the *ratio absentis*, and there are other smaller differences from Caesar's own report of his demands.

Cicero to Tiro, 27 January 49 (*Fam.* 16.12.3–4)

You see the situation we are in. An offer is after all being exten-

---

85. *fore uti . . . componantur*, "will be resolved." *fore ut* + subjunctive replaces the awkward future passive infinitive with *iri* and the supine.

86. This, in fact, is now Caesar's most significant argument: only by direct negotiations with Pompey can civil war be avoided. Certainly, he would not have expected all his terms to be met, any more than Pompey would have expected his reply (in the next chapter) to have settled things. Meanwhile, both sides continue to pursue vigorous military preparations.

87. Caesar is again following his story to its dramatic conclusion in defiance of strict chronology, for he does not report the departure of the consuls for Capua until 1.14, below, where he again has chronological inconsistencies. (The "Caesar" mentioned here as going to Capua with Roscius is of course the Lucius Caesar mentioned above.) Nevertheless, Caesar's aim is not to obfuscate the issues, but to simplify the narrative in traditional historiographic fashion (see above, discussion at 1.6).

88. *scripta . . . mandata*, "proposals in writing," so that they could be circulated among the rest of the aristocracy for propagandistic purposes.

89. *summa*, "the substance."

ded by him: Pompey should go to Spain, the levies that have been held and our garrisons should be discharged; he will surrender Farther Gaul to Domitius and Nearer Gaul to Considius Nonianus (these men have been allotted them as provinces); he will come back for the consular campaign, and he no longer insists that his candidacy be conducted in absentia; he will campaign for the required period of three market days in person. We have accepted the offer,[90] but only if he removes his garrisons from the places he has occupied, so that the Senate may be assembled in Rome to discuss these terms without fear. If he does this, there is hope for peace, but not an honorable one, for the rules are imposed upon us; but anything is better than to be as we are. But if he is unwilling to stand by his own conditions, war has been prepared, but a war of the sort that he cannot hold out against, especially since he will have abandoned his own terms, assuming that we prevent him from being able to reach Rome, and we hope this can be done. For we are holding massive levies, and we think he is afraid that if he begins to go toward Rome he will lose the two Gauls, both of which he now holds in a very hostile state, except for the Transpadanes, and out of Spain he has six legions and large auxiliary forces at his back under Afranius and Petreius. It seems, if he decides to go mad, that he can be crushed—assuming that Rome remains safe. He has received a heavy blow, because the man who commanded the greatest respect among his troops, T. Labienus, has refused to be a partner in his crime. He has abandoned Caesar and is now with us, and many are said to be about to do the same.

Cicero to Atticus, 2 February 49 (*Att.* 7.17.2)

You must already know the answer that L. Caesar is taking back from Pompey, the letter from him that he is taking to Caesar; for it was written and sent in such a way that it could be displayed in public. On this matter I have preferred charges in my own mind

---

90. On 23 January (Cic. *Att.* 7.14.1).

against Pompey, who is a lucid writer, for having given to our friend Sestius such an important job and the writing of a letter that will come into everyone's possession; true to form, I have never read anything more characteristic of Sestius.[91] At any rate, it is easy to see from Pompey's letter that nothing is being denied to Caesar and that all his demands are being given to him in a heap. He would be completely insane not to accept these terms, especially since he has demanded them so shamelessly. Who in the world are you, Caesar, to say "If Pompey goes to Spain" or "If he dismisses his garrisons"? Even so, it is granted, with less honor now, to be sure, since he has violated the Republic and waged war on her, than if he had secured his right to run in absentia beforehand. Nevertheless, I am afraid that he will not be content with these concessions. For after he had given his proposals to L. Caesar, he should have been a little more peaceful until the answer was returned to him; but it is said that he is even now acting quite vigorously.

CAESAR, *DE BELLO CIVILI* 1.11–15

11 Erat iniqua condicio postulare, ut Caesar Arimino excederet atque in provinciam reverteretur, ipsum[92] et provincias et legiones alienas tenere; exercitum Caesaris velle dimitti, dilectus habere; [2] polliceri se in provinciam iturum neque ante quem diem iturus sit definire, ut, si peracto consulatu Caesaris non profectus esset, nulla tamen mendaci religione obstrictus[93] videretur. [3] Tempus[94] vero

---

91. That is, written in ugly Latin. Catullus, punning liberally on *frigiditas* as a symptom both of illness and of bad writing, claims that hearing Sestius recite his own material made him so sick he had to stay in bed in his villa in Tivoli until he could recover (Poem 44). Cicero had groused while out of Rome in 51 that Sestius' jokes were being falsely attributed to him (*Fam.* 7.32.1).

92. *ipsum* = *Pompeium*.

93. *nulla . . . mendaci religione obstrictus*, "unconfined by any scruple about lying." *Mendaci* is genitive of *mendacium*.

94. *tempus* is the direct object of *dare*, which is in turn (with *polliceri*) the subject of *adferebat*; *polliceri* also governs (*Pompeium*) *accessurum* (*esse*), an indirect statement.

colloquio non dare neque accessurum polliceri magnam pacis desperationem adferebat. *[4]* Itaque ab Arimino M. Antonium cum cohortibus V Arretium[95] mittit;[96] ipse Arimini cum duabus subsistit ibique dilectum habere instituit; Pisaurum, Fanum,[97] Anconam[98] singulis cohortibus occupat.

12 Interea certior factus Iguvium[99] Thermum[100] praetorem cohortibus V tenere, oppidum munire, omniumque esse Iguvinorum optimam erga se voluntatem, Curionem cum tribus cohortibus, quas Pisauri et Arimini habebat, mittit. *[2]* Cuius adventu cognito, diffisus municipi voluntati, Thermus cohortis ex urbe reducit et profugit.[101] Milites in itinere ab eo discedunt ac domum revertuntur. *[3]* Curio summa omnium voluntate Iguvium recipit. Quibus rebus cognitis confisus municipiorum voluntatibus[102] Caesar cohortis legionis XIII. ex praesidiis deducit Auximumque[103] proficiscitur; quod oppidum Attius[104] cohortibus introductis tenebat dilectumque toto Piceno circummissis senatoribus habebat.

---

95. A major town of northeast Etruria, commanding the direct road from Ravenna, and in turn from Ariminum to Rome. It also was strategically placed against the valleys of the Tiber and the Arnus, and commanded the northern and western entrances to Italy (Perrin).

96. Again, the chronology is Caesarian. By the time Caesar had received Pompey's reply, Antony had already marched down the coast, and Caesar was raising troops.

97. From Fanum (Fortunae), the Via Flaminia led directly to Rome. Fanum and Pisaurum were large towns in Umbria. Caesar's opponents assumed, when word was received that he had captured these cities, that he would march on Rome.

98. Ancona was a major seaport of Picenum.

99. Another strong town in the heart of Umbria, just off the Via Flaminia.

100. Q. Minucius Thermus was actually propraetor this year (Caesar's sloppy terminology is in fact standard). He had been tribune in 62 and praetor no later than 53. *Thermum* is the subject of *tenere* and *munire*.

101. A bad sign for the Pompeians, who had expected this part of Italy to stand firmly behind Pompey. This is the first sign that Pompey, and with him the Senate, have badly overestimated his position.

102. This support (*voluntas*) is now added to that of his legions.

103. Another stronghold and key site in Picenum.

104. P. Attius Varus, who appears regularly in the early part of this war.

13 Adventu Caesaris cognito decuriones[105] Auximi ad Attium Varum frequentes conveniunt; docent sui iudici rem non esse; neque se neque reliquos municipes pati posse C. Caesarem imperatorem, bene de re publica meritum, tantis rebus gestis, oppido moenibusque prohiberi: proinde habeat rationem posteritatis et periculi sui. *[2]* Quorum oratione permotus Varus praesidium quod introduxerat ex oppido educit ac profugit. *[3]* Hunc[106] ex primo ordine pauci[107] Caesaris consecuti milites consistere coegerunt. *[4]* Commisso proelio deseritur a suis Varus, non nulla pars militum domum discedit; reliqui ad Caesarem perveniunt, atque una cum eis deprensus L. Pupius, primipili centurio,[108] adducitur qui hunc eundem ordinem in exercitu Cn. Pompei antea duxerat. *[5]* Caesar milites Attianos collaudat, Pupium dimittit, Auximatibus agit gratias seque eorum facti[109] memorem fore pollicetur.

14 Quibus rebus Romam nuntiatis[110] tantus repente terror invasit ut, cum Lentulus consul ad aperiendum aerarium venisset ad pecuniamque Pompeio ex senatus consulto proferendam, protinus aperto sanctiore aerario[111] ex urbe profugeret. Caesar

---

105. *decuriones*, "town council."

106. *Hunc* = *Varum*.

107. *ex primo ordine pauci Caesaris . . . milites*, "a few of Caesar's troops from the front ranks."

108. *primipili centurio*, "his highest ranking centurion."

109. *eorum facti: facti* depends on *memorem*, *eorum* is possessive (or subjective) genitive.

110. Caesar now returns to events in the city, around 19 January. The reaction described here, as the letters from Cicero quoted below illustrate, was to the fall of Auximum, Pisaurum, Fanum, Ancona, and Arretium, not the episodes just described. The Senate's reaction to the fall of these cities may also explain its sudden show of being willing to accept Caesar's proposals and conditions, as illustrated by the two letters of Cicero quoted above.

111. *sanctiore aerario* < *sanctius aerarium*, "the inner (holier) treasury." This was a special reserve fund that was only supposed to be opened under the direst emergencies. It is not clear what Caesar means here, other than that Lentulus has panicked, since Lentulus does not seem to have robbed or misappropriated it. Perhaps Caesar found this inner treasury open when he himself later came to Rome, and someone attributed this to Lentulus.

enim adventare iam iamque et adesse eius equites¹¹² falso
nuntiabantur. [2] Hunc Marcellus collega et plerique magistratus
consecuti sunt. [3] Cn. Pompeius pridie eius diei¹¹³ ex urbe
profectus iter ad legiones habebat, quas a Caesare acceptas in Apulia
hibernorum causa disposuerat. Dilectus circa urbem intermittuntur;
[4] nihil citra Capuam tutum esse videtur. Capuae primum sese
confirmant et colligunt dilectumque colonorum qui lege Iulia¹¹⁴
Capuam deducti erant habere instituunt; gladiatoresque, quos ibi
Caesar in ludo habebat, ad forum productos Lentulus libertatis spe
confirmat atque his equos attribuit et se sequi iussit; [5] quos postea
monitus ab suis, quod ea res omnium iudicio reprehendebatur,
circum familias¹¹⁵ conventus Campaniae¹¹⁶ custodiae causa
distribuit.¹¹⁷

15 Auximo Caesar progressus omnem agrum Picenum
percurrit. Cunctae earum regionum praefecturae¹¹⁸ libentissimis
animis eum recipiunt exercitumque eius omnibus rebus iuvant. [2]
Etiam Cingulo, quod oppidum Labienus constituerat suaque
pecunia exaedificaverat, ad eum legati veniunt quaeque imperaverit
se cupidissime facturos pollicentur. Milites imperat: mittunt. [3]

---

112. *equites* here are the actual cavalry in Caesar's army, not the social class
known as the Equites.

113. *pridie eius diei* = *priore die*, a redundancy favored by Caesar (he frequently
uses *postridie eius diei*).

114. Many of Pompey's veterans from the Asian campaign had been settled in
Campania under a Julian law sponsored by Caesar as consul in 59.

115. *familias*, "households," not just slaves.

116. *conventus Campaniae*, "the Campanian Society," a league or confed-
eration of Roman citizens organized for the benefit of the group as a whole.

117. The consuls had left Teanum Sidicinum for Capua no earlier than 23
January, and a meeting of the Senate was held in Capua on the 25th. Meanwhile,
Cicero writes on the 25th that Pompey (not Lentulus) had disposed of Caesar's
gladiators quite nicely (*Att.* 7.14.3). Evidently, "Lentulus took Pompey's
instructions to Capua on the 23d and carried them out on the 24th; and . . .
Caesar's account is based on rumour, possibly arising from an earlier expression of
intention by Lentulus" (Shackleton Bailey). The rumor must have been false, but
it presents Lentulus in a suitably desperate and scurrilous light.

118. Italian towns presided over by annually appointed *praefecti* from Rome but
with rights of Roman citizenship; those towns with their own governing bodies
(*decuriones*) and chief magistrates (variously titled) were *municipia*.

Interea legio XII. Caesarem consequitur. Cum his duabus[119] Asculum Picenum proficiscitur. Id oppidum Lentulus Spinther[120] X cohortibus tenebat; qui Caesaris adventu cognito profugit ex oppido cohortisque secum abducere conatus magna parte militum deseritur. *[4]* Relictus in itinere cum paucis incidit in[121] Vibullium Rufum[122] missum a Pompeio in agrum Picenum confirmandorum hominum causa. A quo factus Vibullius certior quae res in Piceno gererentur, milites ab eo accipit, ipsum dimittit.[123] *[5]* Item ex finitimis regionibus quas potest contrahit cohortis ex dilectibus Pompeianis; in his Camerino fugientem Lucilium Hirrum[124] cum sex cohortibus, quas ibi in praesidio[125] habuerat, excipit; quibus coactis XIII efficit.[126] *[6]* Cum his ad Domitium Ahenobarbum[127] Corfinium[128] magnis itineribus[129] pervenit Caesaremque adesse cum legionibus duabus nuntiat. *[7]* Domitius per se circiter XX

---

119. Caesar eventually has with him the Eighth Legion, in addition to the Twelfth and Thirteenth Legions referred to here, which constitute his three veteran legions at Corfinium (see chapter 3).

120. P. Cornelius Lentulus Spinther had been consul in 57; he should not be confused with the Lentulus Crus who is the present consul (49).

121. *incidit in*, "he joined."

122. L. Vibullius Rufus, a loyal adherent of Pompey, of whom Cicero thought highly.

123. This seems strikingly abrupt and—as Carter notes—a reversal of the roles that would have been anticipated from the social status. But inasmuch as the language is Caesar's, not Vibullius', it is quite possible that Vibullius merely took command of the remnants of Spinther's troops so that Lentulus himself could be released from responsibility and proceed to Corfinium (where we next see him).

124. C. Lucilius Hirrus, who had been tribune in 53.

125. *in praesidio*, "as a garrison."

126. *quibus . . . efficit*, "and when he united them all, he mustered thirteen (cohorts)."

127. L. Domitius Ahenobarbus, who had been consul in 54. An inveterate enemy of Caesar, he had also opposed Pompey until Pompey split with Caesar. He was Cato's brother-in-law.

128. Corfinium was the most important city of the Paeligni and controlled a major road to Rome. During the Social War of the late 90s, Corfinium was the adopted "capital" of the rebellious allies.

129. *magnis itineribus < magnum iter*, "forced march," a military term familiar to readers of *De bello Gallico*.

cohortis Alba,[130] ex[131] Marsis et Paelignis, finitimis ab regionibus coegerat.

We are now in February, but before continuing Caesar's account of the siege at Corfinium, let us read Cicero's reactions in late January to the swift strike by Caesar down the eastern coast of Italy.

LETTERS FROM CICERO TO ATTICUS

Cicero to Atticus, about 21 January 49 (*Att.* 7.11.1, 3–4)

I ask you, what is this? What is happening? I have only darkness. "Our side has Cingulum," he says, "but we have lost Ancona; Labienus has left Caesar." Are we speaking of a Roman general or of Hannibal? O what an insane and wretched man, who has never seen even a shadow of the Good![132] And he says he is doing all these things on behalf of his honor. But where is there honor except where there is right?[133] Is it right, then, to have an army with no authority from the state, to occupy citizens' towns in order to have easier access to Rome, to attempt "cancellations of debts, recall of exiles," and any number of other crimes, "to have the greatest of the gods, Tyranny?"[134] He is welcome to his greatness.[135] . . .

But let us return to our friend. By the vagaries of fortune! What sort of plan do you think Pompey has? I refer to his abandoning the city, for I am thoroughly confused. At the time, nothing was more absurd. You are leaving the city? You would do

---

130. *Alba* is ablative, "from Alba (Fucens)," a town of the Aequi near Lake Fucinus.

131. *ex*, "consisting of."

132. A reference to Plato's Allegory of the Cave (*Rep.* 7.514A–521B), where knowledge of the Truth comes in the form of a shadow on the wall of a cave.

133. "Atque haec ait omnia facere se dignitatis causa. Ubi est autem dignitas nisi ubi honestas?"

134. From Euripides *Phoen.* 506.

135. "Sibi habeat suam fortunam." (The translation of this sentence is Shackleton Bailey's.)

the same, then, if the Gauls were coming? "The Republic," he says, "does not consist of the walls of houses." But it does consist of altars and hearths.[136] "Themistocles did it." Because a single city could not stand up to a wave of all Persia. . . . In the old days our ancestors held on to the citadel even when the rest of the city had been captured. . . . Then again, it seems from the suffering in the outlying towns and the conversations with those I meet that this plan will produce something. The lamentation of everyone here (I don't know about where you are, but you will let me know) is marvelous: that the city is without magistrates, without a Senate. In short, Pompey in flight is stirring people up wonderfully. The point is, the whole case is now different. They think now that nothing should be yielded to Caesar.

Cicero to Atticus, 22 January 49 (*Att.* 7.12.1–3)

Now, since you ask me to help you understand what Pompey is doing, I think he does not know himself; no one of us does. I saw Lentulus the consul at Formiae on the 21st; I saw Libo; I saw everything full of fear and uncertainty. Pompey travels to Larinum, because there he will find some cohorts, as well as at Luceria and Teanum and in the rest of Apulia. From there, whether he plans to make a stand anywhere or to cross the sea, is not known. If he stays, I am afraid that he will be unable to keep his army loyal; but if he leaves, I do not know where he is going or how, or what I should do. For I think that the man whose Phalarism[137] you fear

---

136. As often, Cicero invokes Greek literature for language that will capture his emotions. This conversation with Pompey is purely hypothetical. The dramatic Pompey defends himself by referring to Themistocles' decision to save Greece from the Persians by abandoning Athens and taking to the sea. Cicero counters with *exempla* from Roman history that support the efficacy of (stubbornly) holding the city. He thus illustrates the enormous emotional and symbolic value of the city of Rome in public opinion. (I have omitted a couple of sentences in this paragraph.)

137. Phalaris was a Greek tyrant, a favorite of Cicero's for the stereotype of the despot. Here he means Caesar, whom he expects to become a tyrant or dictator, with bloody consequences.

will behave most abominably in every respect, nor will either the postponement of business, nor the withdrawal of the Senate and the magistrates, nor the closing of the treasury slow him down. But these things, as you write, we shall soon know.

3

The Siege at Corfinium

When Caesar began to move south, there was great anxiety and confusion. Throughout early February of 49, Cicero writes to Atticus expressing disgust at the performance of Pompey and his supporters, and fear that Caesar has become unstoppable. He does not know Pompey's plans but fears that he will abandon Italy. Atticus had expressed the common fear that a victorious Caesar would slaughter his opponents in the manner of Sulla (Cicero says at one point to Atticus, *tu caedem non sine causa times*, *Att.* 7.22), though Cicero correctly hopes that Caesar will know this would not be in his best interests. Such must indeed have been the state of knowledge and expectation of most Romans during February.

By the end of January, Domitius Ahenobarbus, Caesar's intransigent enemy, had occupied Corfinium. He may have been marching through Samnium with the intention of joining Pompey, but he decided to hold up at Corfinium and find out what Caesar intended to do. He was very confident, unjustifiably so, since his previous military experience was at best marginal. But Domitius had land and *clientela* among the Marsi, the tribe, along with the Paeligni, occupying the area nearest Corfinium. This must have been decisive in his mind: he felt that he could best resist Caesar in the area where the local inhabitants were most loyal to him, and that they would not go over to Caesar while he himself was present. This, in effect, was similar to the mistake already made by Pompey, who must have been severely disappointed by the defection of the cities in his home area of Picenum; he, of course, had not actually been present at the crucial moment. Meanwhile, Domitius wrote to Pompey, who had gone to Apulia (on his way, as it turned out, to Brundisium), imploring him to come to Corfinium and thus trap Caesar between them.

CAESAR, *DE BELLO CIVILI*, 1.16–17

16 Recepto Firmo[1] expulsoque Lentulo, Caesar conquiri mili-

---

1. In early February.

tes qui ab eo discesserant, dilectumque institui iubet; ipse unum diem ibi rei frumentariae causa moratus Corfinium contendit. *[2]* Eo cum venisset,² cohortes V praemissae a Domitio ex oppido pontem fluminis³ interrumpebant,⁴ qui erat ab oppido milia passuum circiter III. *[3]* Ibi cum antecursoribus Caesaris proelio commisso, celeriter Domitiani a ponte repulsi se in oppidum receperunt. *[4]* Caesar, legionibus traductis, ad oppidum constitit iuxtaque murum castra posuit.

17   Re cognita Domitius ad Pompeium in Apuliam peritos regionum⁵ magno proposito praemio⁶ cum litteris mittit qui⁷ petant atque orent ut sibi subveniat: Caesarem, duobus exercitibus et locorum angustiis facile intercludi posse frumentoque prohiberi; *[2]* quod nisi fecerit, se cohortisque amplius XXX magnumque numerum senatorum atque equitum Romanorum⁸ in periculum esse venturum.⁹ *[3]* Interim suos¹⁰ cohortatus tormenta in muris

---

2. 15 February.

3. The river Aternus.

4. *interrumpebant*, "were in the process of breaking."

5. *peritos regionum*, "men who knew the territory." The adjective *peritus* takes an objective genitive.

6. *magno proposito praemio*, "with the promise of a great reward."

7. *qui* = *ut ei*, a relative clause of purpose.

8. *equitum Romanorum*, "Roman Knights," the social class, not cavalrymen.

9. The figure of thirty cohorts appears to be in conflict with Caesar's previous estimate of twenty (15.7), but in that passage he was describing the troops that Domitius had raised on his own (*per se*). Caesar here includes the thirteen that Vibullius put together from the scattered troops of Spinther, and the six cohorts from Hirrus (15.5), in addition to those of Domitius himself. Two letters from Pompey preserved by Cicero (*Att.* 8.11A and 8.12A) indicate that Pompey assessed Domitius' cohorts as twelve (he also gives the figure for Vibullius as fourteen, rather than thirteen, and that for Hirrus as five, rather than six). It is possible that Caesar's figure in 1.15.7 should have been XII instead of XX (this could easily be a copyist's error), or that his estimate in that passage is a bit high. In any case, Pompey's letters make clear that Domitius had a total of thirty-one cohorts, just over three legions. The wording here is Caesar's analysis of Domitius' thinking, giving Domitius credit for understanding his plight from the beginning. From the letters of Pompey preserved by Cicero, it is clear that Domitius began the siege with considerably more confidence.

10. *suos*, "his (own) men." The use of this possessive adjective, as well as *nostri*, in this way is quite common.

disponit certasque cuique partis[11] ad custodiam urbis attribuit; *[4]* militibus in contione agros ex suis possessionibus pollicetur, XL in singulos iugera[12] et pro rata parte centurionibus evocatisque.[13]

LETTERS FROM POMPEY

Only rarely do we have authentic examples of Pompey's Latin, for he did not leave his own account of the war. Cicero had a high opinion of his style. Although the letters that follow do not throw any particular light on Caesar, as political documents from Pompey himself they are priceless. In these letters, Pompey expresses his fears about Domitius' situation in Corfinium and confirms finally that he will go to Brundisium. He is quite open about this to the consuls Marcellus and Lentulus. In his letters to Domitius, the first of which was written a bit before the one to Marcellus and Lentulus, he is rather vague. Domitius' situation is getting worse by the day.

Pompey to Gaius Marcellus and Lucius Lentulus, mid-February 49 (Cic. *Att*. 8.12A)

1 Ego, quod existimabam dispersos nos neque rei publicae utilis[14] neque nobis praesidio[15] esse posse, idcirco ad L. Domitium litteras misi, primum ut ipse cum omni copia ad nos veniret; si de se dubitaret, ut cohortis XVIIII quae ex Piceno ad me iter habebant ad nos mitteret. Quod veritus sum factum est:[16] ut Domitius implicaretur, ut neque ipse satis firmus esset ad castra facienda,[17]

---

11. *certas cuique partis*, "fixed positions for everyone."

12. *XL in singulos iugera*, "forty acres per man."

13. Centurions and veterans were paid at a rate double that of ordinary soldiers, so Domitius evidently promised them proportionately (*pro rata parte*) more land.

14. *utilis*, accusative plural, with *nos*.

15. *nobis praesidio*, "a source of protection for ourselves."

16. *factum est*, "has happened," present perfect in sense.

17. *ad castra facienda*, "for taking the field" (Shackleton Bailey), lit., "for pitching camp."

quod meas[18] XVIIII et suas XII cohortis in tribus oppidis distributas haberet[19] (nam partim Albae, partim Sulmone collocavit), neque se, si vellet, expedire posset.

2 Nunc scitote me esse in summa sollicitudine. Nam et tot et talis viros periculo obsidionis liberare cupio neque subsidio[20] ire possum, quod his duabus legionibus non puto esse committendum[21] ut illuc ducantur;[22] ex quibus tamen non amplius XIIII cohortis contrahere potui, quod Brundisium praesidium misi neque Canusium sine praesidio, dum abessem, putavi esse dimittendum. . . .

4 Quam ob rem placitum est mihi (atque ita video censeri[23] M. Marcello et ceteris nostri ordinis qui hic[24] sunt) ut Brundisium ducerem hanc copiam quam mecum habeo. Vos hortor ut quodcumque militum contrahere poteritis contrahatis et eodem Brundisium veniatis quam primum. Arma[25] quae ad me missuri eratis, iis censeo[26] armetis milites quos vobiscum habetis. Quae arma superabunt, ea si Brundisium iumentis deportaritis[27] vehe-

---

18. *meas*: Pompey believes that he has a right to these troops, since they come from Picenum, even though Domitius now commands them. He consistently distinguishes between these nineteen and Domitius' twelve.

19. *distributas haberet*, "he has them deployed." The diction with *habere* + participle is common enough, and in later Romance languages gives rise to the use of *habere* as an auxiliary verb.

20. *subsidio*, dative of purpose, "to reinforce them."

21. *his duabus legionibus . . . esse committendum*: *legionibus* is dative after *committere*, which is here used impersonally: "that these two legions should be trusted."

22. *ut ducantur*, "to be taken."

23. *ita video censeri*, "I observe that this has been agreed to (by)." (The reading *atque ita* is suggested by Shackleton Bailey.)

24. *hic*, i.e., in Luceria.

25. *arma* (accusative) is attracted to the case of *quae*, though it strictly should be parallel to *iis* (ablative of means) in the next clause.

26. *censeo*, "I suggest (that)," followed by the subjunctive *armetis* (without *ut*).

27. *Quae arma superabunt, ea si . . . deportaritis*, "If you bring the weapons that are left." The relative clause anticipates the main clause, and *arma*, the antecedent for *quae*, is attracted into the relative clause. *deportaritis* = *deportaveritis* (future perfect).

menter rei publicae profueritis. De hac re velim nostros[28] certiores
faciatis. Ego ad P. Lupum et C. Coponium praetores nisi ut se
vobis coniungerent et militum quod[29] haberent ad vos deducerent.

Pompey to Lucius Domitius,
11 February 49 (Cic. *Att.* 8.12B)

1 Valde miror te ad me nihil scribere et potius ab aliis quam
a te de re publica me certiorem fieri. Nos disiecta manu[30] pares
adversariis esse non possumus; contractis nostris copiis spero nos et
rei publicae et communi saluti prodesse posse. Quam ob rem cum
constituisses[31] (ut Vibullius mihi scripserat) a.d. V Id. Febr.[32]
Corfinio proficisci cum exercitu et ad me venire, miror quid causae
fuerit qua re[33] consilium mutaris. Nam illa causa, quam mihi
Vibullius scribit, levis est: te propterea moratum esse quod audieris
Caesarem Firmo progressum in Castrum Truentinum venisse.
Quanto enim magis appropinquare adversarius coepit, eo tibi
celerius agendum erat[34] ut te mecum coniungeres prius quam
Caesar aut tuum iter impedire aut me abs te excludere posset.

2 Quam ob rem etiam te rogo et hortor, id quod non destiti
superioribus litteris a te petere, ut primo quoque die[35] Luceriam
ad me venires, ante quam copiae, quas instituit Caesar contrahere,
in unum locum coactae, vos a nobis distrahant. Sed si erunt qui te
impediant ut villas suas servent, aequum est me a te impetrare ut
cohortis quae ex Piceno et Camerino venerunt, quae fortunas suas

---

28. *nostros*, "our supporters."
29. *militum quod*, "as many soldiers as." *Quod* is direct object of *deducerent*.
30. *disiecta manu*, "with our forces separated."
31. *cum constituisses*, "although you had decided."
32. 9 February.
33. *quid causae fuerit qua re*, "why."
34. *eo tibi celerius agendum erat*, "the quicker you should have acted."
35. *primo quoque die* < *primus quisque dies*, all ablative, "on the first possible day."

reliquerunt, ad me missum facias.[36]

In a letter not quoted here (Cic. *Att.* 8.12C), Pompey urges Domitius to make strenuous efforts to join him in Brundisium and not allow himself to be trapped by Caesar; he expresses great lack of confidence in the troops he now has and indicates that he cannot come to Domitius' aid for that reason. But when Domitius received Pompey's next letter, which follows here, he must have known that his situation was hopeless.

Pompey to Lucius Domitius, 17 February 49 (Cic. *Att.* 8.12D)

1 Litterae mihi a te redditae sunt a.d. XIII Kal. Mart.,[37] in quibus scribis Caesarem apud Corfinium castra posuisse. Quod putavi et praemonui fit, ut nec in praesentia committere tecum proelium velit et, omnibus copiis conductis, te implicet ne ad me iter tibi expeditum sit,[38] atque istas copias coniungere optimorum civium possis[39] cum his legionibus de quarum voluntate dubitamus. Quo[40] etiam magis tuis litteris sum commotus: neque enim eorum militum, quos mecum habeo, voluntate[41] satis confido ut de omnibus fortunis rei publicae dimicem, neque etiam qui ex dilectibus conscripti sunt consulibus[42] convenerunt.

2 Qua re da operam, si ulla ratione etiam nunc efficere potes,

---

36. *ad me missum facias*, "that you make sure they are sent to me." Pompey must have believed that Domitius would choose the former option, for to send nineteen of his thirty-one cohorts to Pompey would have been suicidal. But as the previous letter shows, Pompey has already decided to go to Brundisium, plans that he chooses not to share with Domitius until the next letter (not quoted), a reply to Domitius' declaration that he will hold out in Corfinium.

37. 17 February.

38. *ne ad me iter tibi expeditum sit*, "so that you have no unobstructed route to me."

39. Continue *ne* with *possis*, "and you are unable."

40. *Quo*, "Therefore."

41. *voluntate*: the ablative with *confido* is unusual.

42. *consulibus* is dative; construe with *conscripti sunt*.

ut te explices, hoc[43] quam primum venias, ante quam omnes copiae adversarium[44] conveniant. Neque enim celeriter ex dilectibus hoc homines convenire possunt et, si convenient, quantum iis committendum sit,[45] qui inter se ne noti quidem sunt contra veteranas legiones, non te praeterit.

CAESAR, *DE BELLO CIVILI* 1.18-23

18 Interim Caesari nuntiatur Sulmonensis,[46] quod oppidum a Corfinio VII milium intervallo[47] abest, cupere ea facere quae vellet, sed a Q. Lucretio senatore et Attio Paeligno prohiberi, qui id oppidum VII cohortium praesidio tenebant. *[2]* Mittit eo M. Antonium cum legionis XIII. cohortibus V. Sulmonenses simul atque signa nostra viderunt, portas aperuerunt universique, et oppidani et milites, obviam gratulantes Antonio exierunt.[48] *[3]* Lucretius et Attius de muro se deiecerunt.[49] Attius, ad Antonium deductus, petit ut ad Caesarem mitteretur. Antonius cum cohortibus et Attio, eodem die quo profectus erat, revertitur. *[4]* Caesar eas cohortis cum exercitu suo coniunxit Attiumque incolumem dimisit.

Caesar primis diebus castra magnis operibus munire et ex

---

43. *hoc* = *huc* (also in the next sentence), a usage not admitted by Cicero himself but found in the diction of some of his correspondents (see Shackleton Bailey, *Letters to Atticus* 4:352).

44. *adversarium* = *adversariorum*; this form of the genitive is often labeled archaic.

45. *quantum iis committendum sit*, "how much those men should be trusted." This entire clause is the subject of *praeterit*.

46. *Sulmonensis*, accusative, subject of *cupere* in indirect statement, "the people of Sulmo." Sulmo was an important Paelignian town to the southeast of Corfinium.

47. *intervallo* is ablative of degree of difference with *abest*; the genitive *milium* then qualifies *intervallo*. The natural English is, "is seven miles away."

48. *obviam . . . exierunt*, "went out to meet" + dative.

49. That is, they took desperate measures to escape—not to commit suicide, for Attius appears again immediately. Attius and Lucretius could not trust their soldiers to escort them out of the city. Perhaps the phrase means only "came down from (their position on) the walls."

finitimis municipiis frumentum comportare reliquasque copias exspectare instituit. *[5]* Eo triduo legio VIII. ad eum venit cohortesque ex novis Galliae dilectibus XXII equitesque ab rege Norico[50] circiter CCC.[51] Quorum adventu altera castra ad alteram oppidi partem ponit; his castris Curionem praefecit.[52] *[6]* Reliquis diebus oppidum vallo castellisque[53] circumvenire instituit. Cuius operis maxima parte effecta eodem fere tempore missi[54] ad Pompeium revertuntur.

19 Litteris perlectis Domitius dissimulans in consilio pronuntiat Pompeium celeriter subsidio venturum hortaturque eos ne animo deficiant, quaeque[55] usui ad defendendum oppidum sint parent. *[2]* Ipse arcano cum paucis familiaribus suis colloquitur consiliumque fugae capere constituit. *[3]* Cum[56] vultus Domiti cum oratione non consentiret atque omnia trepidantius timidiusque ageret quam superioribus diebus consuesset,[57] multumque[58] cum suis consiliandi causa secreto praeter consuetudinem colloqueretur, concilia conventusque hominum fugeret, res diutius tegi dis-

---

50. *rege Norico*, "the king of Noricum." Noricum was in southern Germany and Austria.

51. The Eighth Legion now joins the Twelfth and the Thirteenth, and together with these twenty-two cohorts from Cisalpine Gaul, Caesar now has a fighting force of over five legions. He had left Ravenna a little more than a month before with only the Thirteenth Legion.

52. Indicative both of the rapid rise of Curio in Caesar's favor and of the paucity of seasoned and reliable commanders among his supporters. On Curio, see chapter 1, n. 29.

53. *vallo castellisque*, "with a rampart and fortified guard posts." The *vallum* was made of the earth dug from the moat in front of it and was strengthened at points by small forts. Caesar's Gallic troops had had plenty of practice with this fortification.

54. *missi*, "the men who had been sent (by Domitius)."

55. *quaeque . . . parent = et ut ea parent quae.*

56. *Cum* governs *consentiret, ageret, colloqueretur,* and *fugeret,* all of which establish the cause for *res* ("the true situation," nominative) . . . *non potuit.*

57. *consuesset = consueverat,* attracted to the subjunctive of the surrounding verbs.

58. *multum* is adverbial; there is a contrast established between the frequency of his secret meetings with his advisers and the increasing rarity of his appearances in public.

simularique non potuit. *[4]* Pompeius enim rescripserat sese rem in summum periculum deducturum non esse, neque suo consilio aut voluntate Domitium se in oppidum Corfinium contulisse: proinde, siqua fuisset facultas, ad se cum omnibus copiis veniret. *[5]* Id[59] ne fieri posset, obsidione atque oppidi circummunitione fiebat.

20 Divulgato Domiti consilio milites qui erant Corfini primo vesperi secessionem faciunt atque ita inter se per tribunum militum centurionesque atque honestissimos sui generis[60] colloquuntur: *[2]* obsideri se a Caesare; opem munitionesque prope esse perfectas; ducem suum Domitium, cuius[61] spe atque fiducia permanserint, proiectis omnibus fugae consilium capere; debere se suae salutis rationem habere. *[3]* Ab his primo[62] Marsi dissentire incipiunt eamque oppidi partem quae munitissima videretur occupant; tantaque inter eos dissensio exsistit ut manum conserere[63] atque armis dimicare conentur; *[4]* post paulo tamen, internuntiis ultro citroque missis, quae[64] ignorabant de L. Domiti fuga cognoscunt. *[5]* Itaque omnes uno consilio Domitium productum in publicum circumsistunt et custodiunt, legatosque ex suo numero ad Caesarem mittunt: sese paratos esse portas aperire quaeque imperaverit facere, et L. Domitium vivum in eius potestatem tradere.

21 Quibus rebus cognitis Caesar, etsi magni interesse[65] arbitrabatur quam primum oppido potiri cohortisque ad se in castra

---

59. *Id . . . fiebat* is not a report of Pompey's statements but an editorial comment by Caesar. The clause *Id . . . posset* is governed by *ne* because it is dependent on the notion of prevention (*obsidione, circummunitione*) found in the next clause; otherwise, the standard construction would have been a result clause with *ut non*. The whole clause is the subject of *fiebat*: "That this could not be done came about because of . . ."

60. *sui generis*, "of their own kind," that is, common soldiers.

61. *cuius*, objective genitive: they had remained in Corfinium because of their hope and trust *in him*. The relative clause is difficult to render smoothly in English.

62. *primo*, "at first," because they were loyal to Domitius and did not know of or believe in his treachery. This situation changes as the sentence progresses.

63. *manum conserere*, "to engage (in battle)," a military idiom: it implies close quarters.

64. *quae = ea quae*.

65. *magni interesse*, "(that) it was of great importance."

traducere, ne[66] qua aut largitionibus aut animi confirmatione aut
falsis nuntiis commutatio fieret voluntatis, *[2]* quod[67] saepe in bello
parvis momentis magni casus intercederent, tamen[68] veritus ne
militum introitu et nocturni temporis licentia oppidum
diriperetur,[69] eos qui venerant[70] collaudat atque in oppidum
dimittit, portas murosque asservari iubet. *[3]* Ipse in eis operibus[71]
quae facere instituerat milites disponit, non certis spatiis intermissis,
ut erat superiorum dierum consuetudo, sed perpetuis vigiliis
stationibusque,[72] ut contingant inter se atque omnem munitionem
expleant; *[4]* tribunos militum et praefectos circummittit atque
hortatur non solum ab eruptionibus caveant[73] sed etiam
singulorum hominum occultos exitus asservent. *[5]* Neque vero tam
remisso ac languido animo quisquam omnium fuit qui[74] ea nocte
conquieverit. *[6]* Tanta erat summae rerum exspectatio[75] ut alius in
aliam partem mente atque animo traheretur: quid[76] ipsis
Corfiniensibus, quid Domitio, quid Lentulo, quid reliquis
accideret, qui quosque eventus exciperent.[77]

   22 Quarta vigilia[78] circiter Lentulus Spinther de muro cum

---

66. *ne*: the purpose clauses explain why Caesar thought it was important *quam
primum . . . potiri . . . (et) traducere.*

67. *quod*, "because."

68. *tamen*, "even so," answering *etsi* above. Caesar knew that speed in taking
over Corfinium was important, but other concerns intervened.

69. *veritus ne . . . oppidum diriperetur*, "fearing that the town would be
sacked." As we shall see, Caesar had other plans for Corfinium.

70. *eos qui venerant*: these were the delegation from Domitius' mutinous
soldiers.

71. *in eis operibus*, "on the siege works."

72. *perpetuis vigiliis stationibusque*, "in a continuous line of watches and guard
posts."

73. *eruptionibus caveant*, "to watch for (attempts to) break out." *cavere* +
ablative is as common as *cavere* + accusative.

74. *qui = ut*: the relative clause shows both characteristic and result (after *tam*).

75. *summae rerum exspectatio*, "the anticipation of the final outcome."

76. *quid . . . accideret, qui . . . exciperent*: the indirect questions reflect the
direction of everyone's thoughts from the previous clause.

77. *qui quosque eventus exciperent*, "what consequences would greet each."

78. The night was divided into four watches (*vigiliae*) from sundown to sunrise.

vigiliis custodibusque nostris colloquitur: velle, si sibi fiat potestas, Caesarem convenire. *[2]* Facta potestate ex oppido mittitur, neque ab eo prius[79] Domitiani milites discedunt quam in conspectum Caesaris deducatur. *[3]* Cum eo[80] de salute sua orat atque obsecrat ut sibi parcat veteremque amicitiam commemorat, Caesarisque in se beneficia exponit,[81] quae erant maxima: *[4]* quod per eum in collegium pontificum[82] venerat, quod provinciam Hispaniam ex praetura[83] habuerat, quod in petitione consulatus[84] erat sublevatus. *[5]* Cuius orationem Caesar interpellat: se non malefici causa ex provincia egressum sed uti se a contumeliis inimicorum defenderet, ut tribunos plebis in ea re[85] ex civitate expulsos in suam dignitatem restitueret, ut se et populum Romanum[86] factione[87] paucorum oppressum in libertatem vindicaret.[88] *[6]*

---

79. *prius*: take together with *quam* in the next clause: the soldiers (who were guarding him as he went out) did not leave Domitius *until* he was in Caesar's sight.

80. *eo* = *Caesare*.

81. A remarkable example of the functioning of Roman *amicitia*: in order to persuade Caesar to be merciful, Spinther reminds him of favors Caesar has done for Spinther, not the other way around.

82. The Pontifical College was the most important of the Roman priestly colleges, and a position there had political implications. Caesar had become pontifex maximus in 63 and was therefore instrumental in confirming other appointments to that college.

83. Spinther had been praetor urbanus in 60 and became governor of Nearer Spain in 59, the year of Caesar's consulship.

84. *in petitione consulatus*, "in his campaign for the consulship" during 58 for the consulship of 57.

85. *in ea re*, "as a result of that process."

86. *se et populum Romanum*: this combination occurs regularly in Caesar's account of the Gallic War and illustrates the degree to which any general, and Caesar in particular, could associate his own will and status with that of the Roman People. "For Caesar there is no discrepancy, certainly no antagonism, between his self-respect and the public interest" (Raditsa, 451). Ironically or not, Cicero imitates this usage in a letter of 20 March to Caesar (*tibi et rei publicae*, *Att.* 9.11A.2).

87. *factione*, "by the power" (not "faction").

88. *in libertatem vindicare*, "reassert the freedom of," lit., "to claim for freedom." This is the formal wording for freeing a slave, especially (in theory) one who had been or was actually a free person.

Cuius oratione confirmatus Lentulus ut in oppidum reverti liceat petit: quod de sua salute impetraverit[89] fore etiam reliquis ad suam[90] spem solacio; adeo esse perterritos non nullos ut suae vitae durius consulere[91] cogantur. Facta potestate discedit.

23 Caesar, ubi luxit, omnis senatores senatorumque liberos, tribunos militum equitesque Romanos ad se produci iubet. [2] Erant quinque senatorii ordinis: L. Domitius, P. Lentulus Spinther, L. Caecilius Rufus, Sex. Quintilius Varus quaestor, L. Rubrius; praeterea filius Domiti aliique complures adulescentes et magnus numerus equitum Romanorum et decurionum,[92] quos ex municipiis Domitius evocaverat. [3] Hos omnis productos a contumeliis militum conviciisque prohibet;[93] pauca apud eos loquitur, quod[94] sibi a parte eorum gratia relata non sit pro[95] suis in eos maximis beneficiis; dimittit omnis incolumis.[96] [4] HS LX,[97]

---

89. *quod . . . impetraverit*, "his successful plea." The whole clause, considered neuter, is the subject of *fore* (= *futurum esse*). That clause, in turn, employs a double dative (*reliquis . . . solacio*, "a source of comfort for the others").

90. *suam*, "their."

91. *durius consulere*, lit., "to make rather severe plans for" + dative; this is a euphemistic phrase for "destroy."

92. *decurionum*, "nobles from surrounding towns," i.e., important Italians who did not live in Rome. *Decuriones* is frequently used for members of municipal town councils.

93. *prohibet*, "he protected."

94. *quod*, "to the effect that."

95. *pro*, "in proportion to."

96. One of history's greatest diplomatic coups. Caesar, who has taken Corfinium without the loss of a single life, here exercises abnormal restraint against his bitterest enemies, whom he chides in traditional terms (*gratia pro beneficiis*) but constrains neither physically (most of them went elsewhere to continue fighting against him) nor even morally (by requiring an oath not to serve against him). Thus he refutes the claims that he would become another Sulla, and much of the resistance to him now collapses.

97. *HS LX*, "6 million sesterces." "HS" is the standard abbreviation for sesterces (here = *sestertiorum*). The sestertius, though the standard unit of accounting, was worth only one-fourth of a denarius, which was the silver coin in common usage. Prices and wages so greatly exceeded the small value of the sestertius that significant sums were abbreviated: hence, LX (i.e., 60) stood for 60 (× 100) × 1,000, or *sexagies* (*centena milia*), or 6 million. Because of fluctuations in currency and fundamental differences in price structures, monetary equivalencies

quod[98] advexerat Domitius atque in publico deposuerat, allatum ad se ab IIIIviris[99] Corfiniensibus Domitio reddit, ne continentior in vita hominum quam in pecunia fuisse videatur, etsi eam pecuniam publicam esse constabat[100] datamque a Pompeio in stipendium. *[5]* Milites Domitianos sacramentum[101] apud se dicere iubet atque eo die castra movet[102] iustumque iter[103] conficit VII omnino dies ad Corfinium commoratus,[104] et per finis Marrucinorum, Frentanorum, Larinatium in Apuliam pervenit.

But Pompey has already proceeded to Brundisium, enabled to march there by the delay that Domitius caused Caesar to endure at Corfinium. Cicero makes clear that Pompey had started from Luceria for Brundisium before the fate of Corfinium was known; it is apparent that Pompey had decided to sacrifice those at Corfinium so that he could reach the port without having to confront Caesar. Militarily, this was of course the most prudent course, but Cicero and other supporters of Pompey were altogether disgusted by his action.

LETTERS FROM JULIUS CAESAR

Two letters from Caesar (quoted here in English), one to his generals Oppius and Cornelius and another to Cicero himself are preserved in

---

between ancient Rome and modern America are notoriously inaccurate. A talent was considered a very large amount of money and was reckoned at HS 2,400, or 600 denarii. An indication of the size of the figure of HS 6 million (2,500 talents) in the text may be inferred from the fact that Caesar had introduced a standard pay for ordinary soldiers of HS 900 per year during the Gallic campaign: HS 6 million was therefore enough to pay a whole legion (6,000 troops) for a year.

98. *quod*, "a sum which."

99. *IIIIviris*, "the Commission of Four," the title of the magistrates in Corfinium.

100. *constabat*, "it was generally agreed," that is, it was not just Caesar's opinion.

101. *sacramentum*, "oath (of loyalty)."

102. *castra movet*, "broke camp," standard military terminology.

103. *iustum iter*, "an ordinary day's march," about twenty miles, as opposed to a *magnum iter*, which is considered about twice that distance.

104. From 15 February to 21 February.

Cicero's correspondence. They illustrate the satisfaction felt by Caesar both with the outcome at Corfinium and with his policy of *clementia*.

Caesar to Oppius and Cornelius, early March 49 (*Att.* 9.7C.1)

By Hercules, I am heartened by your comment in your letter on how thoroughly you approve of the actions that were taken at Corfinium. I shall use your advice gladly, and all the more so because I had decided on my own account to present myself as lenient as possible and to take pains to reconcile Pompey. Let us try in this way to regain, if we can, the good will of all and to have a lasting victory, since the rest have not been able to escape hatred by cruelty or to hold their victory for any length of time, except for L. Sulla, whom I do not intend to imitate. Let this be a new method for conquest, to protect ourselves with compassion and generosity.[105] As to how that can be done, several ideas come to mind and many devices can be found. I ask you both to begin thinking about these things.

Caesar to Cicero, a little before 26 March 49 (*Att.* 9.16.2–3)

Your conjecture about me is right—for I am well known to you—that nothing is more alien to me than cruelty.[106] And not only am I getting great good will from the deed itself, but I am exultant with the joy that comes from your approval. Nor is it of much interest to me that those whom I have released are said to have gone off to renew their war against me. For nothing pleases

---

105. "Haec nova sit ratio vincendi, ut misericordia et liberalitate nos muniamus."

106. Cicero has just mentioned that he had written to praise Caesar for *eius clementiam Corfiniensem illam* (*Att.* 9.16.1).

me better than that I should be true to my nature and they to theirs.[107]

If only you could be at hand for me in the city so that I could, as has become my habit, make use of your counsels and resources in all things.

---

107. "Nihil enim malo quam et me mei similem esse et illos sui." The translation is Shackleton Bailey's. This extraordinary sentence illustrates clearly Caesar's sense of his individuality and special character.

4

Departure of Pompey from Italy

Caesar's victory and *clementia* at Corfinium have for the time being turned the tide of the conflict. The confidence of many nobles was severely shaken, and the opposition to Caesar now seems to lack direction. Pompey, under no illusions about his newly recruited soldiers, realizes that Caesar cannot be met in Italy because Caesar has with him experienced troops from his Gallic campaigns; but this politically unpopular analysis could not be widely disseminated. Pompey therefore keeps everyone uncertain of his plans, while actively preparing to leave Italy. Caesar goes on to illustrate the low quality of the legions, and more particularly of the generals, that oppose him by telling of the desertions described below. Pursuing Pompey to Brundisium, Caesar continues to work for a peaceful settlement.

CAESAR, *DE BELLO CIVILI* 1.24–26

24 Pompeius his rebus cognitis quae erant ad Corfinium gestae Luceria proficiscitur Canusium[1] atque inde Brundisium. *[2]* Copias undique omnis ex novis dilectibus ad se cogi iubet; servos, pastores armat[2] atque eis equos attribuit; ex his circiter CCC equites conficit. *[3]* L. Manlius praetor Alba cum cohortibus sex profugit,

---

1. On 17 February. Corfinium, as we have seen, did not actually fall until the 21st.

2. It seems highly improbable that this statement should be taken at face value, though Caesar is not likely to have made a claim that had no possible basis in events. Perhaps Pompey enlisted some gladiators or some others of sufficiently low standing or scurrilous character that a Roman noble would not object to calling them *servi* (see chapter 1, n. 125, on *BC* 1.14.5). "Arming the slaves" is standard invective against a violent rival. The *pastores* may simply be local inhabitants drafted into Pompey's levy.

Rutilius Lupus praetor Tarracina cum tribus; quae procul
equitatum Caesaris conspicatae, cui praeerat Vibius Curius, relicto
praetore signa ad Curium transferunt atque ad eum transeunt. *[4]*
Item reliquis itineribus non nullae cohortes in agmen Caesaris, aliae
in equites incidunt. Reducitur ad eum deprensus ex itinere N.
Magius Cremona, praefectus fabrum Cn. Pompei.³ *[5]* Quem Caesar
ad eum⁴ remittit cum mandatis: quoniam ad id tempus facultas
colloquendi non fuerit atque ipse Brundisium sit venturus, interesse
rei publicae et communis salutis se cum Pompeio colloqui; neque
vero idem profici⁵ longo itineris spatio, cum per alios condiciones
ferantur, ac si⁶ coram de omnibus condicionibus disceptetur.⁷

25 His datis mandatis Brundisium cum legionibus VI
pervenit,⁸ veteranis III et reliquis, quas ex novo dilectu confecerat
atque in itinere compleverat; Domitianas enim cohortis protinus a
Corfinio in Siciliam miserat. *[2]* Repperit consules Dyrrachium
profectos cum magna parte exercitus, Pompeium remanere Brundisi
cum cohortibus XX; *[3]* neque certum inveniri poterat, obtinendine
Brundisi causa⁹ ibi remansisset, quo¹⁰ facilius omne Hadriaticum
mare ex ultimis Italiae partibus regionibusque Graeciae in potestate
haberet¹¹ atque ex utraque parte¹² bellum administrare posset, an
inopia navium ibi restitisset; *[4]* veritusque ne ille Italiam

---

3. *deprensus ex itinere N. Magius Cremona, praefectus fabrum Cn. Pompei,*
"Pompey's chief of engineers, Numerius Magius of Cremona, who was captured
on the march." *Cremona* is ablative of place from which.

4. *eum = Pompeium.*

5. *neque vero idem profici,* (and he said that) "the same advantage would not
arise."

6. *ac si,* "as if," answering *idem* (see previous note).

7. *disceptetur,* "they should negotiate." *Disceptetur* is an impersonal passive,
with Pompey and Caesar implied as agents.

8. 9 March.

9. *obtinendi Brundisi causa,* "to hold Brundisium." The enclitic *-ne* introduces
the first of two indirect questions (the second comes below, introduced by *an*) and
is equivalent to *utrum,* "whether."

10. *quo = ut* (purpose), the usual construction in association with a
comparative word (here *facilius*).

11. *in potestate haberet,* "he might keep under his control."

12. *ex utraque parte,* "from both sides" (of the Adriatic).

dimittendam non existimaret,[13] exitus administrationesque[14] Brundisini portus impedire instituit. *[5]* Quorum operum haec erat ratio: qua fauces erant angustissimae portus, moles atque aggerem[15] ab utraque parte litoris iaciebat, quod his locis erat vadosum mare. *[6]* Longius progressus, cum agger altiore aqua contineri non posset,[16] ratis duplices quoquo versus pedum XXX[17] e regione[18] molis collocabat. *[7]* Has quaternis ancoris ex IIII angulis destinabat, ne fluctibus moverentur. *[8]* His perfectis collocatisque alias deinceps pari magnitudine ratis iungebat. *[9]* Has terra atque aggere integebat, ne aditus atque incursus ad defendendum impediretur; a fronte atque ab utroque latere cratibus ac pluteis protegebat;[19] *[10]* in quarta quaque earum[20] turris[21] binorum tabulatorum excitabat, quo[22] commodius ab impetu navium incendiisque defenderet.

26 Contra haec Pompeius navis magnas onerarias, quas in portu Brundisino deprenderat, adornabat. Ibi turris cum ternis tabulatis erigebat easque multis tormentis et omni genere telorum completas ad opera Caesaris appellebat,[23] ut ratis perrumperet atque opera disturbaret. Sic cotidie utrimque eminus fundis, sagittis

---

13. *ne ille Italiam dimittendam non existimaret*: *ne* introduces the clause of fearing, which is then negated by *non* ("fearing that . . . not"). The standard diction for a negative fear would have been *ut* instead of *ne . . . non*. *Italiam dimittendam* (*esse*) ("that Italy ought to be abandoned") is indirect statement depending on *existimaret*, the subject of which is Pompey (*ille*).

14. *administrationes*, "normal operations."

15. *moles atque aggerem*, i.e., a dam: the base (*moles*) was made up of large rocks and the superstructure of a mixture of earth, wood, and stone (*agger*).

16. *altiore aqua contineri non posset*, "could not be held together because of the increasing deepness of the water."

17. *quoquo versus pedum XXX*, "thirty feet in every direction," i.e., square.

18. *e regione*, "in a line with." The rafts thus became an extension of the dam (Perrin).

19. *cratibus ac pluteis protegebat*, "he covered (the rafts) with wicker and sheds."

20. *in quarta quaque earum*, "on every fourth one of them."

21. *turris* is accusative plural.

22. *quo = ut*, as in n. 10, above.

23. *appellebat* < *appellere* (not *appellare*).

reliquisque telis pugnabatur. *[2]* Atque haec Caesar ita administrabat, ut condiciones pacis dimittendas²⁴ non existimaret; ac tametsi magnopere admirabatur Magium, quem ad Pompeium cum mandatis miserat, ad se non remitti,²⁵ atque ea res saepe temptata, etsi impetus eius consiliaque tardabat, tamen omnibus rebus in eo perseverandum putabat. *[3]* Itaque Caninium Rebilum legatum, familiarem necessariumque Scriboni Libonis,²⁶ mittit ad eum²⁷ colloqui causa; mandat ut Libonem de concilianda pace hortetur; in primis ut ipse²⁸ cum Pompeio colloqueretur postulat; *[4]* magnopere sese confidere demonstrat, si eius rei sit potestas facta, fore ut aequis condicionibus ab armis discedatur;²⁹ cuius rei magnam partem laudis atque existimationis ad Libonem

---

24. *condiciones pacis dimittendas*, "negotiations for peace should be abandoned."

25. This appears to be untrue: a letter from Caesar to Cicero (*Att.* 9.13A) indicates that Magius had been sent by Pompey and that Caesar sent a reply. It is not absolutely clear, on the other hand, that Magius was sent as soon as Caesar arrived. Further, Caesar's infinitive is present (*remitti*), not perfect; he may mean that Magius was not being (repeatedly) sent back and forth, despite his own continual efforts at negotiation. In any case, Pompey's reluctance to negotiate satisfactorily has been a constant theme, and Caesar here exploits Pompey's dilatoriness to explain his own inability to capture him in Brundisium. According to his presentation, he slowed up his efforts to give Pompey a chance to negotiate, and he was unsure of Pompey's intentions. But since Pompey would leave Brundisium only eight days after Caesar's arrival (Cic. *Att.* 9.15A, quoted below), his preparations for departure must have begun before Caesar had even arrived.

26. L. Scribonius Libo was closely connected with Pompey, to whose son Sextus Pompeius Libo's daughter was married, and he was the brother of the Scribonia who, in a brief political match, became Octavian's wife and mother of his only child, Julia. Octavian divorced her soon after 40 to marry Livia. C. Caninius Rebilus was a legate for Caesar in Gaul in the 50s and later was to go to Africa with Curio. Unlike Curio, he survived that experience and fought with Caesar there in 45, a year in which he became consul for a single day by Caesar's appointment when the consul Fabius died suddenly on 31 December.

27. *eum = Libonem.*

28. *ipse = Caesar.*

29. *fore ut . . . discedatur*: the future passive infinitive was commonly avoided by this construction: the impersonal infinitive *fore* supplies the future tense and the indirect statement, and the following *ut* clause (with the subjunctive) expresses the actual action of the verb. Here the verb *discedatur* is also impersonal, "(that) they would give up their arms."

perventuram,[30] si illo auctore atque agente ab armis sit discessum. [5] Libo a colloquio Canini digressus ad Pompeium proficiscitur. Paulo post renuntiat, quod consules absint,[31] sine illis non posse agi de compositione. [6] Ita saepius rem frustra temptatam Caesar aliquando dimittendam sibi iudicat et de bello agendum.

ATTICUS AND CICERO ON CAESAR'S PROSPECTS

Cicero exchanged a stream of letters, especially with his friend Atticus, as he awaited news of the outcome at Brundisium and sought advice on what he should do himself. We have already cited one of these above, in the Introduction, from Balbus and Oppius. In the letter quoted here, Cicero expresses disgust at Caesar's new popularity, tempered by a too optimistic hope for peace if Caesar and Pompey can confer.

Cicero to Atticus, 1 March 49 (*Att.* 8.13)

Let the handwriting of my clerk be a sign for you of my ophthalmia as well as a cause for my brevity; even if at this moment there is nothing to write. All my anticipation is on news from Brundisium. If Caesar has found our Gnaeus there, I have a wavering hope for peace, but if he has already crossed over, only the fear of ruinous war.

But do you see what man the Republic has fallen to, how sharp, how vigilant, how ready? By Hercules, if he kills no one and takes nothing away from anyone, he will be beloved by those who had feared him the most. The local townspeople talk to me a lot, so do the country dwellers; they care for nothing beyond their fields, their little estates, their bits of cash. And look how the tide has turned: they fear the man whom they once trusted, they love him whom they once feared. I cannot think without agony of the

---

30. *perventuram* (*esse*), "would devolve (upon)" (indirect statement).

31. *quod . . . absint*: this is part of the reply (*non posse agi*) reported in indirect statement; the subjunctive is used in a subordinate clause in indirect statement. Here the subjunctive might also have been used to show that *quod . . . absint* was the reason alleged by the speaker, not the reason claimed by the narrator.

degree to which this has come about through our mistakes and flaws. What I think is looming I have already written to you, and I am still waiting for your letter.

Atticus shows himself a hardheaded analyst of Pompey's actions and of the possibility that Cicero can avoid compromising himself, in particular as to whether he should have stayed in Italy or tried to escape to join Pompey. His attitude also represents a visible shift in the attitudes of several prominent nobles, who are now, as we have seen, more inclined to deal with Caesar, about which Cicero complains bitterly and often.

Atticus to Cicero, 5 March 49 (*Att.* 9.10.9)

And yet I am not unhappy that you are not with Pompey. Later, if need be, your presence will not be difficult, and it will be acceptable to Pompey whenever it happens. But I mean by this that if Caesar conducts the rest of these affairs as he has begun, with sincerity, with moderation, and with wisdom, I shall take a good look and consider our welfare more deliberately.

CAESAR, *DE BELLO CIVILI* 1.27

27 Prope dimidia parte operis a Caesare effecta diebusque in ea re consumptis VIIII, naves a consulibus Dyrrachio remissae, quae priorem partem exercitus eo deportaverant, Brundisium revertuntur. *[2]* Pompeius, sive operibus Caesaris permotus sive etiam quod ab initio Italia excedere constituerat, adventu navium profectionem parare incipit et, *[3]* quo facilius impetum Caesaris tardaret, ne sub ipsa profectione[32] milites oppidum irrumperent, portas obstruit, vicos plateasque inaedificat,[33] fossas transversas viis praeducit atque ibi sudis stipitesque praeacutos defigit. *[4]* Haec levibus cratibus terraque inaequat;[34] aditus autem atque itinera

---

32. *sub ipsa profectione*, "at the very point of departure."
33. *vicos plateasque inaedificat*, "barricaded the blocks (of houses) and side streets," as opposed to the *viae*, "main avenues," of the next clause.
34. *haec (opera)* . . . *inaequat*, "he leveled off these entrenchments."

duo, quae extra murum ad portum ferebant, maximis defixis trabibus atque eis praeacutis praesepit. *[5]* His paratis rebus milites silentio navis conscendere iubet, expeditos[35] autem ex evocatis, sagittariis funditoribusque raros in muro turribusque disponit. *[6]* Hos certo signo revocare constituit, cum omnes milites navis conscendissent, atque eis expedito[36] loco actuaria navigia[37] relinquit.

MATIUS AND TREBATIUS TO CICERO, ABOUT 20 MARCH 49 (*Att.* 9.15A)

When we had left Capua, we heard en route that Pompey had departed from Brundisium on 17 March with all the forces he had, and that Caesar had entered the town on the following day and held an assembly; from there he hurried on to Rome: he wanted to be in the city before the Kalends, spend a few days there, and then set out for Spain. We thought it not inappropriate, since we are certain of Caesar's arrival, to send your messengers back to you so that you would know of this as soon as possible. . . . This letter had already been finished when we were told that Caesar will stay at Beneventum on the 25th, at Capua on the 26th, and at Sinuessa on the 27th; these reports we regard as certain.

CAESAR, *DE BELLO CIVILI* 1.28–32.1

28 Brundisini Pompeianorum militum iniuriis atque ipsius Pompei contumeliis permoti Caesaris rebus[38] favebant. *[2]* Itaque cognita Pompei profectione concursantibus illis[39] atque in ea re occupatis vulgo ex tectis significabant.[40] Per quos re cognita Caesar[41] scalas

---

35. *expeditos*, "lightly armed men," the military idiom (see next note).
36. *expedito*, "(place) free from obstacles."
37. *actuaria navigia*, "fast boats" that could be either rowed or sailed.
38. *Caesaris rebus*, "Caesar's side."
39. *illis* = *militibus Pompeianis*.
40. *significabant*, "they began to signal."
41. *re cognita Caesar*, "Caesar learned what was happening and . . ."

parari militesque armari iubet, ne quam rei gerendae facultatem dimittat. *[3]* Pompeius sub noctem navis solvit. Qui erant in muro custodiae causa collocati eo signo quod convenerat revocantur notisque itineribus ad navis decurrunt. *[4]* Milites, positis scalis, muros ascendunt, sed moniti a Brundisinis ut vallum caecum fossasque[42] caveant, subsistunt et longo itinere ab his[43] circumducti ad portum perveniunt, duasque navis cum militibus, quae ad moles Caesaris adhaeserant, scaphis lintribusque[44] reprehendunt, reprehensas excipiunt.

29 Caesar etsi ad[45] spem conficiendi negoti maxime probabat[46] coactis navibus mare transire et Pompeium sequi priusquam ille sese transmarinis auxiliis confirmaret, tamen eius rei moram temporisque longinquitatem timebat, quod omnibus coactis navibus Pompeius praesentem facultatem[47] insequendi sui ademerat. *[2]* Relinquebatur ut[48] ex longinquioribus regionibus Galliae Picenique et a freto[49] naves essent exspectandae. Id propter anni tempus longum atque impeditum videbatur. *[3]* Interea

---

42. *vallum caecum fossasque*, "the hidden rampart and trenches."

43. *his = Brundisinis.*

44. *scaphis lintribusque*, "with their skiffs and dugouts." Caesar contrasts the large ships (*navis*) that were captured with the small boats that captured them, and emphasizes the speed of the action with the collocation *reprehendunt reprehensas*.

45. *ad*, "with respect to."

46. *maxime probabat*, "thought it by far the best."

47. *praesentem facultatem*, "the immediate opportunity."

48. *Relinquebatur ut . . . essent exspectandae*, lit., "it was left that (ships) had to be awaited," i.e., "his alternative was the necessity to wait for (ships)." Caesar emphasizes the length of time that either choice would take because of the remoteness of naval reinforcements, and explains his decision to go instead to Rome and Spain.

49. Gaul and Picenum refer to the area around Ravenna on the Adriatic and around Ariminum, respectively, through which Caesar had just marched with great speed; the "strait" means the channel between Italy and Sicily. Picenum was Pompey's home ground, and that these areas were far from secure is attested a year later in a letter from Caelius to Cicero (*Fam.* 8.17).

veterem exercitum, duas Hispanias[50] confirmari,[51] quarum erat altera maximis beneficiis Pompei devincta, auxilia, equitatum parari, Galliam Italiamque temptari se absente nolebat.

30 Itaque in praesentia Pompei sequendi rationem omittit, in Hispaniam proficisci constituit. Duumviris municipiorum omnium imperat ut navis conquirant Brundisiumque deducendas curent. *[2]* Mittit in Sardiniam cum legione una Valerium[52] legatum, in Siciliam Curionem[53] pro praetore cum legionibus III; eundem, cum Siciliam recepisset, protinus in Africam traducere exercitum iubet.[54] Sardiniam obtinebat[55] M. Cotta,[56] Siciliam M. Cato;[57] Africam sorte Tubero[58] obtinere debebat.[59] *[3]* Caralitani,[60] simul

---

50. *veterem exercitum, duas Hispanias*: Pompey's "veteran" army in Spain consisted of seven legions that could be very dangerous at Caesar's back. Of the two Spains, Nearer and Farther, Nearer Spain had had close ties of clientship with Pompey ever since the Sertorian War. In Farther Spain, Caesar had forged ties during his governorship there as proconsul in 61.

51. The infinitives *confirmari, parari,* and *temptari* are complementary after *nolebat,* whose subject is still Caesar. The subjects of each of these infinitives, a pair of accusative nouns in all three instances, immediately precede them (the first two pairs lack a copulative).

52. Q. Valerius Orca had been praetor in 57 and proconsul in Africa in 56.

53. C. Scribonius Curio was last seen in Corfinium (*BC* 1.18), but has evidently been with Caesar all through the war thus far. Caesar later describes his tragic African campaign in substantial detail (*BC* 2.23–44). On the number of Curio's legions, see Carter, 181.

54. With Sardinia, Sicily, and Africa, Caesar takes steps to secure the crucial grain-bearing provinces. Pompey, meanwhile, planned to raise a large fleet and cut off all grain convoys to Italy in order to diminish Caesar's popularity there. (This was the beginning of the career of Pompey's son Sextus as a naval commander of some ability; Octavian still had to deal with him a decade later.)

55. *obtinere* is the standard term for being assigned to or being in charge of a province; thus "was governing" rather than "was holding." These are the men that had been appointed by the Senate in January.

56. M. Aurelius Cotta is otherwise unknown.

57. M. Porcius Cato the Younger.

58. L. Aelius Tubero.

59. He had been prevented from taking charge of the province, as Caesar goes on to describe in the next chapter.

60. Caralis was the most important city in the southern part of Sicily.

ad se Valerium mitti audierunt, nondum profecto[61] ex Italia, sua
sponte Cottam ex oppido eiciunt. Ille perterritus, quod omnem
provinciam consentire intellegebat, ex Sardinia in Africam profugit.
[4] Cato in Sicilia navis longas[62] veteres reficiebat, novas civitatibus
imperabat. Haec magno studio agebat. In Lucanis Bruttiisque per
legatos suos civium Romanorum dilectus habebat, equitum
peditumque certum numerum[63] a civitatibus Siciliae exigebat. [5]
Quibus rebus paene perfectis, adventu Curionis cognito, queritur
in contione sese proiectum ac proditum a Cn. Pompeio, qui
omnibus rebus imparatissimis non necessarium bellum suscepisset[64]
et, ab se reliquisque in senatu interrogatus, omnia sibi esse ad
bellum apta ac parata confirmavisset. Haec in contione questus ex
provincia fugit.[65]

31 Nacti vacuas ab imperiis[66] Sardiniam Valerius, Curio
Siciliam, cum exercitibus eo perveniunt. [2] Tubero cum in Africam
venisset, invenit in provincia cum imperio Attium Varum; qui ad
Auximum, ut supra demonstravimus, amissis cohortibus protinus
ex fuga in Africam pervenerat atque eam sua sponte vacuam
occupaverat dilectuque habito duas legiones effecerat, hominum et
locorum notitia et usu eius provinciae nactus aditus[67] ad ea
conanda, quod paucis ante annis ex praetura eam provinciam
obtinuerat. [3] Hic[68] venientem Uticam[69] navibus Tuberonem

---

61. *nondum profecto*, ablative absolute, "although he had not yet set out."
62. *navis longas*, "war ships."
63. *certum numerum*, "a fixed quota."
64. This is an extraordinary argument from the mouth of Cato, if he did
indeed make it, for he had been among the most adamant of those urging no
concessions to Caesar.
65. 23 April.
66. *Nacti vacuas ab imperiis*: *nacti* (< *nanciscor*) is plural to agree with the two
subjects (Valerius and Curio); *vacuas ab imperiis* agrees with the two objects of *nacti*
(Sardinia and Sicily).
67. *hominum et locorum notitia et usu eius provinciae nactus aditus*, "having
acquired the means (*aditus*, accusatuve plural) through his knowledge and
experience of the people and geography of that province."
68. *Hic* = *Attius*.
69. *Uticam*, accusative of motion. Utica was about twenty miles from the site
of Carthage.

portu atque oppido prohibet neque adfectum valetudine[70] filium exponere in terra patitur, sed sublatis ancoris excedere eo loco cogit.

32 His rebus confectis Caesar, ut reliquum tempus a labore intermitteretur, milites in proxima municipia deducit; ipse ad urbem proficiscitur.

CICERO TO ATTICUS, 28 MARCH 49 (*Att.* 9.18.1, 3)

For all his vacillation in private, Cicero had clearly determined not to be bullied by Caesar. The relationship between the two men is interesting, because Cicero evidently disguised his ill will toward Caesar with considerable success: Caesar consistently attempted to maintain a friendly relationship with him; Caesar's supporters (such as Balbus and Oppius) regarded the two as friendly; and Caesar appears in the letter quoted here to have every expectation that Cicero will agree to his proposals. Caesar is of course aware of Cicero's ties of *amicitia* with Pompey, but he seems to be under the impression that he himself has claims of equal or greater value (for example, as recently as 51 Caesar had written to support Cicero's claim for a triumph), and he is making a considerable effort to enlist "respectable" Roman nobles in his cause. When Cicero refuses to comply, Caesar is clearly miffed and departs with a rare display of temper.[71]

In both particulars I followed your advice. My language was such as to earn his respect rather than his thanks and I stood firm against going to Rome. But we were wrong in thinking him accommodating [*facilem*]; I have never found anyone less so. He said I was passing judgment against him, that the rest would be slower to come if I did not. I replied that their position was different. After a long discussion: "Come along then and work for peace." "At my own discretion?" "Naturally," he answered, "Who am I to lay down rules for you?" "Well," I said, "I shall

---

70. *adfectum valetudine*, "seriously ill."

71. This entire selection is quoted in Shackleton Bailey's translation. For a discussion of Cicero's assessment of his own actions, see Brunt, "Cicero's *officium*."

take the line that the Senate does not approve of an expedition to Spain or of the transport of armies into Greece, and," I added, "I shall have much to say in commiseration of Pompey." At that he protested that this was not the sort of thing he wanted said. "So I supposed," I rejoined, "but that is just why I don't want to be present. Either I must speak in that strain or stay away—and much besides which I could not possibly suppress if I were there." The upshot was that he asked me to think the matter over, as though seeking a way to end the talk. I could not refuse. On that note we parted.

So I imagine Caesar is not pleased with me. But I was pleased with myself, an experience I have not had for quite a long time. . . . But I nearly forgot to mention Caesar's disagreeable Parthian shot. If, he said, he could not avail himself of my counsels, he would take those he could get and stop at nothing.

CAESAR, *DE BELLO CIVILI* 1.32.2–33

In an effort to legitimize his position, Caesar called for a meeting of the Senate in Rome on 1 April. He had hoped to induce Cicero to attend and several other consulars with whom he had ties, but in the end he could produce only two. Symbolically, this meeting could have had great value for Caesar, giving him legal status while Pompey was still at large, and validating both the actions he had already taken and those he would take soon. Caesar reports this meeting in sketchy terms, highlighting those parts of it that foster his goals and pointing to setbacks to his plans that he construes as reflecting badly on his enemies.

32 . . . *[2]* Coacto senatu[72] iniurias inimicorum commemorat. Docet se nullum extraordinarium honorem appetisse, sed exspectato legitimo tempore[73] consulatus eo fuisse contentum

---

72. Cassius Dio (41.15) informs us that the meeting was called by Antony and Cassius, as tribunes, in the absence of the two consuls. The meeting was held outside the formal city limit (*pomerium*) so that Caesar, who was now acting as though still in possession of proconsular *imperium*, could legally attend. Attendance was sparse, but form was observed.

73. *legitimo tempore*, "the legal time limit," i.e., ten years between offices.

quod omnibus civibus pateret. *[3]* Latum[74] ab X tribunis plebis, contradicentibus inimicis, Catone vero acerrime repugnante et pristina consuetudine dicendi mora dies extrahente,[75] ut sui ratio absentis[76] haberetur, ipso consule Pompeio;[77] qui si improbasset, cur ferri passus esset? Si probasset, cur se uti populi beneficio prohibuisset? *[4]* Patientiam proponit suam, cum[78] de exercitibus dimittendis ultro postulavisset in quo iacturam dignitatis atque honoris ipse facturus esset. *[5]* Acerbitatem inimicorum docet, qui quod ab altero postularent in se recusarent[79] atque omnia permisceri mallent quam imperium exercitusque dimittere. *[6]* Iniuriam in eripiendis legionibus praedicat, crudelitatem et insolentiam in circumscribendis tribunis plebis; condiciones a se latas, expetita[80] colloquia et denegata commemorat. *[7]* Pro quibus rebus hortatur ac postulat ut rem publicam suscipiant atque una secum administrent. Sin timore defugiant illis se oneri non futurum[81] et per se rem publicam administraturum.[82] *[8]* Legatos

---

74. *latum* (*esse*) . . . *ut* . . . *haberetur*, "a law had been passed . . . that . . . (his right) should be kept."

75. *extrahente* concludes the ablative absolute (continuing from *Catone*), with *dies* (accusative plural) as its object; *pristina consuetudine* is ablative of manner (the genitive *dicendi* defines *consuetudine*); and *mora* is ablative of means.

76. *sui ratio absentis*, "his right (to run for the consulship) in absentia."

77. In 52. Caesar now recalls the main points of the constitutional basis of his position and his grievances against his enemies (for a review of these matters, refer to the Introduction). It is quite likely that Caesar's actual speech closely reflected the version he gives here, for his position on these issues remained constant. He also gave a similar speech to a popular assembly, adding the promise of a distribution of grain and a cash gift of seventy-five denarii (a month's wages on a soldier's pay scale) per man.

78. *cum* here is causal: since he (Caesar) had made the proposal (*postulavisset*).

79. *qui quod ab altero postularent in se recusarent*, "since they refused in their own case what they were requiring of another."

80. *latas*, "proposed." *expetita*, "requested."

81. *illis se oneri non futurum*: *se* . . . *non futurum* (*esse*) is indirect statement, "he would not be"; *illis* . . . *oneri* is double dative (dative of reference and predicate dative, or dative of purpose), "a (source of) burden for them."

82. Caesar characterizes his words as a temperate offer for joint responsibility for the Republic to be shared among the Senate, the People, and Caesar. Curio, as we shall see in Cicero's letter quoted below (*Att.* 10.4.8), heard a rather different message, ensconced in a threat to operate as he wished.

ad Pompeium de compositione mitti oportere, neque se reformidare quod in senatu Pompeius paulo ante dixisset, ad quos[83] legati mitterentur, his auctoritatem attribui timoremque eorum qui mitterent significari. *[9]* Tenuis atque infirmi haec animi videri.[84] Se vero, ut[85] operibus anteire studuerit, sic iustitia et aequitate velle superare.

33 Probat rem senatus de mittendis legatis; sed qui mitterentur[86] non reperiebantur, maximeque timoris causa pro se quisque id munus legationis[87] recusabat. *[2]* Pompeius enim discedens ab urbe in senatu dixerat eodem se habiturum loco qui Romae remansissent et qui in castris Caesaris fuissent. *[3]* Sic triduum disputationibus excusationibusque extrahitur. Subicitur etiam L. Metellus tribunus plebis ab inimicis Caesaris, qui[88] hanc rem distrahat reliquasque res[89] quascumque agere instituerit impediat.[90] *[4]* Cuius cognito consilio Caesar, frustra diebus aliquot consumptis, ne reliquum tempus dimittat, infectis eis quae agere destinaverat ab urbe proficiscitur atque in ulteriorem Galliam pervenit.

---

83. *ad quos . . . significari*: this is the content of what Pompey had said, an argument for not sending ambassadors to Caesar. The relative clause (subjunctive in indirect statement) precedes its antecedent, *his*, which is dative with *attribui* (passive infinitive), of which the subject is *auctoritatem*; *timorem* is the subject of *significari*. Pompey had made much of the symbolism in who would be sending and who would be receiving ambassadors: sending concedes fear, receiving confers *auctoritas*.

84. *Tenuis atque infirmi haec animi videri*: Caesar's rejoinder to Pompey. *Animi* is a genitive of characteristic.

85. *ut*, "just as," looking forward to *sic* in the next clause.

86. *qui mitterentur*, "men who could be sent."

87. *id munus legationis*, "the responsibility for this delegation."

88. *qui* (referring to Marcellus) = *ut* (*distrahat . . . impediat*) relative clauses of purpose.

89. *reliquasque res*: the most important of which was Caesar's taking control of the public treasury.

90. A clever ploy, for Caesar had made much of respecting the *dignitas* of the tribunes. We read in Cicero's letter quoted next, however, that he did not react well in this situation and made his anger obvious, incurring some bad feeling among the populace. In the end, Caesar simply ignored Metellus' attempt to prohibit him from the treasury. It is unclear what, if any, other plans Caesar is referring to here.

CICERO TO ATTICUS, 14 APRIL 49 (*Att*. 10.4.8)

A rather different assessment of this meeting is provided by this excerpt from a letter to Atticus in which Cicero reports on a lengthy conversation he has had that day with C. Scribonius Curio, now among Caesar's closest associates and an eyewitness to events in the city, but perhaps not an altogether reliable interpreter of Caesar's mind. Cicero portrays Curio as babbling on incessantly about Caesar's feelings and goals. Accurately reported or not, these sentiments reproduce Cicero's own fears and biases.

Curio passed by my estate, gave instructions that I be informed that he would come soon, and ran to Puteoli to give a speech there. He made his speech, came back, and stayed with me quite a long while. O what a foul experience! You know the man. He concealed nothing: he bragged above all that nothing is more certain than the restoration of all those condemned by the *Lex Pompeia*; he will therefore employ their services in Sicily.[91] As for the two Spains, he did not doubt that they are Caesar's. Caesar himself will go from there with his army wherever Pompey is. Pompey's death will be the end of it: nothing had been more nearly realized.[92] And Caesar, visibly transported with rage, wanted the tribune Metellus to be killed,[93] and if that had happened there would have been a great slaughter. There were numerous advocates of the slaughter, but Caesar avoided cruelty not because of his nature or from conviction but because he thought clemency appealed to the people. But if he lost the backing of the People, he would be cruel, and he was upset because he realized that he had caused offense with the masses in the business with the treasury. And so even though he had determined to address the People

---

91. Curio had been granted propraetorian *imperium* at Caesar's 1 April meeting of the Senate and was to go on to Sicily, which Cato had vacated.

92. I.e., at Brundisium.

93. Metellus filibustered Caesar's meeting of the Senate on 1 April and eventually interposed his veto on the proceedings. Moreover, he placed himself physically in front of the gate of the Temple of Saturn, where the treasury was housed, so that Caesar (who had vociferously championed the rights of tribunes) was compelled to remove him by intimidation.

before leaving, he did not venture to do it and set out in a state of thorough exasperation.

CAESAR TO CICERO, 16 APRIL 49 (*Att.* 10.8B)

On the way to Spain, Caesar wrote to Cicero asking him to refrain from direct action and Cicero included that letter in one he himself sent to Atticus. While Caesar was campaigning in Spain, Cicero again was torn about what course he should take, whether to stay in Rome or go to Pompey. It is plain from his letter to Atticus that he was unconvinced by Caesar's show of clemency, and he fully expected that Caesar would fail because of the tyrannical actions he would have to take.[94] Caesar's letter is hastily composed, but in view of his previous interactions with Cicero it is worth reading in full, and it is interesting to compare the somewhat murky style of this letter to the clean exposition of his historical narrative.

Etsi nihil temere, nihil imprudenter facturum iudicaram,[95] tamen, permotus hominum fama, scribendum ad te existimavi et pro nostra benevolentia petendum ne quo progredereris[96] proclinata iam re[97] quo[98] integra etiam[99] progrediendum tibi non existimasses. Namque et amicitiae graviorem iniuriam feceris et tibi

---

94. "For I see slaughter if he wins [in Spain] and an attack on the fortunes of private individuals, and a recall of exiles, cancellation of debts, high office for the most revolting men, and a tyranny that would be intolerable not only to a Roman but even to any Persian" (Cic. *Att.* 10.8.2; also revealing are 10.8.6–8.) He was fostered in this view by Caelius, who had written to him with the assertion that the days of clemency were limited (*Att.* 10.9A, 16 April).

95. (*te*) *facturum* (*esse*) *iudicaram*, "I thought that you would do." *Iudicaram* is contracted from *iudicaveram*, and the tense appears to be "epistolary," i.e., it presumes that Cicero will be reading the letter at a time when past action to the writer will be past perfect to the reader.

96. *ne quo progredereris*, "that you not move in a direction." *Quo* (adverbial) is for *aliquo* after *ne* (introducing indirect command).

97. *proclinata iam re*, ablative absolute, "now that events have taken a turn."

98. *quo*, adverbial again, "in a direction that."

99. (*re*) *integra etiam* resumes the ablative absolute of *proclinata re*, and qualifies (*non*) *progrediendum*.

minus commode consulueris,[100] si non fortunae obsecutus videberis[101] (omnia enim secundissima nobis, adversissima illis accidisse videntur), nec causam secutus (eadem enim tum fuit[102] cum ab eorum consiliis abesse iudicasti), sed meum aliquod factum[103] condemnavisse; quo[104] mihi gravius abs te nihil accidere potest. *[2]* Quod[105] ne facias, pro iure nostrae amicitiae a te peto. Postremo quid viro bono et quieto civi[106] magis convenit quam abesse a civilibus controversiis? Quod non nulli probarent, periculi causa[107] sequi non potuerunt; tu, explorato[108] et vitae meae testimonio et amicitiae iudicio, neque tutius neque honestius reperies quicquam quam ab omni contentione abesse.

But Cicero, despite Caesar's assurances and despite his own doubts about Pompey's strategy for the war and his intentions if he should be victorious, was inclined to believe the dire projections about Caesar offered by volatile men like Scribonius Curio and Caelius Rufus. In the

---

100. *tibi minus commode consulueris*, euphemistic, "you will do yourself no good," lit., "you will have taken less agreeable counsel for yourself." Caesar had put this same euphemism (*consulere* + comparative + dative) into the mouth of Lentulus (see 1.22.6, chapter 3, n. 2) after Corfinium.

101. *videberis*, "you will seem," or better, "it will seem that you," governs three complementary perfect infinitives, the first two being followed by parenthetical interruptions: (a) *non . . . obsecutus* (*esse*) (+ dative); (b) *nec . . . secutus* (*esse*); (c) *sed . . . condemnavisse*.

102. *eadem enim* (*causa*) . . . *fuit*, "for the cause was the same." That is, Cicero is not following any consistent policy or "cause," apart from personal considerations, because the "causes" (his and Pompey's) have not changed.

103. *meum aliquod factum*, "something that I have done."

104. *quo = et . . . eo*, "and . . . than this." *Quo* is comparative with *gravius*.

105. *Quod = Et . . . id.*

106. *viro bono et quieto civi*, "a dependable man and a peaceful citizen." This apparently complimentary phrase has an edge to it: Caesar is reminding Cicero that he chose to stay away from Rome rather than become entangled in a fight between (as Caesar portrays it) two *amici*; he therefore gently but quite firmly suggests that Cicero maintain that course.

107. *periculi causa*, "because of personal risk."

108. *explorato* qualifies both *testimonio* and *iudicio* in ablative absolute. Thus, "when you evaluate the evidence . . . and your decision." Shackleton Bailey explains *amicitiae iudicio* as the result of Cicero's decision to remain *in amicitia* with Caesar (he translates: "the judgement implied in our friendship").

belief that the Republic as he understood it could not survive under Caesar, Cicero left Italy and joined Pompey's camp on 7 June.

5

Caesar in Spain

Now that Pompey had left Italy, it was essential for Caesar to reduce Pompey's bases of support, especially in Spain, where his *legati* L. Afranius and M. Petreius commanded seven legions. Pompey's strategy of attrition was essentially sound: eventually, Caesar would have to fight him in the East, where Pompey's resources were immense. Although men like Cicero despaired over the abandonment of the city of Rome, it was clear that Caesar could concoct no firm basis of support there. Caesar could not afford to follow Pompey to the East until the West was secure.

CAESAR, *DE BELLO CIVILI* 1.34–35, 37–38, 67–72, 84–87

34 Quo[1] cum venisset,[2] cognoscit[3] missum in Hispaniam a Pompeio Vibullium Rufum, quem paucis ante diebus[4] Corfinio captum ipse dimiserat; *[2]* profectum item Domitium ad occupandam Massiliam navibus actuariis VII, quas Igili[5] et in Cosano[6] a privatis coactas servis, libertis, colonis suis compleverat; *[3]* praemissos etiam legatos Massiliensis domum, nobilis

---

1. *Quo = in Galliam Transalpinam*, continuing from the previous narrative.
2. About 19 April.
3. Caesar learns three things: *missum (esse) Vibullium, profectum (esse) Domitium*, and *praemissos (esse) legatos*. None of these is good news for him.
4. Actually closer to two months. Perhaps Caesar means that Pompey had sent Rufus to Spain within a few days of his being released (Carter).
5. *Igili*, "at Igilium" (now Giglio, between Corsica and Italy).
6. *in Cosano (agro)*, "in the territory around Cosa" on the Etruscan coast about sixty miles northwest of Rome.

adulescentis,[7] quos ab urbe discedens Pompeius erat adhortatus ne nova Caesaris officia veterum suorum beneficiorum in eos memoriam expellerent.[8] *[4]* Quibus mandatis acceptis Massilienses[9] portas Caesari clauserant; Albicos, barbaros homines, qui in eorum fide antiquitus erant montisque supra Massiliam incolebant, ad se vocaverant; *[5]* frumentum ex finitimis regionibus atque ex omnibus castellis in urbem convexerant; armorum officinas in urbe instituerant; muros, portas, classem reficiebant.

35 Evocat ad se Caesar Massilia XV primos.[10] Cum his agit ne initium inferendi belli ab Massiliensibus oriatur; debere eos Italiae totius auctoritatem[11] sequi potius quam unius hominis voluntati obtemperare. *[2]* Reliqua quae ad eorum sanandas mentis pertinere arbitrabatur commemorat. *[3]* Cuius orationem legati domum referunt atque ex senatus auctoritate[12] haec Caesari renuntiant: Intellegere se divisum esse populum Romanum in partis duas. Neque sui iudici neque suarum esse virium[13] discernere utra pars iustiorem habeat causam. *[4]* Principes vero esse earum partium patronos civitatis,[14] quorum alter agros Volcarum Arecomicorum

---

7. *praemissos (esse) legatos Massiliensis, nobilis adulescentis*, all accusative in indirect statement. The force of *praemissos* is that the *legati* had been sent back to Massilia (*domum*) ahead of Caesar, bearing Pompey's message.

8. On the difference between *beneficia* and *officia*, see the Introduction. Pompey cleverly implies that Caesar's benefactions were recompense owed to Massilia, while his own were favors that they still must repay.

9. The Massiliotes have taken five actions: *portas clauserant, Albicos ad se vocaverant, frumentum in urbem convexerant, armorum officinas instituerant*, and *classem reficiebant*. On the climactic structure of this sentence, see Carter, 184.

10. *XV primos*, "the Board of Fifteen." The Senate of Massilia consisted of six hundred men, fifteen of which constituted a kind of executive committee. Of these, three were the chief magistrates of the city.

11. *auctoritatem*, "authority," as usual (see Introduction). Caesar contrasts this collective *auctoritas* with the mere *voluntas* of one individual (Pompey).

12. *ex senatus auctoritate*, "officially." The terminology is Roman, but the senate in question is Massiliot.

13. *neque sui iudici neque suarum esse virium*, "it belonged neither to their judgment nor to their abilities."

14. *Principes vero esse earum partium patronos civitatis*, "Indeed, the leaders of those factions were (both) patrons of their city." The Massiliotes use *patroni* in the Roman sense.

et Helviorum publice eis concesserit, alter bello victos Sallyas attribuerit vectigaliaque auxerit.[16] *[5]* Quare paribus eorum beneficiis parem se quoque voluntatem tribuere debere et neutrum eorum contra alterum iuvare aut urbe aut portibus recipere. . . .

Despite these assurances from Massilia, when Domitius Ahenobarbus arrived by sea, the Massiliotes took him in, and he immediately began aggressive defensive naval operations. "The judgment of this free state, an ally of long standing, was the same as that of all others; it felt no confidence in Caesar's prospects" (Gelzer, 212). Caesar therefore laid siege to the city, leaving Gaius Trebonius in charge of that operation, and constructed twelve ships, over which he appointed Decimus Brutus. Caesar goes on to describe the arrangements Pompey had made for the supervision of Spain in his absence.

37 Dum haec parat[16] atque administrat, C. Fabium[17] legatum cum legionibus III, quas Narbone[18] circumque ea loca hiemandi causa disposuerat, in Hispaniam praemittit celeriterque saltus Pyrenaeos occupari iubet, qui eo tempore ab L. Afranio[19] legato

---

15. The events referred to here are not otherwise attested, so that it is impossible to elucidate them or even to decide which Roman benefactor performed which benefaction. (There is a half-hearted consensus that Caesar, who mentions the Volcae and the Helvii in the *Gallic War*, is probably responsible for the first *beneficium* mentioned. But this is far from decisive.)

16. During June of 49.

17. *Fabium*: he had been mentioned by Hirtius (*BG* 8.54.4, quoted in chapter 1) as taking four legions into Aeduan Gaul in late 50. The duty assigned to him here is substantially more significant. This Fabius may be the same man who was tribune in 55.

18. Narbo, also known as Narbo Martius, was a very old commercial town that commanded the main road to Spain from Italy, on the Gallic gulf across from Massilia; it eventually gave its name to the whole Roman province (Gallia Narbonensis).

19. L. Afranius was a veteran commander of considerable skill but a *novus homo*, which retarded his political advancement for some time. He had served with Pompey as *legatus* against Sertorius thirty years before (77–73/2). He was probably praetor in the late 70s, before holding a proconsulship in Spain in the early 60s, as a result of which he celebrated a triumph. He accompanied Pompey to the East in the Mithridatic campaigns, where once again his contribution was substantial. He finally advanced to the consulship under Pompey's patronage in 60.

praesidiis tenebantur. *[2]* Reliquas legiones, quae longius hiemabant, subsequi iubet. *[3]* Fabius, ut erat imperatum, adhibita celeritate praesidium ex saltu[20] deiecit magnisque itineribus ad exercitum Afrani contendit.

38 Adventu L. Vibulli Rufi, quem a Pompeio missum in Hispaniam demonstratum est,[21] Afranius et Petreius[22] et Varro,[23] legati Pompei, quorum unus Hispaniam citeriorem tribus legionibus, alter ulteriorem a saltu Castulonensi[24] ad Anam duabus legionibus, tertius ab Ana Vettonum[25] agrum Lusitaniamque pari numero legionum obtinebat, *[2]* officia inter se partiuntur, uti Petreius ex Lusitania per Vettones cum tribus legionibus, alter omnibus copiis ad Afranium proficiscatur, Varro cum eis quas habebat legionibus omnem ulteriorem Hispaniam tueatur. *[3]* His

---

Appointed *legatus* again by Pompey in 55, he had remained in Spain (with Petreius and Varro) ever since. Pompey, who was nominally governor of the province, had stayed in Rome to supervise the grain supply.

20. This was a small inland pass, not on the main road to Tarraco, leading directly toward Ilerda following the valley of the Sicoris. The Sicoris (now the Segre) is a major tributary of the Ebro, flowing southwest down from its source in the Pyrenees.

21. Above, 1.34.1.

22. M. Petreius was another of Pompey's *legati*, also of great military ability and experience. He is described by Sallust (*Cat.* 59.6) as a military veteran whose career extended over five decades, beginning in the 90s; he had served as military tribune, prefect, and praetor at unknown dates. In 62 he was *legatus* to C. Antonius, Cicero's consular colleague in 63, who turned over operations in the battle against Catiline to Petreius because of an alleged attack of gout. Petreius was also appointed *legatus* to Pompey in Spain in 55.

23. M. Terentius Varro had also served against Sertorius in the 70s and with Pompey in the East in the 60s. This Varro, who had held the praetorship in the 60s and who would throw himself on Caesar's mercy after Pharsalus, was already sixty-seven years old. According to Aulus Gellius (3.10.17), within ten years of these events he had authored nearly five hundred books, fifty-five titles of which are known. Of this voluminous output, only *De re rustica* remains entire, while substantial portions of *De lingua Latina* have also been preserved.

24. Named after the southern Spanish town of Castulo.

25. *Vettonum* is genitive plural. The Vettones lived northeast of the Lusitani.

rebus constitutis, equites auxiliaque toti Lusitaniae²⁶ a Petreio, Celtiberiae, Cantabris barbarisque omnibus qui ad Oceanum pertinent ab Afranio imperantur. *[4]* Quibus coactis celeriter Petreius per Vettones ad Afranium pervenit, constituuntque communi consilio bellum ad Ilerdam²⁷ propter ipsius loci opportunitatem gerere.

Fabius' legions became separated when one of the bridges over the Sicoris was broken. Although the isolated group was immediately attacked, Fabius was able to reinforce it by crossing another bridge. Caesar then arrived (22 June) and, having assumed command, marched to Ilerda, where he entrenched himself safely. But the Spanish style of fighting demoralized Caesar's troops; after pursuing too far in a successful skirmish, they were almost trapped, finally escaping to the camp after a desperate charge. A flood cut Caesar's troops off from supplies, and attempts to bring in provisions from Gaul were repelled by Afranius. Afranius wrote to friends in Rome with such glowing accounts of these events that many felt the war was nearly over. Finally, Caesar built makeshift boats, crossed the river, and set up another camp on the other side, from which he was able to gather supplies; thus he had salvaged a seemingly hopeless situation. Meanwhile, Decimus Brutus had brought the campaign of Massilia to a successful conclusion, and as Caesar's cavalry made movement around Ilerda more and more difficult, surrounding tribes came to his support. When news arrived that Pompey was not in fact marching to assist Ilerda, the Pompeians' morale, already weakened by Caesar's recent successes, sank even further. Afranius and Petreius decided to move into central Celtiberia, where Pompey's Spanish supporters were still loyal, by marching to the Ebro River and sailing downstream. But Caesar, urged on by his troops, managed to ford the Sicoris and pursue closely. Both armies drew up, exhausted, about five miles apart across an open plain that led to the pass through which either would have to march to reach the Ebro. Petreius and Afranius tried

---

26. *toti Lusitaniae*, "from all of Lusitania," dative depending upon *imperantur*, as are *Celtiberiae*, *Cantabris*, and *barbarisque* in the next line. The passive construction renders the datives awkward: in the active the clause would have run *Petreius equites auxiliaque Lusitaniae imperat*.

27. *ad Ilerdam*, "near Ilerda," in northeast Spain (now Lérida). The city was strongly protected by the topography of mountains and rivers.

unsuccessfully to lead their army out during the night (see n. 29 below). Cut off from supplies and unable to advance, Petreius and Afranius were now in serious difficulties.

67 Disputatur in consilio a Petreio atque Afranio, et tempus profectionis quaeritur. Plerique censebant ut noctu iter facerent; posse prius ad angustias veniri quam sentiretur.[28] [2] Alii, quod pridie noctu conclamatum esset[29] a Caesaris castris, argumenti sumebant loco[30] non posse clam exiri: [3] circumfundi[31] noctu equitatum Caesaris atque omnia loca atque itinera obsidere; nocturnaque proelia esse vitanda, quod perterritus miles in civili dissensione timori magis quam religioni consulere consuerit.[32] [4] At lucem[33] multum per se pudorem omnium oculis, multum etiam tribunorum militum et centurionum praesentiam adferre; quibus rebus coerceri milites et in officio contineri soleant. [5] Quare omni ratione esse interdiu perrumpendum: etsi aliquo accepto detrimento, tamen summa exercitus salva[34] locum quem

---

28. *prius . . . veniri quam sentiretur*, "that they could come . . . before it was noticed." *Veniri* is an impersonal passive; the infinitive is due to indirect statement.

29. *conclamatum esset*, "there had been a shout," impersonal passive. About midnight of the previous night, Petreius and Afranius had quietly begun to march out, hoping to beat Caesar's troops to the pass. Caesar had his soldiers raise a clatter as if they too were ready to march, shouting, for example, "*Vasa!*" ("Baggage ready!"); the ruckus convinced Petreius and Afranius that it was not safe to march, and they remained in camp. On the sequence of thought in the next few paragraphs, see Stadter.

30. *argumenti sumebant loco*, "they assumed," lit., "they took in lieu of proof."

31. The infinitive continues the indirect statement, which has been implied by the previous sentences, specifically *censebant*. The indirect statement of the prevailing view among Afranius' advisers continues through section 5 (*capi posse*).

32. *timori magis quam religioni consulere consuerit*, "pays more attention to fear than to obligation." The subjunctive is a characteristic clause, expressing a generic truth.

33. *At lucem multum . . . pudorem, multum (pudorem) etiam . . . praesentiam adferre*, "but (day)light causes much restraint, and so does the presence, etc." *omnium oculis*, "in the sight of everyone."

34. *summa exercitus (parte) salva*, ablative absolute, "as long as most of the army were saved."

The Spanish Campaign

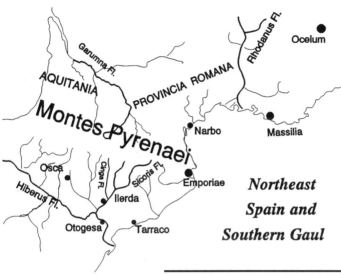

**Northeast
Spain and
Southern Gaul**

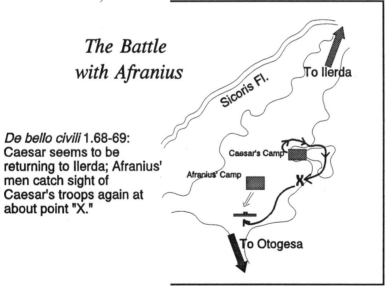

*The Battle
with Afranius*

De bello civili 1.68-69:
Caesar seems to be
returning to Ilerda; Afranius'
men catch sight of
Caesar's troops again at
about point "X."

petant capi posse. *[6]* Haec vincit in consilio sententia, et prima luce postridie constituunt proficisci.

68 Caesar exploratis regionibus albente caelo omnis copias castris educit magnoque circuitu nullo certo itinere[35] exercitum ducit. Namque itinera quae ad Hiberum atque Octogesam[36] pertinebant castris hostium oppositis tenebantur. *[2]* Ipsi[37] erant transcendendae valles maximae ac difficillimae: saxa multis locis praerupta iter impediebant, ut arma per manus necessario traderentur militesque inermes sublevatique alii ab aliis magnam partem itineris conficerent. *[3]* Sed hunc laborem recusabat nemo, quod eum omnium laborum finem fore existimabant, si hostem Hibero intercludere et frumento prohibere potuissent.

69 Ac primo Afraniani milites visendi causa laeti ex castris procurrebant contumeliosisque vocibus prosequebantur nostros: necessarii victus inopia coactos fugere[38] atque ad Ilerdam reverti. Erat enim iter a proposito diversum[39] contrariamque in partem iri videbatur. *[2]* Duces vero eorum consilium suum laudibus ferebant, quod se castris tenuissent; multumque eorum opinionem adiuvabat,[40] quod sine iumentis impedimentisque ad iter profectos videbant, ut non posse inopiam diutius sustinere confiderent. *[3]* Sed ubi paulatim retorqueri agmen ad dexteram[41] conspexerunt

---

35. *nullo certo itinere*, "on an irregular pattern of march" intended to keep Afranius and Petreius from predicting his movements. As Stadter (221) notes, Caesar's use of *albente caelo* here means that it was already full daylight when Caesar began this maneuver.

36. A town whose location and identity are uncertain but presumably the nearest to the Ebro once through the disputed pass. The correct form of the name is probably Otogesa, not Octogesa (Carter).

37. *Ipsi* = *Caesari*, dative of agent with *erant transcendendae*.

38. *coactos (nostros) fugere*, "(that our men) were retreating because they had been compelled." These are examples, in indirect statement, of the *contumeliosae voces*.

39. *a proposito diversum*, "contrary to (our) intention."

40. *multum . . . adiuvabat, quod*, "it greatly supported . . . that."

41. *retorqueri agmen ad dexteram*, "that (Caesar's) line was bending back toward the right." Afranius had stopped somewhat south of Caesar, who had encamped on the nearest hill (*in proximo colle*, 1.65.5). When Caesar marched down from his camp, he apparently moved off the northern (far) slope so that he

iamque primos superare regionem castrorum animadverterunt,
nemo erat adeo tardus aut fugiens laboris quin[42] statim castris
exeundum atque occurrendum putaret. *[4]* Conclamatur ad arma
atque omnes copiae paucis praesidio relictis cohortibus exeunt
rectoque ad Hiberum itinere contendunt.

70 Erat in celeritate omne positum certamen:[43] utri prius
angustias montisque occuparent; sed exercitum Caesaris viarum
difficultates tardabant, Afrani copias equitatus Caesaris insequens
morabatur. *[2]* Res[44] tamen ab Afranianis huc erat necessario
deducta ut, si priores montis quos petebant attigissent, ipsi
periculum vitarent, impedimenta totius exercitus cohortisque in
castris relictas servare non possent; quibus interclusis exercitu
Caesaris auxilium ferri nulla ratione poterat. *[3]* Confecit prior iter
Caesar atque ex magnis rupibus nactus planitiem, in hac contra
hostem aciem instruit. Afranius, cum ab equitatu novissimum
agmen premeretur, ante se hostem videret, collem quendam nactus
ibi constitit. *[4]* Ex eo loco IIII caetratorum cohortis in montem,
qui erat in conspectu omnium excelsissimus, mittit. Hunc magno
cursu concitatos[45] iubet occupare, eo consilio uti ipse eodem[46]
omnibus copiis contenderet et mutato itinere iugis[47] Octogesam
perveniret. *[5]* Hunc cum obliquo itinere caetrati peterent,

---

appeared to be headed toward Ilerda, but then crossed difficult terrain toward the
east while still hidden behind the hill (Perrin). Caesar does not specifically say this,
but it is hard to believe that Afranius would have missed a flanking maneuver
carried out before his eyes. Caesar's line must have been long enough that his rear
troops were still visible on the hill outside his camp while the forward troops were
already crossing toward the east. He did not take his baggage and supplies because
he could not have crossed the steep rocks with them. By the time his front line
reappeared to the east or southeast of the hill, which would have been on
Afranius' right, his troops threatened to outflank Afranius' camp and were already
moving between them and the pass to the Ebro (*superare regionem castrorum*).

42. *quin*, "that he did not."

43. *Erat . . . omne positum certamen*, "The whole match had been wagered."

44. *Res . . . huc erat . . . deducta*, "The situation had been reduced to the
point."

45. *magno cursu concitatos*, "(them) running at full speed."

46. *eodem*, "to that same hill."

47. *iugis*, "along the ridges."

conspicatus equitatus Caesaris in cohortis impetum facit; nec
minimam partem temporis[48] equitum vim caetrati sustinere
potuerunt omnesque ab eis circumventi in conspectu utriusque
exercitus interficiuntur.

71 Erat occasio bene gerendae rei.[49] Neque vero id Caesarem
fugiebat tanto sub oculis accepto detrimento perterritum exercitum
sustinere non posse, praesertim circumdatum undique equitatu,
cum in loco aequo atque aperto confligeretur;[50] idque ex omnibus
partibus ab eo flagitabatur.[51] [2] Concurrebant legati, centuriones
tribunique militum: ne dubitaret[52] proelium committere; omnium
esse militum paratissimos animos. [3] Afranianos contra multis rebus
sui timoris signa misisse: quod suis non subvenissent, quod de colle
non decederent, quod vix equitum incursus sustinerent collatisque
in unum locum signis conferti, neque ordines neque signa[53]
servarent. [4] Quod si iniquitatem loci timeret, datum iri[54] tamen
aliquo loco pugnandi facultatem, quod certe inde decedendum esset
Afranio[55] nec sine aqua permanere posset.

72 Caesar in eam spem venerat[56] se sine pugna et sine vulnere
suorum rem conficere posse, quod re frumentaria adversarios
interclusisset. [2] Cur[57] etiam secundo proelio aliquos ex suis
amitteret? Cur vulnerari pateretur optime meritos de se milites?
Cur denique fortunam periclitaretur, praesertim cum non minus

---

48. *minimam partem temporis*, "for even a moment."

49. *occasio bene gerendae rei*, "opportunity for successfully concluding the war."

50. *cum . . . confligeretur*, "as soon as there could be a conflict."

51. *id . . . ab eo flagitabatur*, "this (i.e., pressuring the enemy into an open
conflict) was demanded of him."

52. *ne dubitaret*: the subjunctive is used in indirect statement to represent an
imperative in direct statement; "Caesar should not hesitate."

53. *neque ordines neque signa*, "neither companies nor cohorts."

54. *datum iri*, future passive infinitive in indirect statement, "would be
provided." More common than this construction is the periphrasis with *fore ut*
(*daretur*).

55. *Afranio*, dative of agent with *decedendum esset*.

56. *in eam spem venerat*, "had begun to hope."

57. Introduces a series of rhetorical questions in the subjunctive.

esset imperatoris[58] consilio superare quam gladio. *[3]* Movebatur etiam misericordia civium, quos interficiendos videbat; quibus salvis atque incolumibus rem obtinere malebat.[59] *[4]* Hoc consilium Caesaris plerisque non probabatur; milites vero palam inter se loquebantur, quoniam talis occasio victoriae dimitteretur, etiam cum vellet Caesar, sese non esse pugnaturos. Ille in sua sententia perseverat et paulum ex eo loco degreditur, ut timorem adversariis minuat; *[5]* Petreius atque Afranius oblata facultate in castra sese referunt. Caesar, praesidiis montibus dispositis omni ad Hiberum intercluso itinere, quam proxime potest hostium castris castra communit.[60]

Petreius and Afranius left the camp to supervise fortifications of their access to water. While they were away, the soldiers of the two armies began to fraternize. The Pompeians were assured of Caesar's good faith and received promises that, if they should surrender, Afranius and Petreius would be spared. Although Afranius was prepared to give up all as lost, Petreius compelled the soldiers to renew their oaths to Pompey. The Pompeians then made a move to return to Ilerda, but Caesar pursued and gradually closed them in. Battle lines were drawn up, but neither side attacked, and at sunset both sides returned to camp.

84 Tandem omnibus rebus obsessi,[61] quartum iam diem sine pabulo retentis iumentis, aquae, lignorum, frumenti inopia colloquium petunt[62] et id, si fieri possit, semoto a militibus loco.

---

58. *imperatoris*, "the duty of a commander," a characteristic genitive.

59. That Caesar was almost certainly motivated by hope of another political coup on the order of Corfinium, allowing him to display his generosity and *clementia*, should in no way damage his claim to sincerity in his desire to avoid loss of life. At the same time, he was taking a great risk, and his soldiers make their irritation over this clear. Caesar hoped that by allowing the Pompeians access to water, they would have time to decide to surrender.

60. His previous camp was now abandoned, since it was too far away to shut the Pompeians off from the pass. Although he had posted guards, he did not want them to consider trying to break through. From his new camp he could harass any enemy movements with ease.

61. *obsessi*, "beleaguered," referring to Afranius and Petreius.

62. About 2 August.

[2] Ubi id a Caesare negatum et, palam si colloqui vellent, concessum est, datur obsidis loco[63] Caesari filius Afrani. *[3]* Venitur in eum locum quem Caesar delegit. Audiente utroque exercitu[64] loquitur Afranius: non esse aut ipsis aut militibus suscensendum,[65] quod fidem erga imperatorem suum Cn. Pompeium conservare voluerint. *[4]* Sed satis iam fecisse officio[66] satisque supplici tulisse perpessos omnium rerum inopiam; nunc vero paene ut feras circummunitos[67] prohiberi aqua, prohiberi ingressu, neque corpore dolorem neque animo ignominiam ferre posse. *[5]* Itaque se victos confiteri; orare atque obsecrare, si qui locus misericordiae relinquatur, ne ad ultimum supplicium progredi necesse habeat. Haec quam potest demississime et subiectissime exponit.

85 Ad ea Caesar respondit:[68] nulli omnium has partis vel

---

63. *obsidis loco,* "as a hostage."

64. This was certainly the point of Caesar's refusal to allow private negotiations. Afranius and Petreius must be discredited as leaders in the eyes of their troops, and the cause of loyalty to Pompey robbed of its value. Once again, Caesar directs his attention to the three targets of his detractors: character, leadership, and patriotism. In terms of narrative style, of course, it makes no difference whether the negotiations were public or private, since Caesar's answering speech would still have the same impact on the reader (as for example his report of the negotiations between the German Ariovistus and himself in the first book of the *Gallic Wars*). But Caesar's arguments here are not merely for rhetorical effect, they are real arguments of constantly present and genuine concern to him.

65. *non esse . . . suscensendum,* impersonal passive infinitive in indirect statement, "(that) there should be no outrage against."

66. *satis iam fecisse officio,* "they had fulfilled the requirements of obligation" as demanded by *fides* (previous sentence). The effect of this plea is to imply that Pompey has been deficient in his duty to protect those loyal to him.

67. *paene ut feras circummunitos,* "almost like caged beasts."

68. Some scholars believe that most of this speech could not have been delivered by Caesar at this time, but rather that he has used the opportunity of presenting his case again to the reader in somewhat modified form (no complaints here of violated tribunes, for example), interpreting all of Pompey's actions since 55 as hostile to him and designed for his destruction. No doubt Caesar has embellished his words, but much of this argument is plausible as a rejustification of his position to *his own* troops, legates, and commanders, who are also in the audience, along with his intended readers. It would be consistent with Caesar's character to treat his soldiers as informed citizens rather than merely as troops.

querimoniae vel miserationis minus convenisse.[69] *[2]* Reliquos enim omnis[70] officium suum[71] praestitisse: se, qui etiam bona condicione et loco et tempore aequo confligere noluerit, ut[72] quam integerrima essent ad pacem omnia; exercitum suum, qui iniuria etiam accepta suisque interfectis, quos in sua potestate habuerit conservarit et texerit; illius denique exercitus milites, qui per se de concilianda pace egerint, qua in re omnium suorum vitae consulendum putarint. *[3]* Sic omnium ordinum partis in misericordia constitisse,[73] ipsos duces a pace abhorruisse; eos neque colloqui neque indutiarum iura servasse[74] et homines imperitos et per colloquium deceptos crudelissime interfecisse. *[4]* Accidisse igitur his, quod plerumque hominibus nimia pertinacia atque arrogantia accidere soleat, uti eo recurrant et id cupidissime petant quod paulo ante contempserint. *[5]* Neque nunc se illorum humilitate[75] neque aliqua temporis opportunitate postulare quibus rebus[76] opes augeantur suae; sed eos exercitus, quos contra se[77] multos iam annos aluerint, velle dimitti. *[6]* Neque enim VI

---

69. *nulli omnium has partis vel querimoniae vel miserationis minus convenisse*: *has partis* (accusative), a metaphor from acting ("these roles"), is the subject of (*minus*) *convenisse*, upon which the dative *nulli* depends: "These roles . . . are less fitting for no one at all (*omnium*)." *Quaerimoniae* and *miserationis* qualify *partis*.

70. *Reliquos omnis*, "Everybody else." These are specified in three subsequent clauses, *se* (= *Caesarem*), *exercitum suum*, and *illius exercitus milites*, each of which is elaborated by an explanatory *qui* clause.

71. *officium suum*: answers Afranius' claim that all requirements of *officium* have been met.

72. *ut*: purpose clause.

73. *constitisse*, "had been consistent."

74. *neque colloqui neque indutiarum iura servasse*: in *BC* 1.75.2 and 1.76.4 (not quoted here) Petreius had fallen upon some of Caesar's men who were fraternizing with members of the Pompeian forces and killed them; he also ordered his soldiers to produce any such that they had in hiding, and executed them as well. Caesar's words (*colloquium, indutiae, iura*) imply much greater formality to these exchanges between soldiers than actually took place, but part of his audience consists of his own soldiers, who would respond warmly to this rhetorical trick.

75. *humilitate* and *opportunitate* are ablatives of cause.

76. *quibus rebus* = *aliquas res quibus*. As often, the antecedent has been attracted into the relative clause.

77. *se* = *Caesarem*.

legiones alia de causa missas in Hispaniam septimamque ibi conscriptam neque tot tantasque classis[78] paratas neque summissos duces rei militaris peritos. *[7]* Nihil horum ad pacandas Hispanias, nihil ad usum provinciae provisum quae propter diuturnitatem pacis[79] nullum auxilium desiderarit. *[8]* Omnia haec iam pridem contra se parari; in se novi generis imperia[80] constitui ut idem ad portas urbanis praesideat rebus et duas bellicosissimas provincias absens tot annos obtineat; *[9]* in se iura magistratuum commutari, ne ex praetura et consulatu,[81] ut semper, sed per paucos probati et electi in provincias mittantur; in se aetatis excusationem nihil valere, quod superioribus bellis probati ad obtinendos exercitus evocentur;[82] *[10]* in se uno[83] non servari quod sit omnibus datum semper imperatoribus, ut rebus feliciter gestis aut cum honore aliquo aut certe sine ignominia domum revertantur exercitumque dimittant.[84] *[11]* Quae tamen omnia et se tulisse patienter et esse

---

78. *tantasque classis*, hyperbolically for the ships sent to Massilia under Domitius.

79. *diuturnitatem pacis*: evidently Caesar means the whole period after the fall of Sertorius in 72 or, alternatively, since the time that he himself campaigned extensively in Spain in 61. In any case, he argues that a continued campaign since 55 was not merited by danger in the province. This argument is of course not consistent with his description below of the two Spains as *bellicosissimae*, unless (as is possible) that is intended as irony.

80. *novi generis imperia*, "(provincial) commands of a new sort," i.e., that of Pompey, who was allowed to hold *imperium* through legates in Spain without actually going there himself, as Caesar goes on to explain.

81. *ex praetura et consulatu*, "(in the years) following the praetorship and consulship."

82. *ad obtinendos exercitus evocentur*, "were called out of retirement in order to compose armies." Caesar has already indicated (1.3.2; chapter 2, n. 19) that Pompey induced these men to return to service for the money and the hope of advancement; here he claims that some or many of them were also too old and feeble.

83. *in se uno*: the other uses of *in se* in this paragraph have been accusative, "against him"; this one (and perhaps, arguably, the one in the previous clause) is of course ablative, "in his case alone."

84. Caesar's complaint here refers to his conclusion of the Gallic Wars. He had been decreed some fifty-five days of thanksgiving by the Senate during the course of that campaign (*BG* 2.35.4, 4.38.5, and 7.90.8) and could reasonably have expected a triumph. The argument seems to reside somewhat strangely in this

laturum; neque nunc id[85] agere ut ab illis abductum exercitum teneat ipse, quod tamen sibi difficile non sit, sed ne illi habeant quo[86] contra se uti possint. *[12]* Proinde,[87] ut esset dictum, provinciis excederent exercitumque dimitterent; si id sit factum, se nociturum nemini. Hanc unam atque extremam esse pacis condicionem.[88]

86 Id vero militibus fuit pergratum et iucundum, ut ex ipsa significatione cognosci potuit ut, qui aliquid iusti incommodi[89] exspectavissent, ultro praemium missionis ferrent. *[2]* Nam cum de loco et de tempore eius rei[90] controversia inferretur, et voce et manibus universi ex vallo, ubi constiterant, significare coeperunt ut statim dimitterentur, neque omni interposita fide[91] firmum esse posse, si in aliud tempus differretur. *[3]* Paucis cum esset in utramque partem verbis[92] disputatum, res huc deducitur ut ei qui habeant domicilium aut possessionem in Hispania statim, reliqui ad

---

speech, unless we recall that Caesar's troops also had a strong interest in Caesar's holding a triumph, in which they would share both the glory and the financial benefits. The Senate's treatment of Caesar earlier in this year, when he had been ordered to release his troops before returning, is portrayed in terms that show the injustice to himself and the implications of that treatment for the soldiers. He omits the violence against tribunes because that theme has less force with this audience.

85. *id* stands for the following *ut* clause, a noun clause used as the direct object which is further qualified by *quod . . . non sit*; *ne*, however, introduces a purpose clause also dependent upon *agere*, "he was acting . . . to prevent."

86. *quo* = (*exercitum*) *quo*, ablative depending upon *uti*.

87. *proinde* suddenly introduces Caesar's actual orders, imperatives in direct speech which become (imperfect) subjunctive in indirect statement.

88. As had been his hope since 1.72 (above), despite the unpopularity of his decision among his own troops at that time.

89. *aliquid iusti incommodi*, "some legitimate suffering."

90. *eius rei*, i.e., their release from service.

91. *omni interposita fide*, ablative absolute with conditional force, "even if every guarantee were provided."

92. *Paucis . . . verbis*, i.e., Caesar did not allow the debate to go on very long but did allow expression of opinion on both sides.

Varum flumen,[93] dimittantur; *[4]* ne[94] quid eis noceatur neu quis invitus sacramentum dicere[95] cogatur, a Caesare cavetur.

87 Caesar ex eo tempore, dum[96] ad flumen Varum veniatur, se frumentum daturum pollicetur. Addit etiam ut, quod quisque eorum in bello amiserit, quae sint penes milites suos eis qui amiserint restituatur; militibus aequa facta aestimatione pecuniam pro his rebus dissolvit.[97] *[2]* Quascumque postea controversias inter se milites habuerunt, sua sponte ad Caesarem in ius adierunt. *[3]* Petreius atque Afranius cum stipendium ab legionibus paene seditione facta flagitarentur,[98] cuius illi diem nondum venisse dicerent, Caesar ut cognosceret postulatum est,[99] eoque utrique quod statuit contenti fuerunt. *[4]* Parte circiter tertia exercitus eo biduo dimissa, duas legiones suas antecedere, reliquas subsequi iussit, ut non longo inter se spatio castra facerent, eique negotio Q. Fufium Calenum legatum praeficit. *[5]* Hoc eius praescripto[100] ex Hispania ad Varum flumen est iter factum atque ibi reliqua pars exercitus dimissa est.[101]

---

93. The river Var was the eastern boundary of Gallia Narbonensis.

94. The two *ne* clauses depend upon *a Caesare cavetur*, "it was pledged by Caesar."

95. *sacramentum dicere*, "swear the (military) oath," i.e., no one would be forced to enlist.

96. *dum*, with the subjunctive = "until."

97. *militibus . . . pecuniam . . . dissolvit*, "(Caesar himself) paid back the funds to (his) soldiers."

98. *flagitarentur*, "were being petitioned (for)." *Flagitare* in the active takes two accusatives, on the pattern *flagitare aliquem aliquid*. In the passive, the person being asked becomes the grammatical subject, but the thing demanded remains in the accusative (here *stipendium*).

99. *Caesar ut cognosceret postulatum est*, "Caesar was asked to look into it."

100. *Hoc eius praescripto*, "Following his instructions."

101. About 2 August. Thus had Caesar demolished Pompey's Spanish base of support in forty days (see *BC* 2.32.10–13), again with minimal loss of life and with another opportunity to display his *clementia*. As we shall see, Pompey's defeated officers continued to show their loyalty to him and joined him in Greece (*BC* 3.88.7–10).

CASSIUS DIO ON A MUTINY OF THE TROOPS
(DIO 41.26, 35)

As Caesar was returning to Italy, his soldiers suddenly mutinied near Placentia. Other sources expand upon Dio's explanation of the mutiny: a lack of booty, a protracted war, and Caesar's failure to pay quickly the reward for victory he had promised.[102] The soldiers had already complained, as we have seen, of Caesar's failure to deliver the crushing blow when the opportunity was presented; they were unimpressed by his desire to show clemency for political reasons. Caesar does not report this incident, perhaps because he thought it detracted from his image as an effective leader. In fact, it illustrates, much as his dealing with his terrified legions before the campaign with the German Ariovistus, how he could command the respect and obedience of recalcitrant troops by sheer force of personality. Similar tactics, if tried by a lesser leader, would have been disastrous.

Now in Placentia some of the soldiers began to mutiny and were unwilling to follow him any longer, offering the explanation that they were exhausted, whereas in truth it was because he was not releasing them either to ravage the land or to do other things that they wished (indeed, they were expecting not to be kept from anything at all by Caesar, inasmuch as he needed them so badly). But Caesar did not give in; rather he called together both the mutineers and the others, both as a source of protection against the mutineers and so that when they heard what he had to say and saw that there would be punishment, they would not try to do anything contrary to proper conduct. [Dio inserts a lengthy speech here, of his own invention] . . . After speaking in this way, he designated them by lot for death, and punished the boldest of these, for they had been chosen by prearrangement; the others he dismissed, on the grounds that he had no need of them.[103] The

---

102. Suet. *Caes.* 69; Appian *BC* 2.191; Lucan 5.246.
103. This is in accordance with the ancient custom of decimation: one of every ten (mutinous) soldiers was chosen by lot for execution; Caesar announced his intention of dismissing the rest as unworthy. The soldiers selected in this way were all from the Ninth Legion, which then begged to be allowed to continue in

soldiers then had a change of heart at what they had done, and were now willing to renew the campaign.

This was far from the first time that Caesar had reacted to recalcitrance from his troops by insisting on firm discipline, backed up primarily by his personal *dignitas* when their respect for official power had lagged. It was through actions of this kind, where the risks were quite real, in addition to his more overtly political deeds, that Caesar demonstrated his commitment to his *dignitas* as *vita potior*.

---

service. Caesar then solicited the names of 120 ringleaders as a condition of leniency, and had twelve (again, one in ten) of those executed instead of one-tenth of the Ninth Legion as a whole (see Gelzer 219).

6

Caesar's Pursuit of Pompey to Greece

After describing the final reduction of Spain (2.17–22) and after a long digression on events in Africa, Caesar returns in Book 3 to his own actions against Pompey. Caesar has come back to Italy and assembled ships to transport his army to Greece from Brundisium, a task to which he assigned Fufius Calenus. Because the number of ships was limited, the troops had to be transported in shifts. M. Calpurnius Bibulus (on whom see n. 61 below, on 3.16.3), Caesar's bitter enemy and now a supporter of Pompey, was at Corcyra and managed to sail out and capture about thirty of these ships in transit, although they were empty of troops at the time. In frustration, Bibulus burned the ships and their crews and stationed ships all along the coast of Greece, hoping to get to Caesar himself. Meanwhile, M. Octavius had tried to stir up sentiment against Caesar in the towns of western Greece, with mixed success. At Salonae, support for Caesar was so strong that Octavius laid siege to the town; even though they were hard pressed by lack of food, the inhabitants held out, and finally broke the siege by a daring breakout into Octavius' camps. Octavius was forced to give up the siege and, in view of the onset of winter (48), moved on to join Pompey at Dyrrachium.

CAESAR, *DE BELLO CIVILI* 3.10–19

10 Demonstravimus L. Vibullium Rufum, Pompei praefectum, bis in potestatem pervenisse Caesaris atque ab eo esse dimissum, semel ad Corfinium, iterum in Hispania.[1] *[2]* Hunc pro suis beneficiis Caesar idoneum iudicaverat quem cum mandatis ad Cn. Pompeium mitteret,[2] eundemque apud Cn. Pompeium auctoritatem habere intellegebat. *[3]* Erat autem haec summa mandatorum:[3]

Debere utrumque pertinaciae finem facere et ab armis discedere neque amplius fortunam periclitari. *[4]* Satis esse magna utrimque incommoda accepta, quae[4] pro[5] disciplina et praeceptis habere possent, ut reliquos casus timerent: *[5]* illum[6] Italia expulsum, amissa Sicilia et Sardinia duabusque Hispaniis, et cohortibus in Italia atque Hispania civium Romanorum centum atque XXX; se[7] morte Curionis et detrimento Africani exercitus et Antoni militumque deditione ad Curictam.[8] *[6]* Proinde sibi ac rei publicae parcerent,[9] cum[10] quantum in bello fortuna[11] posset iam ipsi

---

1. *semel ad Corfinium, iterum in Hispania*: Corfinium: 1.15.4, 1.34.1; Spain: 1.38.1 (where he is called *legatus*) and presumably at the end of that campaign, though he is not mentioned there.

2. *idoneum . . . quem . . . mitteret*, characteristic subjunctive, "a suitable man to send."

3. There is nothing new in this message, which Pompey has previously ignored or rejected on numerous occasions, and Caesar could not have seriously expected him to agree to it. But Caesar demonstrates here that he has not ceased to make overtures to end the war. Once again, his hope in principle would be to avoid actual bloodshed, as at Corfinium and in Spain.

4. *quae* introduces a relative characteristic clause. *Quae* (= *et ea*) is the direct object of *habere possent*, of which the subjects are Caesar and Pompey, the plural implied by *utrimque*.

5. *pro*, "as" (to serve as).

6. *illum* = Pompeium.

7. *se* = *Caesarem*.

8. Caesar refers to C. Antonius, the younger brother of Mark Antony, who had been defeated in 49 by M. Octavius and L. Scribonius Libo off the island of Curicta, which is located in the gulf off the coast, between Istria and Dalmatia.

9. *parcerent*: again, the subjunctive is used in indirect statement to reflect an imperative in direct statement, "they should spare" or "let them spare."

10. *cum* goes with the verb *essent*.

11. There has been much scholarly discussion of Caesar's view of the role of Fortuna in human affairs. Whether or not he intended it to be personified, it need mean no more than "luck," and his statements about its influence, including this one, are commonplace enough.

incommodis suis satis essent documento.[12] *[7]* Hoc unum esse tempus de pace agendi, dum sibi uterque confideret et pares ambo viderentur; si vero alteri paulum[13] modo tribuisset fortuna, non esse usurum condicionibus pacis eum qui superior videretur, neque fore aequa parte contentum qui se omnia habiturum confideret. *[8]* Condiciones pacis, quoniam antea convenire non potuissent,[14] Romae ab senatu et a populo peti debere. *[9]* Interea et rei publicae et ipsis placere oportere, si uterque in contione statim iuravisset se triduo proximo exercitum dimissurum; *[10]* depositis armis auxiliisque[15] quibus nunc confiderent, necessario populi senatusque iudicio fore utrumque contentum. *[11]* Haec quo facilius Pompeio probari possent, omnis suas terrestris copias dimissurum.[16]

11 Vibullius expositus Corcyrae[17] non minus necessarium esse existimavit de repentino adventu Caesaris Pompeium fieri certiorem, uti ad id[18] consilium capere posset antequam de mandatis agi inciperetur, atque ideo continuato nocte ac die itinere atque omnibus oppidis mutatis ad celeritatem iumentis[19] ad

---

12. *ipsi . . . satis essent documento*: *documento* is dative of purpose or predicate dative. *Incommodis suis*, then, is ablative of cause. Caesar has strikingly personalized this common construction by making *ipsi* (= *Caesar et Pompeius*) the subject that is predicated by the dative: "they themselves are sufficient proof." Usually, the person(s) most concerned are also in the dative: a more "normal" diction would have been *ipsis incommoda sua essent documento*.

13. *paulum*, "a little advantage" (accusative, direct object of *tribuisset*).

14. *convenire non potuissent*, "could not be agreed upon."

15. *depositis armis auxiliisque*, an example of zeugma: *depositis* strictly applies only to *armis*, but is taken by extension with *auxiliis* as well (for which the usual verb would be *dimissis*).

16. (*se*) *dimissurum* (*esse*), "he (Caesar) would release."

17. *expositus Corcyrae*, "upon landing at Corcyra."

18. *ad id*, "in view of this." Somewhat sloppily, *id* does not modify *consilium*, which is to be taken closely with *capere*. The *ut(i)* clause shows purpose.

19. *continuato . . . itinere atque mutatis . . . iumentis*, ablative absolutes. *Omnibus oppidis* is ablative of place, again somewhat awkwardly located within the absolute construction. In spite of the awkwardness, Caesar may have planned this combination of ambiguous inflections: assuming the apparent jumble of ablatives is intentional, the effect is to emphasize the haste and urgency of, and to suggest a bit of hysteria in, Vibullius' journey. The repeated *atque* in this phrase (also *nocte ac die*) grates a bit after the use of *atque* to introduce the whole clause.

Dyrrachium

Asparagium

MACEDONIA

Amphipolis

Heraclea

Apollonia

Via Egnatia

THRACE

Oricum

Larisa

Corcyra

Pharsalus

ACHAIA

Greece
in the
Civil War

Pompeium contendit, ut adesse Caesarem nuntiaret. *[2]* Pompeius erat eo tempore in Candavia[20] iterque ex Macedonia in hiberna Apolloniam Dyrrachiumque[21] habebat. Sed re nova perturbatus maioribus itineribus Apolloniam petere coepit, ne Caesar orae maritimae civitates occuparet. *[3]* At ille expositis militibus eodem die[22] Oricum[23] proficiscitur. Quo cum venisset, L. Torquatus,[24] qui iussu Pompei oppido praeerat praesidiumque ibi Parthinorum[25] habebat, conatus portis clausis oppidum defendere, *[4]* cum Graecos murum ascendere atque arma capere iuberet, illi autem se contra imperium populi Romani pugnaturos negarent, oppidani autem etiam sua sponte Caesarem recipere conarentur, desperatis omnibus auxiliis[26] portas aperuit et se atque oppidum Caesari dedidit incolumisque ab eo conservatus est.

12 Recepto Caesar Orico nulla interposita mora Apolloniam proficiscitur. Eius adventu audito L. Staberius, qui ibi praeerat, aquam comportare in arcem atque eam munire obsidesque ab

---

20. *Candavia*, a mountainous district on the Via Egnatia just east of Dyrrachium.

21. *Apolloniam Dyrrachiumque*, accusatives of motion after *iter habebat*. Apollonia, on the coast of Illyria at the Aous River, was to become Caesar's headquarters in this campaign. It had become a Roman ally as early as 229 and was one of the terminal points of the Via Egnatia. Dyrrachium (now called Durazzo), which was located below old Epidamnus and terminated the northern fork of the Via Egnatia, became Pompey's main base.

22. *eodem die*, probably 5 January (see next note).

23. After leaving Brundisium on 4 January (3.6.1, not quoted here), Caesar had landed at Palaeste (3.6.3), a convenient seaport of Epirus. Oricum (now Paleo-Kastro) was at the southern end of the Bay of Aulon, just north of the landing point.

24. L. Manlius Torquatus was praetor for 49 and, despite his Epicurean sentiments, a friend of Cicero's. After Pharsalus he made his way to Pompeian forces in Africa, where he was eventually killed trying to go to Spain. Cicero makes him his spokesman for Epicureanism in the first book of *De finibus*.

25. *Parthinorum*, "inhabitants of Parthus," a small city of Greeks, not Parthians.

26. *desperatis omnibus auxiliis*, ablative absolute, "giving up hope of reinforcement."

Apolloniatibus exigere coepit. *[2]* Illi vero daturos se negare[27] neque portas consuli praeclusuros neque sibi iudicium sumpturos contra atque[28] omnis Italia populusque Romanus iudicavisset. *[3]* Quorum cognita voluntate clam profugit Apollonia Staberius. Illi ad Caesarem legatos mittunt oppidoque recipiunt. *[4]* Hos sequuntur Byllidenses et Amantini et reliquae finitimae civitates totaque Epirus et, legatis ad Caesarem missis, quae[29] imperaret facturos pollicentur.

13 At Pompeius, cognitis his rebus quae erant Orici atque Apolloniae gestae, Dyrrachio[30] timens diurnis eo nocturnisque itineribus contendit. *[2]* Simul Caesar appropinquare dicebatur; tantusque terror incidit eius[31] exercitui, quod[32] properans noctem diei coniunxerat neque iter intermiserat, ut paene omnes ex Epiro finitimisque regionibus signa relinquerent, complures arma proicerent, ac fugae simile iter videretur. *[3]* Sed cum prope Dyrrachium Pompeius constitisset castraque metari iussisset, perterrito etiam tum exercitu princeps Labienus[33] procedit

---

27. **daturos se negare** = *negabant se daturos esse. Negare* is a historical or narrative infinitive used in place of the indicative. It governs *daturos (esse)*, *praeclusuros (esse)*, and *sumpturos (esse)*, all in indirect statement.

28. **neque sibi iudicium sumpturos contra atque**, "nor would they judge otherwise than."

29. **quae** = *ea quae*.

30. *Dyrrachio* is dative, with *timens*.

31. **eius** = *Pompei*.

32. **quod**, "inasmuch as." The causal connection is loose, since the soldiers' fear arose from the rumors of Caesar's approach to Dyrrachium, where Pompey's supplies were located, not from their own forced marches. The subject of *coniunxerat* and of *intermiserat* is Pompey.

33. **princeps Labienus**, "Labienus first of all." T. Atius Labienus (see chapter 1, n. 21) was last heard from in 1.15: he had been in charge of one of the two legions that Pompey had "loaned" to Caesar for the Gallic Wars and reclaimed early in 49 on the pretext of preparing for a war with Parthia. Labienus' devotion to Pompey now becomes increasingly clear, manifested in the most bitter opposition to Caesar, whom he had served so well in Gaul. But as Brunt, "Cicero's *officium*," suggests, perhaps he simply thought that Pompey's cause was more honorable or, like many others, that Caesar could not ultimately win.

iuratque[34] se eum[35] non deserturum eundemque casum subiturum, quemcumque ei fortuna tribuisset. *[4]* Hoc idem reliqui iurant legati; hos tribuni militum centurionesque sequuntur, atque idem omnis exercitus iurat. *[5]* Caesar praecepto itinere ad Dyrrachium finem properandi facit, castraque ad flumen Apsum ponit[36] in finibus Apolloniatium, ut castellis vigiliisque bene meritae civitates tutae essent, ibique reliquarum ex Italia legionum adventum exspectare et sub pellibus[37] hiemare constituit. *[6]* Hoc idem Pompeius fecit et trans flumen Apsum positis castris eo copias omnis auxiliaque conduxit.

14 Calenus legionibus equitibusque Brundisi in navis impositis, ut erat praeceptum a Caesare,[38] quantum[39] navium facultatem habebat, navis solvit paulumque a portu progressus litteras a Caesare accepit, quibus est certior factus portus litoraque omnia classibus adversariorum teneri. *[2]* Quo cognito se in portum recipit navisque omnis revocat. Una ex his, quae perseveravit neque imperio Caleni obtemperavit, quod erat sine militibus privatoque consilio administrabatur,[40] delata Oricum atque a Bibulo expugnata est; *[3]* qui[41] de servis liberisque omnibus ad[42]

---

34. *iurat*: the officers and soldiers had already sworn such an oath before, the *sacramentum* that bound them to (Rome and) their general; the renewal of that oath in effect is a renewal of their loyalty. Petreius in Spain had used this same moral tactic to strengthen the resolve of his and Afranius' troops.

35. *se* = *Labienum*; *eum* = *Pompeium*.

36. About 11 January.

37. *sub pellibus*, "in (tents made of) skins," rather than the semipermanent barracks of a usual Roman winter camp.

38. Recounted in 3.8.2, not quoted here, but see introductory remarks on this section.

39. *quantum*, "to the extent that."

40. *privatoque consilio administrabatur*, "and was being run by private management." An entrepreneurial captain had presumably leased his ship to the army.

41. *qui* = *et Bibulus*.

42. *ad*, "including even." These *impuberes* would not be children but very young men hiring themselves out as sailors.

impuberes supplicium sumit et ad unum interficit.[43] Ita in exiguo tempore magnoque casu[44] totius exercitus salus constitit.[45]

15 Bibulus, ut supra demonstratum est, erat cum classe ad Oricum et, sicuti mari portibusque Caesarem prohibebat, ita ipse omni terra earum regionum prohibebatur. *[2]* Praesidiis enim dispositis omnia litora a Caesare tenebantur, neque lignandi atque aquandi neque navis ad terram religandi potestas fiebat. *[3]* Erat res[46] in magna difficultate, summisque angustiis rerum necessariarum premebantur adeo ut cogerentur sicuti reliquum commeatum ita ligna atque aquam Corcyra navibus onerariis supportare, *[4]* atque etiam uno tempore[47] accidit ut difficilioribus usi tempestatibus[48] ex pellibus quibus erant tectae naves nocturnum excipere rorem[49] cogerentur; *[5]* quas tamen difficultates patienter atque aequo animo ferebant neque sibi nudanda litora et relinquendos portus existimabant. *[6]* Sed cum essent in quibus demonstravi angustiis[50] ac se Libo[51] cum Bibulo coniunxisset, loquuntur ambo ex navibus cum M'. Acilio[52] et Statio Murco[53] legatis, quorum alter oppidi muris, alter praesidiis

---

43. Caesar has already told of Bibulus' atrocities above (3.8.3, not quoted)—the burning of captured ships and crews. Thus he maintains his emphasis on the character of his opponents, as well as on the cruelty of their actions. The contrast with his own fairness and *clementia* is left implicit.

44. *casu*, "luck." Unlike here, the word usually has a negative connotation.

45. *constitit*, "depended upon" (< *consistere*, not *constare*).

46. That is, from Bibulus' point of view.

47. *uno tempore* = *simul*, as frequently in Caesar.

48. *difficilioribus usi tempestatibus*, "encountering very severe weather." This is a good example of the idiomatic use of the verb *utor*, for which "use" is often a poor or risky translation.

49. Because they could not get water from any other source.

50. *in quibus demonstravi angustiis* = *in eis angustiis quas demonstravi*.

51. L. Scribonius Libo, a loyal Pompeian, on whom see chapter 4, n. 26.

52. M'. Acilius Glabrio. A supporter of Caesar, he was the son of Pompey's former wife (and Sulla's stepdaughter) Aemilia, and a friend of Cicero's, by whom he was twice defended in court.

53. L. Statius Murcus, here a Caesarian supporter, went over to the Pompeians in 45 while praetor.

terrestribus praeerat: velle se[54] de maximis rebus cum Caesare loqui, si sibi eius facultas[55] detur. *[7]* Huc addunt pauca rei confirmandae causa, ut de compositione acturi viderentur.[56] Interim postulant ut sint indutiae, atque ab eis impetrant. *[8]* Magnum enim quod adferebant videbatur,[57] et Caesarem id summe sciebant cupere, et profectum aliquid Vibulli mandatis existimabatur.[58]

16 Caesar eo tempore cum legione una profectus ad recipiendas ulteriores civitates et rem frumentariam expediendam qua anguste utebatur,[59] erat ad Buthrotum oppidum oppositum Corcyrae. *[2]* Ibi certior ab Acilio et Murco per litteras factus de postulatis Libonis et Bibuli legionem relinquit; ipse Oricum revertitur. *[3]* Eo cum venisset, evocantur illi ad colloquium. Prodit[60] Libo atque excusat Bibulum, quod is iracundia summa erat inimicitiasque habebat etiam privatas cum Caesare ex aedilitate et praetura conceptas;[61] ob eam causam colloquium vitasse, ne res maximae spei maximaeque utilitatis eius iracundia impedirentur. *[4]* Pompei summam esse ac fuisse semper voluntatem[62] ut componeretur

---

54. *se* = *Bibulum et Libonem*, subjects of *velle*, in indirect statement.

55. *eius facultas*, "an opportunity for this."

56. *acturi viderentur*: the personal construction (as opposed to the alternative, the impersonal *acturos videretur*, "it would appear that they intended to discuss") strengthens the visibility of their actions: "so that they would clearly be intending to discuss."

57. I.e., to Acilius and Murcus, who are the subjects of *sciebant*.

58. *profectum aliquid . . . existimabatur*, "it was thought that something had been accomplished."

59. *qua anguste utebatur*, "which he was finding in short supply."

60. *prodit* < *prod-ire* (also below, 3.19.5), not < *pro-dere*.

61. Caesar and M. Calpurnius Bibulus were aediles together in 65 and praetors in 62, in addition to sharing the consulship in 59. It is not clear what difficulty Bibulus had with Caesar as praetor, but Suetonius (*Jul.* 10.1) notes that as aediles he and Caesar jointly sponsored games which Caesar so extravagantly embellished that Bibulus' share in the glory was diminished. In their consulship Caesar simply ignored Bibulus, who tried repeatedly to oppose Caesar's actions but was again totally overshadowed by him (see Suet. *Jul.* 20). Bibulus' ploy here is clever: his petulant abstinence from the conference would, he felt, add credibility to Libo's presentation in Caesar's eyes.

62. *Pompei summam . . . voluntatem*, "Pompey's highest intention."

atque ab armis discederetur; se potestatem eius rei nullam habere,[63] propterea quod, de consili sententia,[64] summam belli[65] rerumque omnium Pompeio permiserint.[66] *[5]* Sed postulatis Caesaris cognitis[67] missuros ad Pompeium, atque illum reliqua per se acturum hortantibus ipsis. Interea manerent indutiae, dum ab illo rediri posset, neve alter alteri noceret. Huc addit pauca de causa et de copiis auxiliisque suis.

17 Quibus rebus[68] neque tum respondendum Caesar existimavit neque nunc ut[69] memoriae prodantur satis causae putamus.[70] *[2]* Postulabat Caesar ut legatos sibi ad Pompeium sine periculo mittere liceret,[71] idque ipsi fore reciperent[72] aut acceptos per se ad eum perducerent. *[3]* Quod ad indutias pertineret, sic belli rationem esse divisam ut illi classe navis auxiliaque sua[73] impedirent, ipse ut aqua terraque eos prohiberet. *[4]* Si hoc sibi remitti vellent, remitterent ipsi de maritimis custodiis; si illud

---

63. *se potestatem . . . nullam habere*, "(but) they (themselves) had no power (over)."

64. *de consili sententia*, "by the decision of the (war) council." These were the senators who were now with Pompey in Greece and who claimed to be the only legitimate source of governmental authority, now that Caesar had taken control of Italy and Rome. The wording (*consilium* rather than *senatus*) reflects Caesar's point of view, and is rhetorically neat if it belonged to Libo.

65. *summam belli*, "the overall command of the war."

66. *permiserint*, construction by sense rather than strict grammar: the subject is the implied group of senators in *consili*.

67. *postulatis Caesaris cognitis*, perhaps conditional, "if Caesar's demands were made known." Vibullius had not yet been able to deliver his message to Pompey, as will become clear below.

68. *Quibus rebus*, i.e., the comments made by Libo at the end of his speech *de causa*, etc.

69. *ut* explains *satis causae* (*esse*), which is indirect statement with *putamus*.

70. *putamus*: "Observe that Caesar uses the third person singular speaking of himself as an actor in the past, but changes to the first person plural when speaking in the capacity of the historian" (Peskett).

71. *sibi . . . mittere liceret*, "he should be allowed to send."

72. *ipsi . . . reciperent*, "they themselves (Libo and Bibulus) should take the responsibility (for ensuring)"; this is a special sense of *recipere*. *id . . . fore*, "that this would occur."

73. *sua* = *Caesaris*.

tenerent, se quoque id retenturum. Nihilo minus tamen agi posse[74] dc compositione, ut[75] haec non remitterentur, neque hanc rem illi[76] esse impedimento. *[5]* Libo[77] neque legatos Caesaris recipere neque periculum praestare eorum, sed totam rem ad Pompeium reicere; unum[78] instare de indutiis vehementissimeque contendere. *[6]* Quem[79] ubi Caesar intellexit praesentis periculi atque inopiae vitandae causa omnem orationem instituisse neque ullam spem aut condicionem pacis adferre, ad reliquam cogitationem belli sese recepit.

18 Bibulus multos dies terra prohibitus et graviore morbo ex frigore ac labore implicitus, cum neque curari posset neque susceptum officium deserere vellet, vim morbi sustinere[80] non potuit. *[2]* Eo mortuo, ad neminem unum summa imperi rediit, sed separatim suam quisque classem ad arbitrium suum administrabat. *[3]* Vibullius, sedato tumultu quem repentinus adventus Caesaris concitaverat, ubi primum reversus est,[81] adhibito Libone et L. Lucceio[82]

---

74. *agi posse*, "discussions could be held," impersonal passive.

75. *ut*, "but although."

76. *neque hanc rem illi esse impedimento*, "(he said that) *this* circumstance (both sides' retaining their tactical advantages) was no impediment to *that* (discussion of peace)."

77. *Libo*, nominative, is the subject of *recipere, praestare, reicere, instare*, and *contendere*, historical infinitives. *Recipere* here is not used as above in the sense of "guarantee" but in its usual sense of "receive."

78. *unum*, direct object: "one thing" he stressed.

79. *Quem* = *Et eum*, subject of *instituisse*, of which *omnem orationem* is the direct object.

80. *sustinere*, "to withstand."

81. *ubi primum reversus est*, "as soon as he returned (to Pompey)," where he had been sent by Caesar to discuss peace negotiations (above, 3.10.1). Events had overtaken Vibullius, for both Caesar and Pompey had in the meantime gone to the west coast by forced marches. Nevertheless, he attempts to carry out the charge given to him by Caesar.

82. L. Lucceius had been praetor in 67 and had run for the consulship with Caesar in 60; he was defeated by Bibulus in that election. Since he was a noted historian, Cicero had asked him to write a history of the year 63, hoping to be cast in the heroic role of savior of the state. Though promised, the work was never written.

et Theophane,[83] quibuscum communicare de maximis rebus Pompeius consueverat, de mandatis Caesaris agere instituit. Quem ingressum in sermonem Pompeius interpellavit et loqui plura prohibuit.

[4] "Quid mihi," inquit, "aut vita aut civitate opus est, quam beneficio Caesaris habere videbor?[84] cuius rei opinio[85] tolli non poterit, cum in Italiam, ex qua profectus sum,[86] reductus existimabor." *[5]* Bello perfecto ab eis Caesar haec facta cognovit qui sermoni interfuerunt;[87] conatus tamen nihilo minus est aliis rationibus per colloquia de pace agere.

19 Inter bina castra Pompei atque Caesaris unum flumen tantum[88] intererat Apsus; crebraque inter se colloquia milites habebant, neque ullum interim telum per pactiones loquentium[89] traiciebatur. *[2]* Mittit[90] P. Vatinium[91] legatum ad ripam ipsam fluminis, qui[92] ea quae maxime ad pacem pertinere viderentur

---

83. Theophanes of Mytilene, another historian, whom Pompey had met in Asia, also mentioned by Cicero (*Pro Archia* 24). He was much admired by Pompey, which earned him a certain influence in Rome, and Pompey sponsored his claim to Roman citizenship.

84. From Pompey's point of view, this is now the telling point: his *dignitas* is at risk, and if he gives it up his life will be meaningless. Thus it is clear that both Caesar and Pompey were operating from essentially the same moral premises, and that for both the issue came down to their own *libertas* and *dignitas*, which was for each of them inseparable from their understanding of the *res publica*.

85. *cuius rei opinio*, "and the general interpretation of this outcome."

86. *profectus sum*, used in the military sense, implying control over his actions.

87. I.e., Lucceius and Theophanes, both of whom Caesar later pardoned.

88. *tantum* is adverbial, "only."

89. *per pactiones loquentium*, "by agreement of those involved in the negotiations."

90. The subject is Caesar.

91. P. Vatinius as tribune in 59 had been the author of the *Lex Vatinia* by which Caesar's province was revised to include Gallia Cisalpina and Illyricum. He had subsequently served as legate and became praetor in 55. In 47, the year after the events recounted here, Vatinius was made temporary consul by Caesar. Vatinius was despised by Cicero, and also came in for brief abuse from Catullus.

92. *qui* (. . . *ageret* . . . *pronuntiaret*) = *ut*, relative clauses of purpose.

ageret et crebro magna voce pronuntiaret, liceretne[93] civibus ad civis de pace legatos mittere, quod etiam fugitivis ab saltu Pyrenaeo[94] praedonibusque[95] licuisset, praesertim cum id agerent ne cives cum civibus armis decertarent? *[3]* Multa suppliciter locutus est, ut de sua atque omnium salute debebat,[96] silentioque ab utrisque militibus auditus. Responsum est ab altera parte A. Varronem[97] profiteri se altera die ad colloquium venturum[98] atque una visurum quem ad modum tuto legati venire et quae vellent exponere possent; certumque ei rei tempus constituitur.

[4] Quo cum esset postero die ventum, magna utrimque multitudo convenit magnaque erat exspectatio eius rei, atque omnium animi intenti esse ad pacem videbantur. *[5]* Qua ex frequentia T. Labienus prodit, summissa oratione loqui de pace atque altercari cum Vatinio incipit. *[6]* Quorum mediam orationem interrumpunt subito undique tela immissa; quae ille obtectus armis militum vitavit; vulnerantur tamen complures, in his Cornelius Balbus, M. Plotius, L. Tiburtius, centuriones militesque non nulli. *[7]* Tum Labienus: "Desinite ergo de compositione loqui; nam nobis nisi Caesaris capite relato pax esse nulla potest."

---

93. *liceretne*, "whether (or not) it should be permitted," i.e., "was it right to allow."

94. *fugitivis ab saltu Pyrenaeo*, "to those trying to escape out of passes in the Pyrenees" during Pompey's war with Sertorius in the 70s. Pompey had allowed some such refugees to found a city in southern Gaul.

95. *praedonibusque*, "pirates" from Cilicia, defeated by Pompey in 67.

96. *debebat*, explains *suppliciter*: he had to adopt the attitude of a suppliant because he was begging for the lives of his fellow citizens (both armies).

97. A. Terentius Varro Murena, son of L. Licinius Murena and adopted by A. Terentius Varro. His sister was the wife of Maecenas, and Horace later addressed an ode to him (2.10). Varro was executed in 23 or 22 after being implicated in the conspiracy of Caepio against Augustus.

98. *profiteri se . . . venturum*, "(Varro) promised that he would come."

7

The Great Confrontation:
Caesar and Pompey at Pharsalus

Caesar has just briefly described events in Italy and Rome, as his
enemies continue to try to undermine his position politically and
militarily. In a vigorous maneuver in early April, Mark Antony has
succeeded in reaching Greece with minimal loss and in joining
forces with Caesar, despite efforts by Pompey to prevent him. Now
Caesar and Pompey are in direct contact for the first time since
Brundisium. In the passages that follow, Caesar is trying to provoke
Pompey into a decisive battle, because he is himself hard pressed by
lack of supplies. Pompey, in turn, hopes that this problem will
finally demoralize Caesar's troops and lead to a mutiny or an easy
victory, and so he avoids a decisive confrontation.

CAESAR, *DE BELLO CIVILI* 3.41–46, 48, 71–72

41 Caesar, postquam Pompeium ad Asparagium[1] esse cognovit,
eodem cum exercitu profectus, expugnato in itinere oppido
Parthinorum,[2] in quo Pompeius praesidium habebat, tertio die ad
Pompeium pervenit iuxtaque eum castra posuit et postridie eductis

---

1. Asparagium was between Apollonia and Dyrrachium on the Genusus River.
Pompey had gone there when his efforts to cut Antony off from Caesar were
unsuccessful (3.30.7, not quoted), evidently intending from this position to
maintain communications with his main camp at Dyrrachium.
2. This *oppidum* was presumably not Parthus itself (see chapter 6, n. 25).

omnibus copiis, acie instructa,³ decernendi potestatem Pompeio
fecit. *[2]* Ubi illum suis locis se tenere animum advertit, reducto in
castra exercitu aliud sibi consilium capiendum existimavit. *[3]* Itaque
postero die omnibus copiis magno circuitu,⁴ difficili angustoque
itinere, Dyrrachium profectus est sperans Pompeium aut
Dyrrachium compelli aut ab eo intercludi posse, quod omnem
commeatum totiusque belli apparatum eo contulisset;⁵ ut accidit.
[4] Pompeius enim primo ignorans eius consilium, quod diverso ab
ea regione itinere⁶ profectum⁷ videbat, angustiis rei frumentariae
compulsum discessisse existimabat; postea per exploratores certior
factus postero die⁸ castra movit, breviore itinere se occurrere ei
posse sperans. *[5]* Quod fore suspicatus Caesar, militesque
adhortatus ut aequo animo laborem ferrent, parva parte noctis
itinere intermisso mane Dyrrachium venit, cum primum agmen
Pompei procul cerneretur, atque ibi castra posuit.

42 Pompeius interclusus Dyrrachio, ubi propositum tenere
non potuit, secundo usus consilio, edito loco qui appellatur Petra⁹
aditumque habet navibus mediocrem atque eas a quibusdam
protegit ventis, castra communit. *[2]* Eo partem navium longarum
convenire, frumentum commeatumque ab Asia¹⁰ atque omnibus

---

3. *aciem instruere* is the technical military idiom for "to draw up the battle
line." Thus Caesar shows Pompey that he will give battle if Pompey also marches
out.

4. *magno circuitu*: evidently, Caesar set off back toward the east, so that
Pompey thought he was moving toward Macedonia for supplies. But once out of
sight he turned north and northwest over rough country toward Dyrrachium.
Caesar could not realistically have expected to beat Pompey there: most estimates
put Caesar's route as 2½ to 3 times the distance covered by Pompey. But he was
sure that Pompey would have to go back to Dyrrachium and that he himself could
not be successfully attacked on route.

5. *quod* . . . (*Pompeius*) *contulisset* explains the basis for *sperans.*

6. *diverso* . . . *itinere*, "in the opposite direction (from Dyrrachium)."

7. *profectum* = *Caesarem profectum esse.*

8. *postero die*, i.e., the day after Caesar had left.

9. Petra (the "Rock") was about five miles southeast of Dyrrachium on a rocky
part of the coast. Caesar's camp was about two miles closer to the town.

10. Asia, as usual in Latin, means Asia Minor. Pompey had substantial
resources in clients and funds there from his wars against the pirates and against
Mithridates in the 60s.

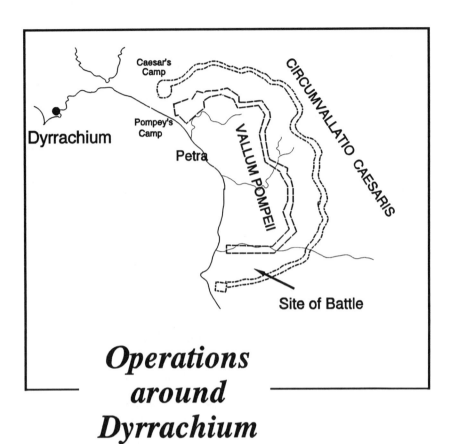

Caesar's
Camp

CIRCUMVALLATIO CAESARIS

Pompey's
Camp

Dyrrachium

Petra

VALLUM POMPEII

Site of Battle

*Operations
around
Dyrrachium*

regionibus quas tenebat comportari imperat. *[3]* Caesar longius
bellum ductum iri[11] existimans et de Italicis commeatibus
desperans, quod[12] tanta diligentia omnia litora a Pompeianis
tenebantur, classesque ipsius[13] quas hieme in Sicilia, Gallia, Italia
fecerat morabantur, in Epirum rei frumentariae causa Q. Tillium et
L. Canuleium legatum misit, *[4]* quodque hae regiones aberant
longius, locis certis horrea constituit vecturasque[14] frumenti
finitimis civitatibus discripsit.[15] Item Lisso Parthinisque et omnibus
castellis quod esset frumenti[16] conquiri iussit. *[5]* Id erat
perexiguum cum[17] ipsius agri natura, quod sunt loca aspera ac
montuosa ac plerumque frumento utuntur importato, tum quod
Pompeius haec providerat et superioribus diebus praedae loco
Parthinos habuerat[18] frumentumque omne conquisitum, spoliatis
effossisque eorum domibus, per equites in Petram comportarat.

43 Quibus rebus cognitis Caesar consilium capit ex loci natura.
Erant enim circum castra Pompei permulti editi atque asperi colles.
Hos primum praesidiis tenuit castellaque ibi communiit. *[2]* Inde,
ut loci cuiusque natura ferebat,[19] ex castello in castellum perducta
munitione, circumvallare Pompeium instituit, haec spectans,[20]
quod angusta re frumentaria utebatur, quodque Pompeius

---

11. ***ductum iri***: future passive infinitive, "was going to be drawn out."

12. Caesar explains his thinking in two clauses, *quod litora tenebantur, classesque
. . . morabantur*, which leads to his first decision (*misit*), and *quodque . . . aberant*,
which leads to his second (*constituit* and *discripsit*).

13. ***ipsius** = Caesaris*.

14. ***vecturasque***, "(responsibility for) transportation."

15. ***discripsit***, "assigned."

16. ***quod esset frumenti***, "whatever grain there was."

17. ***cum***, "both," correlative with *tum* ("and") below.

18. ***praedae loco Parthinos habuerat***, "had regarded the Parthini as booty," i.e.,
had plundered.

19. ***ferebat***, "suggested" or "required." *Natura* is nominative.

20. ***haec spectans***, "with these intentions," is answered below by *uti . . .
prohiberet*, (*uti*) *efficeret*, and *tertio ut . . . minueret*. The reasons for this plan are
explained in two *quod* clauses, *quod . . .* (*Caesar*) *utebatur* and *quod . . . valebat*.
Quo (= *ut*) *. . .* (*Caesar*) *posset* gives the immediate military purpose behind
Caesar's plans and is in a sense parenthetical to the statements of his three
decisions that follow, a reaction to Pompey's numerical superiority in cavalry.

multitudine equitum valebat — quo minore periculo undique frumentum commeatumque exercitui supportare posset — *[3]* simul uti pabulatione Pompeium prohiberet equitatumque eius ad rem gerendam inutilem[21] efficeret, tertio ut auctoritatem, qua ille maxime apud exteras nationes[22] niti videbatur, minueret, cum fama per orbem terrarum percrebruisset illum a Caesare obsideri neque audere proelio dimicare.

44 Pompeius neque a mari Dyrrachioque discedere volebat, quod omnem apparatum belli, tela, arma, tormenta ibi collocaverat frumentumque exercitui navibus supportabat, neque munitiones Caesaris prohibere poterat,[23] nisi proelio decertare vellet; quod eo tempore statuerat non esse faciendum. *[2]* Relinquebatur ut, extremam[24] rationem belli sequens, quam plurimos collis occuparet et quam latissimas regiones praesidiis teneret Caesarisque copias quam maxime posset distineret; idque accidit. *[3]* Castellis enim XXIIII effectis, XV milia passuum circuitu amplexus,[25] hoc spatio pabulabatur; multaque erant intra eum locum manu sata,[26] quibus interim iumenta pasceret. *[4]* Atque ut[27] nostri perpetuas

---

21. *inutilem* modifies *equitatum* and is itself qualified or explained by the gerundive phrase.

22. *exteras nationes*: Caesar means especially the eastern part of the empire, but Spain was also very much a part of Pompey's worldwide *auctoritas*. In recognition of this, Caesar now tries to use Pompey's delaying military strategy against him, to make him look weak.

23. *prohibere poterat* (instead of *prohibere posset*): the indicative of *possum* is regularly used in the apodosis of a subjunctive condition (here the protasis is *nisi . . . vellet*).

24. *extremam*: hyperbolic, at best. Pompey's strategy was fundamentally sound. Caesar was hard pressed by lack of supplies, and Pompey's *auctoritas* was keeping most cities loyal. Though Caesar had outmaneuvered him in marching toward Dyrrachium, he had neither the resources nor the time to lay siege to the town with Pompey at his rear; meanwhile, Pompey could continue to receive supplies by sea. The general perception of Pompey's competence, however, was now becoming the crucial factor, as Caesar continued to exploit tactical coups, none more spectacular than this circumvallation of Pompey's army against the shore, which lasted more than two months.

25. *amplexus*, perfect active (deponent) participle < *amplecti*.

26. *sata*, perfect passive participle < *serere*.

27. *ut*, "just as," with the indicative *habebant*, anticipating *ita* (below).

munitiones habebant perductas ex castellis in proxima castella, ne quo loco erumperent Pompeiani ac nostros post tergum adorirentur, ita illi[28] interiore spatio perpetuas munitiones efficiebant, ne quem locum nostri intrare atque ipsos a tergo circumvenire possent. *[5]* Sed illi operibus vincebant, quod et numero militum praestabant et interiore spatio minorem circuitum habebant. *[6]* Quae[29] cum erant loca Caesari capienda, etsi prohibere Pompeius totis copiis et dimicare non constituerat,[30] tamen suis locis[31] sagittarios funditoresque mittebat, quorum magnum habebat numerum, *[7]* multique ex nostris vulnerabantur, magnusque incesserat timor sagittarum, atque onmes fere milites aut ex coactis[32] aut ex centonibus aut ex coriis tunicas aut tegimenta fecerant quibus[33] tela vitarent.

45 In occupandis praesidiis magna vi uterque nitebatur: Caesar, ut quam angustissime Pompeium contineret, Pompeius, ut quam plurimos collis quam maximo circuitu occuparet; crebraque ob eam causam proelia fiebant. *[2]* In his cum legio Caesaris nona praesidium quoddam occupavisset et munire coepisset, huic loco propinquum et contrarium collem Pompeius occupavit nostrosque opere prohibere coepit. *[3]* Et, cum una ex parte prope aequum[34] aditum haberet, primum sagittariis funditoribusque circumiectis, postea levis armaturae magna multitudine missa tormentisque prolatis, munitiones impediebat; neque erat facile nostris uno tempore propugnare et munire. *[4]* Caesar, cum suos ex omnibus partibus vulnerari videret, recipere se iussit et loco excedere. Erat

---

28. *illi* = *Pompeiani.*
29. *Quae cum erant loca Caesari capienda* = *et cum ea loca Caesari capienda erant.*
30. *non constituerat,* "had decided not (to)."
31. *suis locis,* "from his own positions."
32. *coactis,* "(cloth made of) felt," perfect passive participle < *cogere,* used as a noun. Several layers of cloth were "pressed" together (*coacta*); the word for "fuller" is *coactor.*
33. *quibus* = *ut eis,* relative clause of purpose.
34. *prope aequum,* "almost level."

per declive receptus.³⁵ *[5]* Illi autem hoc acrius³⁶ instabant neque regredi nostros patiebantur quod timore adducti locum relinquere videbantur. *[6]* Dicitur eo tempore glorians apud suos Pompeius dixisse non recusare se quin³⁷ nullius usus³⁸ imperator existimaretur, si sine maximo detrimento legiones Caesaris sese recepissent inde quo temere essent progressae.

46 Caesar receptui³⁹ suorum timens, cratis⁴⁰ ad extremum⁴¹ tumulum contra hostem proferri et adversas locari; intra has mediocri latitudine fossam, tectis militibus,⁴² obduci iussit locumque in omnis partis quam maxime impediri.⁴³ *[2]* Ipse idoneis locis funditores instruxit, ut praesidio nostris se recipientibus essent. His rebus completis, legionem reduci iussit. *[3]* Pompeiani hoc⁴⁴ insolentius atque audacius nostros premere et instare coeperunt, cratisque pro munitione obiectas⁴⁵ propulerunt, ut fossas transcenderent. *[4]* Quod cum animadvertisset Caesar, veritus ne non reducti sed deiecti viderentur maiusque detrimentum caperetur, a medio fere spatio⁴⁶ suos per Antonium,⁴⁷ qui ei legioni praeerat, cohortatus tuba signum dari atque in hostis

---

35. *receptus,* "the (path for) retreat." Caesar had ordered the soldiers *se recipere,* of which the noun is *receptus.*

36. *hoc acrius . . . quod,* "the more fiercely . . . because."

37. *non recusare se quin . . . existimaretur,* "that he did not object to being thought." *Quin* (along with *quominus*) is the regular introductory word after *recusare.*

38. *nullius usus,* "ineffectual."

39. *receptui* is dative with *timens.*

40. *cratis,* "(screens made of) wickerwork."

41. *extremum,* "the farthest (edge of)."

42. *tectis militibus,* ablative absolute, "now that the troops were hidden."

43. *locumque . . . quam maxime impediri,* "the position to be equipped with as many obstacles as possible."

44. *hoc,* "because of this."

45. *pro munitione obiectas,* "(which had been) thrown up as a defense."

46. *a medio fere spatio,* "about halfway (down the hill)," referring to the soldiers (*suos*).

47. Mark Antony had been left in charge of Italy while Caesar was campaigning in Spain, and will command the left wing later this year when Caesar and Pompey at last fight it out at Pharsalus. On Antony's earlier career, see chapter 1, n. 2.

impetum fieri iussit. *[5]* Milites legionis VIIII., subito conspirati, pila coniecerunt et ex inferiore loco adversus clivum incitati cursu, praecipites Pompeianos egerunt et terga vertere coegerunt; quibus ad recipiendum crates derectae, longuriique obiecti,[48] et institutae fossae magno impedimento fuerunt. *[6]* Nostri vero, qui satis habebant[49] sine detrimento discedere, compluribus interfectis,[50] V omnino suorum amissis, quietissime se receperunt pauloque citra eum locum, aliis comprehensis collibus, munitiones perfecerunt.[51] . . .

48 Est etiam genus radicis, inventum ab eis qui fuerant in alaribus,[52] quod appellatur "chara," quod admixtum lacte multum inopiam levabat. Id ad similitudinem panis efficiebant. *[2]* Eius erat magna copia. Ex hoc effectos panis,[53] cum in colloquiis Pompeiani famem nostris obiectarent, vulgo in eos iaciebant ut spem eorum minuerent. . . .

Thus matters continued for some time. But then two Gauls who had been raised to positions of honor in Caesar's army were brought into disgrace for embezzling the pay of some of the cavalry, and even though Caesar tried to smooth the situation over, the two men deserted to Pompey. This event proved disastrous, for they were very well informed about Caesar's position and provided Pompey with precise and precious intelligence. As a result, on about 17 July, Pompey was able to find a weak point in the fortifications, break out, and set up a camp at the southern extremity of the hills being contested. An attempt mainly by Caesar's Ninth Legion to storm Pompey's new camp led to a full-scale assault, which was completely unsuccessful: unfamiliarity with the terrain

---

48. *longurii obiecti*, "the support stakes (for the screens) that had been set up."

49. *satis habebant*, "were content."

50. I.e., of the Pompeians, contrasted immediately with only five losses for Caesar.

51. The date is about 8 July. Although Caesar won the skirmish, Pompey nevertheless gained an important point, compelling Caesar to extend the circuit of his fortification and preventing him from cutting Pompey's troops off from fresh water. The tactical success and courage of the Ninth Legion, however, added to Caesar's propaganda campaign against Pompey's leadership.

52. *in alaribus*, "among the auxiliary troops."

53. *panis*, accusative, "(loaves of) bread."

and bad communications led one part of the army to panic, and thus the rest of the troops also broke and ran. Caesar's troops were saved from total destruction only because Pompey, wary of an ambush, was slow to pursue his advantage, and his cavalry was unable to follow through the narrow gates.[54]

71 Duobus his unius diei proeliis Caesar desideravit milites DCCCCLX, et notos equites Romanos: Tuticanum Gallum, senatoris filium, C. Fleginatem Placentia,[55] A. Granium Puteolis, M. Sacrativirum Capua, tribunos militum et centuriones XXXII; [2] sed horum omnium pars magna, in fossis munitionibusque et fluminis ripis oppressa,[56] suorum in terrore ac fuga sine ullo vulnere interiit; signaque sunt militaria amissa XXXII. [3] Pompeius eo proelio "imperator" est appellatus.[57] Hoc nomen obtinuit[58] atque ita se postea salutari passus est, sed neque in litteris praescribere est solitus neque in fascibus insignia laureae praetulit.[59] [4] At Labienus, cum ab eo impetravisset ut sibi captivos tradi iuberet, omnis productos ostentationis ut videbatur causa,[60] quo[61]

---

54. It was in this situation that Caesar is supposed to have said, "Today the war would have been won by the enemy if they had a man who knew how to conquer" (Suet. *Jul.* 36).

55. *Placentia*, ablative, "from Placentia," as also each of the places of origin that follow, *Puteolis* and *Capua*. The nominative of this man's name is Fleginas. None of those named here is otherwise known.

56. The first of Caesar's troops to break had jumped from the rampart of the camp into the surrounding *fossa* and were then crushed by those coming behind them (3.69.3, not quoted).

57. I.e., by the soldiers as a title of honor.

58. *obtinuit*, "he kept."

59. Pompey did not officially adopt this title, either because it had been gained in a civil war or because he did not yet regard victory as assured, though he had often enough overrated his own position. Ordinarily, he would have included it in his salutations on letters ("Cn. Pompeius Imperator") and had the *fasces* of his lictors (to which he was entitled as a magistrate with *imperium*) wreathed with laurel.

60. *ostentationis ut videbatur causa*, "apparently in order to display them" (to the rest of the army).

61. *quo* = *ut* (purpose).

maior perfugae[62] fides haberetur, "commilitones" appellans et, magna verborum contumelia interrogans solerentne[63] veterani milites fugere, in omnium conspectu interfecit.[64]

72 His rebus tantum fiduciae ac spiritus[65] Pompeianis accessit ut non de ratione belli cogitarent, sed vicisse iam sibi viderentur. *[2]* Non[66] illi paucitatem nostrorum militum, non iniquitatem loci atque angustias praeoccupatis castris[67] et ancipitem terrorem intra extraque munitiones, non abscisum in duas partis exercitum,[68] cum altera[69] alteri auxilium ferre non posset, causae[70] fuisse cogitabant. *[3]* Non ad haec addebant[71] non ex concursu acri facto, non proelio dimicatum,[72] sibique ipsos[73] multitudine atque angustiis maius attulisse detrimentum quam ab hoste accepissent. *[4]* Non denique communis belli casus[74] recordabantur, quam parvulae saepe

---

62. *perfugae*, genitive, "of a deserter." This whole sentence, of course, portrays Caesar's point of view. Caesar explains Labienus' vicious behavior as overcompensation (in modern terms) for abandoning Caesar.

63. *solerentne*, indirect question, "whether (*-ne*) . . . were accustomed."

64. Labienus is archetypical of the character of Caesar's enemies. In victory they are arrogant, cruel, and contemptuous of the rights of others. By contrast, Caesar is magnanimous and considerate of his opponents' *dignitas*.

65. *tantum fiduciae ac spiritus*, "so much (of) confidence and pride."

66. *Non . . . non . . . non*: a nice example of anaphora, carried on into the next two main sentences as well: Caesar lectures Pompey's troops ex post facto. The following accusatives, *paucitatem . . . iniquitatem atque angustias . . . terrorem . . . exercitum*, are all subjects in indirect statement of *fuisse*, below.

67. *praeoccupatis castris*, temporal, "when they had taken the camp ahead of us."

68. *abscisum . . . exercitum*, "the separation . . . of the army." This use of the perfect passive participle to describe a noun where English would use one noun to qualify another is quite common, e.g., *ab urbe condita*, "from the founding of the city." Caesar refers to the separation of the right from the left wing in the battle for the camp described in 3.69.3–4 (summarized but not quoted above).

69. *altera (pars)*.

70. *causae (cur Caesaris milites fugissent)* is predicate dative (or dative of purpose).

71. *Non ad haec addebant*, "They also failed to consider."

72. *non proelio dimicatum*, "that it had not been a pitched battle."

73. *sibique ipsos . . . maius attulisse detrimentum*, "that Caesar's men had caused more damage to themselves."

74. *communis . . . casus*, accusative, "ordinary (mis)fortunes."

causae,[75] vel falsae suspicionis vel terroris repentini vel obiectae
religionis, magna detrimenta intulissent, quotiens vel ducis vitio vel
culpa tribuni in exercitu esset offensum;[76] sed proinde ac si virtute
vicissent neque ulla commutatio rerum posset accidere, per orbem
terrarum fama ac litteris victoriam eius diei concelebrabant.

CASSIUS DIO'S COMPARISON OF CAESAR
AND POMPEY (DIO 41.53–54)

Dio evaluates the two generals just before his account of the battle at
Pharsalus, giving an assessment of their motives and their actions. His
point of view is essentially that of most Romans of the time. He
concludes that ultimately peace was unattainable for personal reasons.

When they had encamped facing one another, the appearance
of the camps bore some similarity to war, but their disposition of
weapons suggested that they were at rest in peacetime. They
realized the greatness of the danger, and they looked ahead toward
an unclear and uncertain outcome; moreover, they still had some
respect for their shared lineage and kinship, and so they kept on
putting things off. For this reason they kept sending proposals for
friendship back and forth, and some people thought that they
would actually come to a hollow agreement. The cause of the
present difficulties was that they were both longing for total power
and they both had much inborn ambition as well as acquired
competitiveness—for some men can least endure getting the worst
in comparison to their equals and to those closest to them. They
were unwilling to yield any ground to each other, because they
both had the ability to dominate, nor were they able to trust, even
if an agreement were reached, that they would not be continually
grasping at the stronger position and fall into discord again over the
whole. They differed from one another in intention to the extent
that Pompey yearned to be second to no man, Caesar to be first of

75. *causae*, nominative, subject of *intulissent*. The nouns set off by *vel*
(*suspicionis . . . terroris . . . religionis*) are genitive of source, all qualifying *causae*.
76. *esset offensum*, impersonal passive, "disaster had been incurred."

all. Pompey was eager to be honored by consenting people and to command and be liked by men who were willing; but to Caesar it was of no concern if he ruled over even unwilling people, administered those who hated him, and handed out his own honors to himself. In the deeds, however, through which they hoped to bring to pass all the things that they wished, they were both inevitably acting in the same way; for it was impossible for anyone to achieve these things without fighting his own people and leading foreigners against his kinsmen, without acquiring great sums of money unjustly, and without killing illegally many of his closest friends. And so, while they differed in their goals, they were alike in the methods by which they hoped to fulfill them. And because they would not give in to each other on anything, even though they extended many justifications, they ended by coming to blows.

CAESAR, *DE BELLO CIVILI* 3.73, 82–83

73 Caesar ab superioribus consiliis depulsus, omnem sibi commutandam belli rationem existimavit. *[2]* Itaque, uno tempore praesidiis[77] omnibus deductis et oppugnatione dimissa coactoque in unum locum exercitu, contionem apud milites habuit[78] hortatusque est ne ea quae accidissent graviter ferrent, neve his rebus terrerentur, multisque secundis proeliis unum adversum—et id mediocre—opponerent.[79] *[3]* Habendam fortunae gratiam, quod

---

77. *praesidiis*, i.e., the garrisons on the fortification at Dyrrachium.

78. By including this speech in this context, Caesar intends to illustrate both his character, which is sufficient to weather such a disaster, and his leadership, by which he raises the morale of his troops when total defeat seems imminent. The contrast to his enemies is stark, and later highlighted once again by Pompey's actions at Pharsalus (below, 3.96).

79. *opponerent*, "(they should) balance . . . (*unum adversum*, accusative direct object) against (*multis secundis proeliis*, dative with the prefix *ob*-)." Thus Caesar, fully aware of the magnitude of this defeat, which has forced him to change his entire strategy, minimizes its importance to his soldiers; no doubt he included in his exhortation some of the reflections on the importance of luck that he elaborated just above.

Italiam sine aliquo vulnere[80] cepissent, quod duas Hispanias bellicosissimorum hominum[81] peritissimis atque exercitatissimis ducibus[82] pacavissent, quod finitimas frumentariasque provincias[83] in potestatem redegissent; denique recordari debere qua felicitate inter medias hostium classes, oppletis non solum portibus sed etiam litoribus, omnes incolumes essent transportati. *[4]* Si non omnia caderent secunda, fortunam esse industria sublevandam. Quod esset acceptum detrimenti, cuiusvis potius quam suae culpae debere tribui:[84] *[5]* locum se aequum ad dimicandum dedisse, potitum se esse hostium castris, expulisse ac superasse pugnantis. Sed sive ipsorum perturbatio sive error aliquis sive etiam fortuna partam[85] iam praesentemque victoriam interpellavisset,[86] dandam omnibus operam ut[87] acceptum incommodum virtute sarciretur. *[6]* Quod si esset factum, futurum ut detrimentum in bonum verteret,[88] uti ad Gergoviam[89] accidisset, atque ei, qui ante dimicare timuissent, ultro se proelio offerrent. . . .

Despite the opinion of some of his officers that he should stay and fight with Pompey immediately, Caesar had no confidence in his demoralized troops and decided to draw Pompey away from his supplies in

---

80. *sine aliquo vulnere*, "without much damage."

81. *bellicosissimorum hominum*, descriptive genitive qualifying *duas Hispanias.*

82. *peritissimis . . . ducibus*, ablative absolute with concessive force: "although the generals were most experienced."

83. *provincias*: Sicily and Sardinia.

84. *cuiusvis potius quam suae culpae debere tribui*, "should be attributed to anything other than Caesar's failure." Caesar is not trying to shift blame to another person but to bad luck: *cuiusvis . . . culpae* ("to the fault of any*one*) virtually means "of any*thing*." This sentiment picks up Caesar's notion from the previous sentence that luck has to be reinforced by hard work; hence, he goes on to detail the efforts he has made to do so.

85. *partam* < *pario*, describing *victoriam* (see also below, 3.82.1, *parta . . . victoria*).

86. *interpellavisset*, "had intervened against."

87. *dandam* (*esse*) *omnibus operam ut*, "(that) they all had to exert themselves."

88. *futurum ut detrimentum in bonum verteret*, "(that) a loss would change to a benefit."

89. *ad Gergoviam*: in Gaul during the campaign of 52 Caesar had suffered a serious setback at Gergovia, soon followed by a decisive victory at Alesia.

Dyrrachium. He therefore sent out his baggage and most of the army during the night, and himself set out near daybreak with lightly armed troops. Pompey once again hesitated. Though in the end he pursued vigorously, he let Caesar get a head start and, now unable to catch up with Caesar's entire army, decided to move toward Macedonia. Caesar in turn had wanted to keep Pompey from reaching and defeating Cn. Domitius Calvinus, who was at Heraclea on the Via Egnatia, but he was forced to detour to Apollonia to tend to the wounded, pay his troops, and replenish his supplies. Eventually, he decided to march from Apollonia to Thessaly, where supplies might be more plentiful. Calvinus, meanwhile, unaware of Pompey's approach, was nearly trapped but escaped with just hours to spare and was finally able to join Caesar on the way to Thessaly.

Pompey's agents busily spread the news of Caesar's recent defeat at Dyrrachium, and Caesar found that a number of the Greek cities had defected to Pompey's cause. When Caesar and Calvinus arrived at Gomphi, which had sought alliance with him a short while before, they found the gates closed to them. Wishing to make an example and to reinspire his troops, Caesar immediately laid siege to the town and sacked it within a day, allowing his troops to plunder it. He then marched quickly to Metropolis and, when that city surrendered, made sure that it remained unharmed. These lessons were not lost on the Thessalians, all of whom except Larisa, where Pompey's legate Scipio had set up operations, now cooperated with Caesar.

82 Pompeius paucis post diebus in Thessaliam pervenit, contionatusque apud cunctum exercitum, suis agit gratias, Scipionis milites cohortatur ut, parta iam victoria, praedae ac praemiorum velint esse[90] participes, receptisque omnibus in una castra legionibus, suum cum Scipione honorem partitur,[91] classicumque

---

90. (*ut*) . . . *velint esse*, a polite form of request. Pompey was strictly following form: Scipio's soldiers are not his, and he cannot in theory order them to participate. This is not to say, of course, that anyone would consider not following Pompey's decisions, or that the soldiers were envisioned as possibly reluctant to share the spoils. For Scipio's background, see chapter 2, n. 6.

91. Scipio and Pompey were both proconsuls and thus technically of equal rank. When the armies joined forces, it was normal to form one camp (*in una castra*, above).

apud eum cani[92] et alterum illi iubet praetorium tendi.[93] *[2]* Auctis copiis Pompei, duobusque magnis exercitibus coniunctis, pristina omnium confirmatur opinio et spes victoriae augetur adeo ut quidquid[94] intercederet temporis, id morari reditum in Italiam videretur et, si quando quid[95] Pompeius tardius aut consideratius faceret, unius esse negotium diei, sed illum delectari imperio et consularis praetoriosque servorum[96] habere numero dicerent. *[3]* Iamque inter se palam de praemiis ac de sacerdotiis[97] contendebant in annosque[98] consulatum definiebant, alii domos bonaque eorum qui in castris erant Caesaris petebant. *[4]* Magnaque inter eos in consilio fuit controversia, oporteretne Lucili Hirri,[99] quod is a Pompeio ad Parthos missus esset, proximis comitiis praetoriis

---

92. *classicum apud eum cani*, "(that) the trumpet call be blown at his tent." See next note.

93. *alterum illi . . . praetorium tendi*, "(that) a second command tent be pitched for him." In other words, Scipio was to continue to be treated like a commanding officer.

94. *quicquid intercederet temporis* is the antecedent of *id* (and thus equivalent to the subject) in the next clause, which completes the *ut* result clause (*ut . . . morari videretur*).

95. *quando quid* for *aliquando* and *aliquid*, after *si*. The protasis of this condition (*si . . . faceret*) is answered in the apodosis by (*homines*) *dicerent*, a present unreal (or contrary-to-fact) condition. The verb *dicerent*, in turn, introduces two indirect statements: (a) *esse negotium* and (b) *illum* (= *Pompeium*) *delectari . . . et habere*.

96. *servorum habere numero*, "(that he) was treating . . . as slaves."

97. Priesthoods were important political offices. The details of some of this debate are elaborated in the next chapter.

98. *in annosque*, "year by year."

99. *oporteretne Lucili Hirri . . . absentis rationem haberi*, "whether Lucilius Hirrus should have the privilege of running in absentia." The same privilege, in other words, that had become such a point of contention with respect to Caesar, who had by any measure done more to earn it than Hirrus. C. Lucilius Hirrus had been tribune in 53 but had subsequently failed in his campaign for the aedileship. Pompey had promised, as the next clause makes clear, to accelerate his path up the ladder by skipping him over the aedileship and by sponsoring his candidacy directly for praetor. Cicero mocks Hirrus for a speech impairment, referring to him as "Hillus" (perhaps Hirrus could not trill an "r"). On the embassy referred to here, he was thrown into prison by the Parthian king.

absentis rationem haberi, cum[100] eius necessarii fidem implorarent[101] Pompei, praestaret[102] quod proficiscenti recepisset,[103] ne per eius auctoritatem deceptus videretur, reliqui[104] in labore pari ac periculo, ne unus omnis antecederet, recusarent.

83 Iam de sacerdotio Caesaris[105] Domitius,[106] Scipio, Spintherque Lentulus[107] cotidianis contentionibus ad gravissimas verborum contumelias palam descenderunt, cum Lentulus aetatis honorem ostentaret, Domitius urbanam gratiam dignitatemque iactaret, Scipio adfinitate Pompei confideret. *[2]* Postulavit[108] etiam L. Afranium proditionis exercitus Acutius Rufus apud Pompeium, quod gestum[109] in Hispania diceret. *[3]* Et L. Domitius in consilio dixit placere sibi, bello confecto, ternas tabellas[110] dari ad

---

100. *cum*, "since." This conjunction governs both *necessarii implorarent* and *reliqui recusarent*.

101. *fidem implorare* means, specifically, "to pray for (the fulfillment of) a pledge."

102. *praestaret*, "(saying that Pompey) should make good."

103. *proficiscenti recepisset*: for the meaning of *recipere* as "guarantee," see chapter 6, n. 72. *Proficiscenti* is the dative of the present participle, "to him (Hirrus) as he was leaving."

104. *reliqui . . . recusarent*, "(and since) the rest were objecting." *Recusare* is regularly followed by *quominus* or *quin* (see above, n. 37, on 3.45.6) when the objection is stated positively; *ne* states it negatively, "that he should not."

105. *de sacerdotio Caesaris*: Caesar had been pontifex maximus since 63, a post now coveted by partisans of Pompey.

106. L. Domitius Ahenobarbus, who had survived Corfinium through Caesar's *clementia* (1.23.2, quoted in chapter 3), not to be confused with Caesar's ally Domitius Calvinus.

107. *Spinther Lentulus* = P. Cornelius Lentulus Spinther (see chapter 2, n. 120).

108. *Postulavit . . . proditionis exercitus*, "accused . . . of betraying the army." *Proditionis* is genitive of the charge; *exercitus* is objective genitive.

109. *quod gestum = id quod gestum esse*.

110. *ternas tabellas*, "three tablets each." In the criminal courts, jurors were given three tablets with which to cast their vote; the *tabellae* were marked *A* for acquittal (= *absolvo*), *C* for conviction (= *condemno*), and *NL* (= *non liquet*) for not proven. If most of the votes turned out "not proven," equivalent to a hung jury in American law, the trial was continued for successive hearings until a decision could in fact be reached. Domitius suggests a different set of *tabellae. Ternus* is a

iudicandum[111] eis qui ordinis essent senatorii belloque una cum ipsis interfuissent:[112] sententiasque de singulis ferrent,[113] qui Romae remansissent quique intra praesidia Pompei fuissent neque operam in re militari praestitissent: unam fore tabellam, qui[114] liberandos omni periculo censerent, alteram, qui capitis[115] damnarent, tertiam, qui pecunia multarent. *[4]* Postremo omnes aut de honoribus suis aut de praemiis pecuniae aut de persequendis inimicitiis agebant, nec[116] quibus rationibus superare possent, sed quem ad modum uti[117] victoria deberent, cogitabant. . . .

Thus are Pompey's supporters shown to have failed not only militarily, by underestimating the enemy, but morally, in their arrogance toward each other and toward others in their cause. Caesar, who has been severely criticized for the low character of his own supporters, for his lack of patriotism, and (most recently) for his leadership, hammers these themes home against his opponents, as he has in fact done since the opening chapters. As we have seen, these themes unify his entire narrative and provide the rationale both for the selection and for the manner of presentation of his material. But while in the early part of his narrative he

---

"distributive" numeral, like *singulus* and *binus*, indicating "how many each." These adjectives are also used instead of cardinal numerals if the noun is regularly plural, like *castra* or *milia*. A list of these adjectives and a brief note on their usage may be found in most Latin grammars, including Allen and Greenough §136–37.

111. *ad iudicandum*, "with which to cast their verdict."

112. I.e., not to all of the senatorial order, or even to all who had crossed with him to Greece, but only to those who had actually participated in the war (*bello . . . interfuissent*) on Pompey's side.

113. *sententiasque de singulis ferrent*, "they should pass judgment on them one by one."

114. *qui*, repeated three times, is the archaic ablative (not the nominative) used as a conjunction, meaning "with which." Perhaps Caesar (or Domitius) is imitating the technical legal phraseology defining the *tabellae*.

115. *capitis*, "to reduction in civil status," the legal definition of *caput*. Conceivably this could mean death, but it probably does not. The penalties envisioned by Domitius seem to progress in severity from absolution to monetary fine, and he is thinking of slapping the hands of people like Cicero—who wavered so long that he was not involved in the actual fighting—not of killing lukewarm supporters.

116. *nec . . . cogitabant*.

117. *uti* < *utor*.

could claim only injustice, here he can clearly illustrate the character flaws of his opponents and, in the following chapters, the consequences of those flaws. In a short passage omitted here, Caesar now begins to provoke Pompey and to raise the morale of his own troops by drawing up his battle line closer to Pompey and farther from his own camp each day. As indicated above, Pompey's senatorial advisers want a quick finish. Pompey's slower strategy is sound, but in the end he cannot resist the pressure from his advisers and Caesar's provocations.

CICERO ON POMPEY'S CAMP IN GREECE

The situation in Pompey's camp at this crucial time is revealed in these passages from two of Cicero's letters, the first written shortly after the end of the war.

Cicero to Atticus, 27 November 48 (*Att.* 11.6.2, 6)

My leaving the war has never caused me any regret. So great was the level of cruelty among those men, so great was the association with barbarian nations, that a proscription list had been drawn up not by individual names but by whole families, that it had already been determined by everyone's agreement that property belonging to all of you was the booty of that victory. I say "you" advisedly, for there were never any but the cruelest thoughts of you yourself. For this reason my choice has never caused me regret, though my actual plan does now.[118] I would prefer to have stayed put in some little town until I was summoned: I would have endured less talk, suffered less pain, and my present situation would not be so distressful. . . . Would you like some consolation about Fannius?[119] He used to say vicious things about your staying

---

118. Cicero is writing from Brundisium, where he was forced to spend several months after the Battle of Pharsalus, both because he was unsure of how Caesar would treat him and because Caesar had given orders that no one should return to Rome without his permission.

119. Presumably the C. Fannius who had been tribune in 59; evidently he had been (falsely) reported killed. It was a long time before it was clear who had and who had not survived the defeat in Greece.

in Rome. L. Lentulus on the other hand had laid claim to the house of Hortensius and to Caesar's Roman gardens and his place at Baiae. To be sure, all these dealings happen in the same way on this side, except that over there it was endless: all the people who had stayed in Italy were considered enemies. Well, I should like to talk about these things someday when my mind is freer.

Cicero is even more candid in this second letter, written two years later to M. Marius.

Cicero to Marius, mid-46 (*Fam.* 7.3.2–3)

I now regret what I did,[120] not so much because of the risk to me as because of the many defects that I encountered where I had come: first, there were not many troops and they were not ready for war; second, other than the general and a few others (I mean the leaders) the rest were insatiable in the war itself and so cruel in their speech that I shuddered at the very thought of victory; in addition, there was massive debt among the most distinguished men. The point is, there was nothing good but the cause. When I saw this, I gave up hope for victory and began first to argue for peace, of which I had always been a proponent; then, since Pompey was strongly opposed to that idea, I started arguing that he should draw out the war. For a while he approved of this and it seemed that he was about to stand by that plan; and he perhaps would have, except that as a result of a certain scuffle[121] he began to have confidence in his troops. From that moment that excellent man was no general. He joined battle, leading a cobbled together army of beginners, against the most powerful legions. Defeated, he even lost his camp and shamefully fled alone.

I considered this the end of the war for me, and I did not think that broken forces would be superior when they were not equal while intact. I gave up a war in which I had to choose among

---

120. He means his decision to join Pompey's forces in Greece in June 48.
121. Cicero is referring to the success at Dyrrachium in July 48.

falling in battle, falling into some trap, coming into the hands of the conqueror, taking refuge with Juba,[122] accepting a position very like exile, or resolving upon voluntary death. There was definitely nothing else, if you were unwilling or lacked the courage to entrust yourself to the conqueror. Of all these undesirable courses I have mentioned, nothing is more bearable than exile, especially a harmless one, where no disgrace is attached, and where, I might add, you are deprived of a city where there is nothing you can see without pain.

CAESAR, *DE BELLO CIVILI* 3.85-87, 89, 92, 96

85 Pompeius, qui castra in colle habebat, ad infimas radices montis aciem instruebat, semper (ut videbatur) exspectans si[123] iniquis locis Caesar se subiceret. *[2]* Caesar nulla ratione ad pugnam elici posse Pompeium existimans, hanc[124] sibi commodissimam belli rationem iudicavit uti castra ex eo loco moveret semperque esset in itineribus, haec spectans[125] ut, movendis castris pluribusque adeundis locis, commodiore frumentaria re uteretur simulque in itinere ut aliquam occasionem dimicandi nancisceretur[126] et insolitum ad laborem Pompei exercitum[127] cotidianis itineribus defatigaret. *[3]* His constitutis rebus, signo iam profectionis dato

---

122. Cicero consistently portrays the African allies as barbarians and regarded it as disgraceful that Romans should have to seek refuge there.

123. *exspectans si*, "waiting in case." Caesar also had a good position by his own camp, with the river to support it and with access at his rear to the Pharsalian plains for forage; but to approach Pompey, he would have to fight from lower ground. The two camps were three or four miles apart.

124. *hanc* . . . *(rationem)* looks forward to the clause introduced by *uti*.

125. *haec spectans*, "with these aims," lit., "looking toward these (goals)," *haec* being explained by the following *ut* clauses.

126. *nancisceretur*: the word implies "getting by chance, happening upon." Caesar would look for an opportunity for battle, but he would not approach Pompey's currently stronger position.

127. *insolitum ad laborem Pompei exercitum*, "Pompey's army, which was not used to such hard work."

tabernaculisque detensis,[128] animum adversum est paulo ante extra cotidianam consuetudinem longius a vallo esse aciem Pompei progressam, ut non iniquo loco posse dimicari videretur.[129] *[4]* Tunc Caesar apud suos, cum iam esset agmen in portis,[130] "Differendum est," inquit, "iter[131] in praesentia nobis et de proelio cogitandum, sicut semper depoposcimus. Animo sumus ad dimicandum parati; non facile occasionem postea reperiemus." Confestimque expeditas copias educit.

86 Pompeius quoque, ut postea cognitum est, suorum omnium hortatu statuerat proelio decertare.[132] Namque etiam in

---

128. *detensis*, "struck," lit., "unstretched" (< *detendere*), since the word for setting up the tents is *tendere* (see above, 3.82.1 and n. 93 on *tendi*). The tents were covered with skins (see 3.13.5, quoted in chapter 6), which had to be stretched over the support poles.

129. 9 August.

130. *in portis*, that is, the gates of his camp. Caesar's lines had already been formed and were in the process of marching out.

131. *Differendum est . . . iter*, "the march must be postponed." The second gerundive, *cogitandum*, does not have *iter* as its subject but is impersonal, a slight example of *inconcinnitas*.

132. This explains why Pompey's line had advanced out further than usual: Caesar had not taken the bait to fight on uneven ground, so Pompey advanced out to where the terrain was more even. As becomes clear, Pompey was confident because he expected his cavalry, in which he had a great numerical superiority, to decide the issue early in the battle. It would be interesting to know something of the historicity of the speech that follows: Pompey has already been shown in Caesar's narrative (especially 3.83, above) to be hampered by the willfulness of his noble advisers. In his portrait of Pompey's sketch of his plan before his *consilium*, Caesar characterizes him as "persuading" the cavalry of his plan, perhaps a jab at Pompey's ability to command, or perhaps a reflection of Pompey's diplomatic use of language. Though he must have done so, at no time do we see Caesar debating his strategy with advisers; his plans are presented fully formed, ready for execution. Pompey, by contrast, must explain himself before battle to those who should be waiting to obey his commands. Finally, Pompey's plan seems amazingly simpleminded in view of the quality of his opponent. He counts on overwhelming Caesar's right wing and surrounding the army as they march across the plain and presents no plan of action in case this does not quite work. Thus Caesar continues to stress two of his main themes—character and leadership.

consilio superioribus diebus dixerat, prius quam[133] concurrerent acies, fore uti exercitus Caesaris pelleretur. *[2]* Id cum essent plerique admirati, "Scio me," inquit, "paene incredibilem rem polliceri; sed rationem consili mei accipite, quo firmiore animo in proelium prodeatis. *[3]* Persuasi[134] equitibus nostris, idque mihi facturos confirmaverunt, ut, cum propius sit accessum, dextrum Caesaris cornu ab latere aperto[135] aggrederentur et, circumventa ab tergo acie, prius[136] perturbatum exercitum pellerent quam a nobis telum in hostem iaceretur.[137] *[4]* Ita sine periculo legionum et paene sine vulnere bellum conficiemus. Id autem difficile non est, cum tantum equitatu valeamus."[138] *[5]* Simul denuntiavit[139] ut essent animo parati in posterum et, quoniam fieret dimicandi potestas, ut saepe cogitavissent, ne usu manuque[140] reliquorum opinionem fallerent.

87 Hunc Labienus excepit[141] et, cum Caesaris copias despiceret, Pompei consilium summis laudibus efferret,[142] "Noli," inquit, "existimare, Pompei, hunc esse exercitum qui Galliam

---

133. *prius quam*: this clause is logically and grammatically dependent on the next one, *fore uti . . . pelleretur*, but placed first by Caesar (or Pompey) for emphasis.

134. *persuasi*, instead of *imperavi*, for rhetorical effect.

135. *ab latere aperto*, "on the open flank," open because Caesar's left wing and Pompey's right would be covered by the stream with an impassable river bank. In general, the phrase *latus apertum* should refer to the right, since the shield was carried in the left hand; but here Pompey refers to the topographical possibilities offered by having Caesar wedged against the stream. Maneuverability on Pompey's left (Caesar's right) could also have been somewhat restricted by the mountains, but the open ground of the battle site extended for two or three miles.

136. *prius*: take with *quam* in the next clause.

137. Because they will not yet have gotten close enough for a spear cast.

138. *tantum . . . valeamus*, "we are so superior." Caesar began the campaign with eight hundred cavalry, Pompey with seven thousand.

139. *denuntiavit*, "he stressed." His points are given in two clauses, *ut essent parati* and *ne . . . fallerent*.

140. *usu manuque*, "in the reality of hand-to-hand combat," an example of hendiadys. Pompey contrasts *usus* with their often expressed plans, implied in *ut saepe cogitavissent*.

141. *excepit*, "followed," lit., "took up."

142. *efferret*, "he extolled."

Germaniamque devicerit. *[2]* Omnibus interfui proeliis, neque temere incognitam rem pronuntio. Perexigua pars illius exercitus superest; magna pars deperiit, quod accidere tot proeliis fuit necesse,[143] multos autumni pestilentia[144] in Italia consumpsit, multi domum discesserunt, multi sunt relicti in continenti.[145] *[3]* An non audistis ex eis qui per causam valetudinis remanserunt cohortis esse Brundisi factas? *[4]* Hae copiae quas videtis ex dilectibus horum annorum[146] in citeriore Gallia sunt refectae,[147] et plerique sunt ex coloniis Transpadanis. Ac tamen[148] quod fuit roboris[149] duobus proeliis Dyrrachinis interiit." *[5]* Haec cum dixisset, iuravit se nisi victorem in castra non reversurum reliquosque ut idem facerent hortatus est. *[6]* Hoc laudans Pompeius idem iuravit; nec vero ex reliquis fuit quisquam qui iurare dubitaret. *[7]* Haec cum facta sunt in consilio, magna spe et laetitia omnium discessum est; ac iam animo victoriam praecipiebant,[150] quod de re tanta et a tam perito imperatore nihil frustra confirmari[151] videbatur. . . .

Caesar goes on to describe the deployment of Pompey's troops: Pompey himself was on the left with the cavalry, where he expected to flank Caesar's right wing, along with the two legions, probably commanded by Labienus, that Caesar had surrendered at the beginning of the war; Scipio was in the center, and a combined group of troops under Afranius were

---

143. For this and the next remark, Labienus could have cited Caesar's own analysis in 3.2.3 (not quoted), where he notes the depletion of his forces from the battles in Gaul and Spain and from the general unhealthiness of the region around Brundisium.

144. *autumni pestilentia*, i.e., malaria.

145. *continenti*, "the continent," here = Italy.

146. *horum annorum*, "of these (last two) years."

147. Caesar had raised twenty-two cohorts from Cisalpine Gaul just before Corfinium: see above, 1.18.5, chapter 3, n. 51.

148. *tamen* is a little unexpected; the strict logic of the argument would suggest *etiam*, or some other strong positive. The thought seems to be, "and (although there are a lot of them,) *nevertheless*."

149. *quod fuit roboris*, "the strongest part of them."

150. *animo . . . praecipiebant*, "they were mentally anticipating" (Gardner).

151. *nihil frustra confirmari*, "(that) no empty assertions were being made."

on the right. Pompey's combined forces came to over 45,000 men. It is of some interest that all other accounts of the battle, including some clearly derived from eyewitnesses like Asinius Pollio, differ both among themselves and with Caesar's description.

89 Caesar superius institutum[152] servans, X. legionem in dextro cornu, nonam in sinistro collocaverat, tametsi erat Dyrrachinis proeliis vehementer attenuata, et huic sic adiunxit octavam ut paene unam ex duabus efficeret,[153] atque alteram alteri praesidio esse iusserat. [2] Cohortis in acie LXXX constitutas habebat, quae summa erat milium XXII;[154] cohortis II castris praesidio reliquerat.

[3] Sinistro cornu Antonium, dextro P. Sullam,[155] media acie Cn. Domitium[156] praeposuerat. Ipse contra Pompeium constitit. [4] Simul his rebus animadversis quas demonstravimus,[157] timens ne a multitudine equitum dextrum cornu circumveniretur, celeriter ex tertia acie singulas cohortis[158] detraxit atque ex his quartam[159]

---

152. *superius institutum*, "his former practice" of putting the Tenth Legion in the place of honor.

153. Labienus' arguments above about the strength of Caesar's troops are substantiated by these tactics. As indicated below, Mark Antony, who had commanded the Ninth Legion at Dyrrachium, was placed in charge of this combined force.

154. This gives an average of 275 men per cohort, and only half the total fighting force of Pompey; Pompey's 110 cohorts averaged over 400 men per cohort.

155. P. Cornelius Sulla, a nephew of the former dictator, had been praetor no later than 68. He ran successfully in 66 for the consulship of 65, but both elected consuls were convicted of bribery and forced to resign before taking office. Nearly convicted as a coconspirator of Catiline's in 63, his political fortunes had never recovered.

156. I.e., Calvinus.

157. I.e., the deployment of Pompey's troops.

158. *ex tertia acie singulas cohortis*, "one cohort from (each legion of) the third line." Thus he scraped together six cohorts (none were taken from the Eighth and Ninth Legions, which were already shorthanded). The triple line was the usual battle formation; Caesar, as we shall see, attacked only with the first two, holding the third line in reserve either for emergency support or, as actually happened, as fresh reinforcements for a successful charge.

159. *quartam* (*aciem*).

instituit equitatuique opposuit, et quid fieri vellet ostendit,[160] monuitque eius diei victoriam in earum cohortium virtute constare. *[5]* Simul tertiae aciei totique exercitui imperavit ne iniussu suo concurrerent; se, cum id fieri vellet, vexillo[161] signum daturum. . . .

92 Inter duas acies tantum erat relictum spati ut satis esset ad concursum utriusque exercitus.[162] *[2]* Sed Pompeius suis praedixerat ut Caesaris impetum exciperent, neve se loco moverent, aciemque eius[163] distrahi paterentur; idque admonitu C. Triari fecisse dicebatur, ut primus excursus visque militum infringeretur, aciesque distenderetur, atque in suis ordinibus dispositi dispersos adorirentur; *[3]* leviusque casura pila[164] sperabat in loco retentis militibus[165] quam si ipsi immissis telis occurrissent, simul fore ut duplicato cursu[166] Caesaris milites exanimarentur et lassitudine conficerentur. *[4]* Quod nobis[167] quidem nulla ratione factum a Pompeio videtur, propterea quod est quaedam animi incitatio atque alacritas, naturaliter innata omnibus, quae studio pugnae incenditur. *[5]* Hanc non reprimere sed augere imperatores debent; neque frustra antiquitus institutum est ut signa undique

---

160. According to Plutarch's *Life of Pompey* (69), they were instructed to strike at the faces of the enemy cavalry.

161. *vexillo*, "by (waving) the flag." This was evidently the red flag that normally stood over the general's tent. The signal to attack was usually given by the *tuba*.

162. *ad concursum utriusque exercitus*, "for the charge of the two armies." *Concursus* means that both armies attacked one another; if only one army charged, the word was *incursus*. *Impetus* was the general word for attack, or else referred specifically to the "shock" of the onslaught (Perrin). *Excursus*, used below (only here in Caesar), is the *incursus* seen from the other point of view.

163. *eius = Caesaris.*

164. *leviusque casura (esse) pila*, indirect statement, "that the missiles (of Caesar's men) would fall more lightly."

165. *retentis militibus*, ablative absolute = *si milites retinerentur.*

166. *duplicato cursu*, "after running twice the distance" because Pompey's troops had not charged.

167. *nobis*: again, Caesar preserves the distinction of his role as historical author, in which he speaks in the first person, from that of a character in the narrative, where he uses the third person.

concinerent[168] clamoremque universi tollerent. Quibus rebus et hostis terreri et suos incitari existimaverunt. . . .

Caesar proceeded to outmaneuver Pompey during the battle. His first two lines charged until they saw that Pompey's forces had not also done so, upon which Caesar's men slowed and regained their breath. They then charged again, and a fierce battle ensued. Meanwhile, Pompey's cavalry charged Caesar's right wing, followed by an outpouring of archers. Caesar's cavalry was not able to hold its position against this charge, and Pompey's cavalry began its planned flanking maneuver. At this point, Caesar gave the signal for his fourth line to move forward, and their charge was so fierce (and unexpected) that Pompey's cavalry broke ranks and fled. The archers were thus left exposed and were wiped out. In a final irony, Caesar's fourth line proceeded to flank Pompey's left wing, as Pompey had planned to do to Caesar, and began attacking the rest from the rear. At that same moment, Caesar brought up his third line, which he had withheld till now, and these fresh troops overwhelmed Pompey's demoralized legions, who now all broke and ran, and Caesar's men stormed Pompey's camp.

96 In castris Pompei videre licuit trichilas structas,[169] magnum argenti pondus expositum, recentibus caespitibus[170] tabernacula constrata, L. etiam Lentuli et non nullorum[171] tabernacula protecta hedera,[172] multaque praeterea quae nimiam luxuriam et victoriae fiduciam designarent, ut facile existimari posset nihil eos de eventu eius diei timuisse, qui non necessarias conquirerent[173] voluptates. *[2]* At hi miserrimo ac patientissimo exercitui Caesaris luxuriem obiciebant,[174] cui semper omnia ad necessarium usum

---

168. *signa . . . concinerent*, "(that) the (trumpet) signals should be sounded."

169. *trichilas structas*, indirect statement, "(that) arbors (of interlaced branches) had been built" instead of tents.

170. *recentibus caespitibus*, "fresh-cut turf."

171. *non nullorum*, "of no few others."

172. *protecta* (accusative) modifies *tabernacula*; *hedera* is ablative.

173. *conquirerent* is subjunctive as a subordinate verb in indirect statement.

174. *obiciebant*, "used to reproach."

defuissent.[175] *[3]* Pompeius,[176] iam cum intra vallum nostri
versarentur, equum nactus, detractis insignibus imperatoris,
decumana porta[177] se ex castris eiecit protinusque equo citato
Larisam[178] contendit. *[4]* Neque ibi constitit, sed eadem celeritate
paucos suos ex fuga[179] nactus, nocturno itinere non intermisso,
comitatu equitum XXX ad mare pervenit navemque frumentariam
conscendit saepe, ut dicebatur, querens tantum se opinionem[180]
fefellisse ut, a quo genere hominum victoriam sperasset, ab eo initio
fugae facto[181] paene proditus[182] videretur.

Caesar himself does not draw out the obvious differences between himself
and Pompey in the face of defeat. Caesar's situation after Dyrrachium was
objectively much worse than Pompey's after the first moments of defeat
at Pharsalus. Pompey's army, still numerically much superior, had by no
means been destroyed, as subsequent events proved. Naval operations in
the West were going very much in the favor of the Pompeians, and the
battle in Sicily would have been lost if not for the timely arrival of word
of Caesar's victory at Pharsalus. By his defeat at Dyrrachium, Caesar was
led to embark upon a new plan of action; after Pharsalus, Pompey
appeared to give up hope entirely. Nor is Pompey's personal withdrawal
from the battle to his credit, especially in comparison with the numerous
occasions when Caesar had risked his own person to rally his troops from

---

175. *defuissent*: the subjunctive is concessive, "although . . . had been
lacking."

176. Caesar emphasizes Pompey's haste with *nactus*, which implies that he took
whatever horse was handy, and with *equo citato*. He inserts a small note of irony
with *detractis insignibus imperatoris*, reminiscent of Pompey's having been acclaimed
"imperator" after Dyrrachium. Plutarch portrays Pompey in dismay at the breach
of his camp (he supposedly exclaimed, "Into the camp as well?") and indicates that
Pompey did not wear the commander's insignia because it was no longer
appropriate to do so.

177. *decumana porta*, "by the rear gate."

178. About thirty miles away.

179. *ex fuga*, "in the course of his escape."

180. *opinionem*, subject of the indirect statement, "his expectation(s)." Recall
Pompey's exhortation to his advisory council above, 3.86.5.

181. *initio . . . facto*, ablative absolute.

182. *proditus*, a telling choice of words, reflecting once again the personal and
moral basis for the alliances of these politicians.

the brink of disaster. Even so, Pompey doubtless had plans to continue the war, and Caesar could not have thought that the war was over. His estimate of his position improved dramatically within a few days, for he received the surrender of about twenty-four thousand Pompeian soldiers and officers, and reckoned the losses in the battle to Pompey's forces at over fifteen thousand, including his old enemy L. Domitius Ahenobarbus. Caesar himself lost only about two hundred men.

8

The Death of Pompey

While the victory at Pharsalus and its aftermath were crushing enough, it was the death of Pompey that for practical purposes decided the war. The proximity of his death to Pharsalus, and the fact that nothing much was accomplished by his forces thereafter made the battle take on even more importance. Of course, Caesar's military problems were not over: his enemies continued to fight, having assembled an army in Africa, and he would have a closer call than expected in Alexandria. But few now doubted that Caesar would eventually prevail. Pompey's end is described below.

CAESAR, *DE BELLO CIVILI* 3.102–4, 106

102 Caesar omnibus rebus relictis¹ persequendum sibi Pompeium existimavit quascumque in partis se ex fuga² recepisset, ne rursus copias comparare alias et bellum renovare posset; et quantumcumque itineris equitatu efficere poterat³ cotidie progrediebatur, legionemque unam minoribus itineribus subsequi iussit. *[2]* Erat edictum Pompei nomine Amphipoli⁴ propositum, uti omnes eius provinciae iuniores,⁵ Graeci civesque Romani,

---

1. ***omnibus rebus relictis***, ablative absolute, takes on the force of the gerundive of obligation that follows and is virtually the same as *omnes res relinquendas (esse)* et.
2. ***ex fuga***, "in the course of his escape." The phrase was used above, 3.96.4, and occurs again below, 3.102.6.
3. ***quantumcumque itineris equitatu efficere poterat***, "as much distance as he could manage with the cavalry."
4. Amphipolis was the most important town in Macedonia.
5. ***iuniores***, "men of military age."

iurandi⁶ causa convenirent. *[3]* Sed utrum⁷ avertendae suspicionis causa Pompeius proposuisset, ut quam diutissime longioris fugae consilium occultaret, an novis dilectibus,⁸ si nemo premeret, Macedoniam tenere conaretur,⁹ existimari non poterat. *[4]* Ipse¹⁰ ad ancoram una nocte constitit et vocatis ad se Amphipoli hospitibus, et pecunia ad necessarios sumptus corrogata, cognitoque Caesaris adventu, ex eo loco discessit et Mytilenas¹¹ paucis diebus venit. *[5]* Biduum tempestate retentus, navibusque aliis additis actuariis,¹² in Ciliciam atque inde Cyprum pervenit.¹³

[6] Ibi cognoscit, consensu omnium Antiochensium¹⁴ civiumque Romanorum qui illic negotiarentur,¹⁵ arcem captam esse excludendi sui causa, nuntiosque dimissos ad eos qui se ex fuga in finitimas civitates recepisse dicerentur, ne Antiochiam adirent; id si fecissent, magno eorum capitis periculo futurum.¹⁶ *[7]* Idem hoc L. Lentulo,¹⁷ qui superiore anno consul fuerat, et P.

---

6. *iurandi*, "swearing (the military oath of enlistment)."

7. *utrum*, followed by *an*, introduces alternative indirect questions, "whether . . . or."

8. *novis dilectibus* is probably dative of purpose, "for new levies."

9. *tenere conaretur*, "he was trying to hold."

10. *Ipse = Pompeius.*

11. Mytilene was the capital city of Lesbos. In 49 Pompey had left there his wife, Cornelia, the daughter of Scipio, and his youngest son, Sextus, who was now about nineteen, the son of Pompey's third wife, Mucia.

12. *navibus . . . actuariis*, "small (fast) ships." See above, chapter 4, n. 37.

13. Plutarch (*Pomp.* 76.1) tells us that Pompey was joined by sixty senators upon landing in Cilicia, and that a debate took place over whether Pompey should go to the Parthians (which he himself favored), to Juba in Africa, or to the young Ptolemy in Egypt. On the advice of Theophanes (see above, chapter 6, n. 83) Pompey decided that Egypt was most likely to be mindful of his past favors.

14. *Antiochensium*, "inhabitants of Antioch." Antioch was the capital city of Seleucid Syria, founded in 300 by Seleucus I on the river Orontes. Pompey had given the city its independence when Syria became a Roman province in 64, but the city had suffered under A. Gabinius, who was governor of Syria (see below, n. 32), and considered Pompey's agent.

15. *qui illic negotiarentur*, i.e., mostly moneylenders.

16. *magno eorum capitis periculo futurum (esse)*, "(that) this would be a great danger to their lives." *Magno periculo* is predicate dative or dative of purpose.

17. L. Cornelius Lentulus Crus, consul in 49, who had been so active against Caesar and in support of Pompey in the opening chapters of the *Civil War*.

Lentulo[18] consulari ac non nullis aliis acciderat Rhodi;[19] qui[20] cum ex fuga Pompeium sequerentur atque in insulam venissent, oppido ac portu recepti non erant, missisque ad eos nuntiis ut ex his locis discederent, contra voluntatem suam navis solverunt. *[8]* Iamque de Caesaris adventu fama ad civitates perferebatur.

103 Quibus cognitis rebus Pompeius, deposito adeundae Syriae consilio, pecunia societatis[21] sublata[22] et a quibusdam privatis sumpta,[23] et aeris[24] magno pondere ad militarem usum in navis imposito, duobusque milibus hominum armatis, partim quos ex familiis[25] societatum delegerat, partim a negotiatoribus coegerat, quosque[26] ex suis quisque ad hanc rem idoneos existimabat, Pelusium[27] pervenit. *[2]* Ibi casu rex erat Ptolomaeus, puer aetate,[28] magnis copiis cum sorore Cleopatra[29] bellum gerens, quam paucis ante mensibus per suos propinquos atque amicos regno expulerat; castraque Cleopatrae non longo spatio ab eius

---

18. P. Cornelius Lentulus Spinther, consul in 57. See chapter 3, n. 36 on 1.22.4.

19. Rhodes had been independent since 84, a reward for loyalty in the Mithridatic Wars. It has been favorable to Caesar throughout the Civil War. In 3.106.2, below, they will supply him with ten warships.

20. *qui* = the two Lentuli.

21. *societatis*, "of the (tax) association." Roman taxes were let out by the state on bids to private corporations, or *societates*, who were then responsible for collecting the money. The tax collectors for these *societates* were called *publicani*.

22. *sublata* < *tollere*.

23. *sumpta*, "borrowed."

24. *aeris*, "of bronze (coinage)." Military pay was still figured in bronze, even though the soldiers were no longer actually paid with bronze. Originally, one *as* was equal to a pound of bronze; the "pound" was gradually devalued to two ounces, then to one ounce, and even to a quarter ounce.

25. *familiis*, "slaves."

26. *quosque* = *partim eos quos*.

27. Pelusium was on the east mouth of the Nile.

28. Ptolemy was now about thirteen, son of Ptolemy Auletes ("Flute Player"). When Auletes was in exile in the 50s, he took refuge in Pompey's house (though it should be noted that at the time Pompey was married to Caesar's daughter Julia); he was restored to his throne by A. Gabinius in 55 (see below, n. 32).

29. Cleopatra VII, now about nineteen, had quarreled with her brother and was now in Syria raising an army on her own. This is the famous Cleopatra who was to become Caesar's mistress and Antony's wife.

castris distabant. *[3]* Ad eum Pompeius misit, ut pro hospitio atque amicitia patris Alexandria[30] reciperetur atque illius opibus in calamitate tegeretur. *[4]* Sed qui ab eo missi erant, confecto legationis officio, liberius cum militibus regis colloqui coeperunt, eosque hortari ut suum officium Pompeio praestarent[31] neve eius fortunam despicerent. *[5]* In hoc erant numero complures Pompei milites, quos ex eius exercitu acceptos in Syria Gabinius[32] Alexandriam traduxerat, belloque confecto, apud Ptolomaeum, patrem pueri, reliquerat.

104 His tunc cognitis rebus, amici regis,[33] qui propter aetatem eius in procuratione erant regni, sive timore adducti, ut postea praedicabant, sollicitato exercitu regio[34] ne Pompeius Alexandriam Aegyptumque occuparet, sive despecta eius fortuna, ut plerumque in calamitate ex amicis inimici exsistunt, eis qui erant ab eo missi palam liberaliter[35] responderunt eumque ad regem venire iusserunt; *[2]* ipsi clam consilio inito[36] Achillam, praefectum regium, singulari hominem audacia, et L. Septimium,[37] tribunum militum, ad

---

30. The ablative is not infrequently used instead of the locative with names of cities.

31. *ut suum officium Pompeio praestarent*, "to fulfill their obligation to Pompey." This is explained in the next sentence.

32. A. Gabinius, as tribune in 66, proposed the law that gave Pompey his command against the pirates. He was consul in 58 and became proconsul in Syria 57–55. In Egypt in 55, with Pompey's support, Gabinius reinstated Ptolemy Auletes, expelled by the Alexandrians in 58; some of Pompey's own troops were transferred by Gabinius to Alexandria. Gabinius was prosecuted in 54 as a result of all these machinations in the East, first for *maiestas*, for which he was acquitted, then for extortion (*repetundae*), for which he was convicted and exiled. During the Civil War he fought for Caesar, who might restore his civil status, despite his long record in service to Pompey's interests, for Pompey was now the executive of the conservative element within the Senate by whom Gabinius had been exiled.

33. *amici regis*, including Pothinus, the king's guardian; Theodotus of Chios, his tutor; and Achillas, the prefect named below.

34. *sollicitato exercitu regio*, ablative absolute, belongs in sense within the following *ne* clause that explains the fear of the king's advisers.

35. *palam liberaliter*, "generously in public." As opposed to *clam*, below.

36. *clam consilio inito*, ablative absolute, "under a plan instigated in secret."

37. L. Septimius had originally served under Pompey as a centurion in the war against the pirates, as Caesar notes below.

interficiendum Pompeium miserunt. *[3]* Ab his liberaliter ipse appellatus et quadam notitia Septimi[38] productus, quod bello praedonum apud eum ordinem duxerat,[39] naviculam parvulam conscendit cum paucis suis; ibi ab Achilla et Septimio interficitur.[40] Item L. Lentulus[41] comprehenditur ab rege et in custodia necatur. . . .

106 Caesar paucos dies in Asia moratus, cum audisset Pompeium Cypri visum, coniectans eum Aegyptum[42] propter necessitudines regni[43] reliquasque eius loci opportunitates, cum legione una, quam se ex Thessalia sequi iusserat, et altera, quam ex Achaia a Q. Fufio[44] legato evocaverat, equiti[45] usque DCCC et navibus longis Rhodiis X et Asiaticis paucis Alexandriam pervenit.[46] *[2]* In his erant legionibus hominum milia III CC;[47] reliqui, vulneribus ex proeliis et labore ac magnitudine itineris confecti, consequi non potuerant. *[3]* Sed Caesar, confisus fama rerum gestarum, infirmis auxiliis proficisci non dubitaverat, aeque omnem

---

38. *quadam notitia Septimi*, "by some acquaintance with Septimius."

39. *ordinem duxerat*, "he had commanded a century," i.e., had been a centurion.

40. 28 September. The scene is described by Plutarch: "As Pompey took Philip's hand in order to get to his feet more easily, Septimius began the assault by stabbing him from behind with his sword, after which Salvius and Achillas drew their knives. Pompey pulled his toga over his face with both hands and withstood their blows, neither saying nor doing anything unworthy of himself. He did groan a little, and so died in his sixtieth year, just one day after his fifty-ninth birthday" (*Pomp.* 79.3–4). (There is a striking similarity between this account of Pompey's death by Plutarch, and the account of Caesar's death by Suetonius.)

41. On Lentulus Crus, see n. 17 above.

42. *Aegyptum*: the omission of *ad* is unusual; before names of countries this construction is not found in Cicero, and in Caesar only with Egypt.

43. *necessitudines regni*, "his close connections to the kingdom" (see above, nn. 28, 32).

44. Q. Fufius Calenus had been sent to Achaea just before Dyrrachium (3.56, not quoted).

45. *equiti*, genitive of *equitum*.

46. 2 October.

47. Three thousand two hundred men in two legions was just over half the strength of a single full legion.

sibi locum tutum fore[48] existimans. *[4]* Alexandriae de Pompei morte cognoscit,[49] atque ibi primum e navi egrediens clamorem militum audit, quos rex in oppido praesidi causa reliquerat, et concursum ad se fieri[50] videt, quod fasces anteferrentur.[51] In hoc omnis multitudo maiestatem regiam minui[52] praedicabat. *[5]* Hoc sedato tumultu crebrae continuis diebus ex concursu multitudinis concitationes fiebant compluresque milites huius urbis omnibus partibus interficiebantur.

Thus the climax of the story, the death of Pompey, is quickly subordinated to the diversion of continuing pragmatic concerns. Caesar goes on to tell of his decision to settle the Egyptian situation by placing Ptolemy and Cleopatra back in joint power. On Pompey's death, Cicero's summation to Atticus in November of 48 was stunningly lukewarm: "As for Pompey's demise, I was never in any doubt:[53] the desperation of his position had so completely seized the attention of all kings and nations that I knew this would happen no matter where he went. I cannot avoid grieving for his fall; I knew him as an honest [*integrum*], decent [*castum*], and thoughtful [*gravem*] person" (*Att.* 11.6.5). Shackleton Bailey's insightful comment on this obituary is worth quoting: "It represents what really drew Cicero towards Pompey. Pompey might be cruel, deceitful,

---

48. *aeque omnem sibi locum tutum fore*, "that every (= any) place would be equally safe for him."

49. From Theodotus, according to Plutarch: "A short time later Caesar arrived in Egypt, which had been polluted by such a base deed. One of the Egyptians had been sent to Caesar bearing Pompey's head: Caesar turned away from the messenger in disgust, as if from the face of an assassin. When he was given Pompey's ring . . ., he burst into tears" (*Pomp.* 80.7).

50. *concursum ad se fieri*, "a rush was being made at him."

51. *anteferrentur*, "were being carried ahead (of him)." Caesar was consul for the year 48 and was entitled to the full array of lictors.

52. *maiestatem regiam minui*, indirect statement, "(that) the royal dignity was being diminished." This cry has all the earmarks of a planned riot. Caesar's narrative leaves the role of the king's soldiers unclear, as it may have been to him. The Egyptians, especially those close to the king, had good cause for concern, since they had murdered their nominal patron and were now confronted with a Roman consul who had made plain his displeasure at that deed.

53. I.e., that the story was true. Many people doubted the story when it was first reported.

self-seeking, and incompetent; but he had the domestic virtues . . ., he was conventionally minded, he took serious things seriously."[54]

In another context, we are also given Cicero's summation of Caesar, comparing him to another dictator, which perhaps makes a fitting conclusion to our study.

CICERO, *DE OFFICIIS* 2.27, 29

And so in the case of Sulla, a dishonorable victory followed upon an honorable cause;[55] for he was bold enough to say, after planting his spear,[56] as he was selling off the property of good men—wealthy men, but certainly citizens—"My booty is for sale." But there followed a man who not only confiscated, in a shameless cause and in a victory even more foul, the property of individual citizens, but enveloped entire provinces[57] and districts with a single edict of disaster. . . . From this we must realize that when such rewards are offered civil wars will never be lacking.[58]

---

54. Shackleton Bailey, *Letters to Atticus* 5:274.

55. Sulla's stated program, he claimed, was to restore the traditional authority of the Senate.

56. The spear was a sign of an auction, as if selling booty from a war. Sulla had confiscated private property and now joked about the symbol.

57. Cicero liked this conceit, it evidently having occurred to him as early as 46 (*Fam.* 9.7.2, to Varro: "illud enim adhuc praemium suum non inspexit [Caesar]," referring to the province of Sardinia).

58. "Ex quo debet intellegi, talibus praemiis propositis, numquam defutura bella civilia."

Appendix 1

Chronological Gazette of Relevant Events, 52–48 B.C.

The names of the consuls for each year are given for reference; the student is also referred to the relevant year in T. R. S. Broughton's *Magistrates of the Roman Republic* 2 (Cleveland: The Press of Case Western Reserve University, 1952), for names of additional magistrates and source references. Undated events took place throughout the period or at an unknown point between dated events. This gazette is by no means intended as a complete register of events, but it does reproduce all events that are cited by date in the readings or discussed in the Introduction or Notes.

52 B.C.
Sole consul (March): Cn. Pompeius (III)
Q. Caecilius Metellus Pius Scipio Nasica (final months)

18 January	Murder of P. Clodius by T. Annius Milo. Continued chaos and near anarchy in Rome.
March	Pompey becomes sole consul and restores order in the city. Law of the Ten Tribunes reaffirms Caesar's *ratio absentis*.
April	Pompey's law on provincial commands passed. Trial and condemnation of Milo.
Summer	Pompey takes Scipio as his consular colleague. Pompey marries Cornelia, Scipio's daughter. Regular elections are held for the first time since 54.

51 B.C.
Consuls: M. Claudius Marcellus, Ser. Sulpicius Rufus

June	Marcellus attacks Caesar's special privileges.
	Caesar engaged in general revolution of all Gaul.
September	Pompey declares that no action may be taken on Caesar's provinces until March of the following year.
10 December	The tribunes for 50 take office, including Curio and Caelius.

50 B.C.
Consuls: C. Claudius Marcellus, L. Aemilius Paullus

Winter	Troops are commissioned for a possible war against Parthia.
	Curio tries to promote his legislation.
1 March	Debate on Caesar's provinces begins.
	Curio unexpectedly sides with Caesar.
Late April or May	Decree of the Senate requires both Caesar and Pompey to contribute a legion for the Parthian war.
	Pompey declares that his contribution will be the legion that he has already sent to Caesar; Caesar thus supplies both legions.
Early Summer	Pompey nearly dies of illness but recovers.
September	Antony elected augur. Caesar returns to Italy, begins canvassing in northern Italy for support for prospective consular campaign in the next year.
	Pompey levies troops for the Parthian war.
Early December	Marcellus turns over the two legions from Caesar to Pompey.
	A vote is taken on Caesar's proposals, which would have passed, but the meeting is invalidated by the consuls.

10 December	The tribunes for 49 take office, including Cassius and Mark Antony.

49 B.C.
Consuls: P. Cornelius Lentulus Crus, C. Claudius Marcellus

1 January	Caesar's proposal is brought to the consuls, and read out only after much delay.
	Debate in the Senate continues throughout this period.
2 January	Pompey calls all senators to a special meeting near nightfall, where he intimidates senators reluctant to force Caesar into a war.
4 January	Cicero returns to Rome and works hard for compromise in the interests of peace.
5 January	Caesar's opponents pack the Senate.
7 January	*Senatus consultum ultimum* passed against Caesar.
10 January	Caesar receives word of the events in Rome.
11 or 12 January	Caesar crosses the Rubicon.
	Caesar captures a string of Italian towns on the east coast. There is near panic among Caesar's opponents in Rome and Italy.
	Caesar continues to offer to disband, if Pompey will do likewise.
18 January	L. Caesar the envoy meets Caesar at Ariminum with a private message from Pompey. Pompey leaves Rome and heads for Apulia to join legions quartered there.
19 January	Lentulus leaves Rome after opening the "inner treasury."
23 January	Caesar's offer for peace is "accepted," with conditions that prove unacceptable to him. The consuls head for Capua.
25 January	Meeting of the Senate is held in Capua.
Early February	Caesar takes Firmum.

9 February	Vibullius wrongly tells Pompey that Domitius has decided to leave Corfinium.
	Pompey and Domitius exchange letters; Domitius begs Pompey to come from Canusium to Corfinium, to help in defeating Caesar, Pompey urges Domitius to come to Brundisium.
15 February	Caesar arrives at Corfinium.
17 February	Pompey tells Domitius that he cannot come to Corfinium, and soon thereafter he leaves Canusium and heads for Brundisium.
21 February	Corfinium surrenders. Caesar moves into Apulia.
	Italian resistance to Caesar collapses.
9 March	Caesar arrives at Brundisium with six legions.
	During abortive negotiations, Caesar tries to blockade Pompey in Brundisium.
17 March	Pompey crosses to Greece. Caesar takes Brundisium.
	Caesar returns to Rome, meets Cicero en route just before 28 March.
1 April	Caesar calls a meeting of the Senate.
	Debate is protracted over several days through a filibuster by the tribune L. Metellus. Caesar leaves Rome in frustration, for Transalpine Gaul.
14 April	Curio visits Cicero; his account of Caesar's motives and plans appears to make up Cicero's mind.
16 April	Caesar writes to Cicero, urging a neutral policy.
19 April	Caesar arrives in Transalpine Gaul.
23 April	Cato, who was supposed to be governor in Sicily, flees from his province.
	Caesar leads his army to Spain.
May	Caesar is delayed around Massilia. Massilia offers to remain neutral but opens its gates to Domitius Ahenobarbus and joins the side of

	Pompey. Caesar appoints D. Brutus to take charge of the siege.
7 June	Cicero leaves Italy and joins Pompey's forces in Greece.
	Caesar sets up his supply lines and prepares for the Spanish campaign. He sends C. Fabius ahead into Spain to secure the route to Ilerda.
22 June	Caesar joins his troops in Spain.
July	Caesar wages a dangerous and difficult campaign against Pompey's armies in Spain.
2 August	Afranius and Petreius surrender.
	Massilia surrenders.
	Caesar faces a mutiny of his troops in Placentia.
September	Caesar returns to Rome and is elected dictator pro tem.
	After holding elections, in which he is elected consul for 48, Caesar resigns his dictatorship and prepares to pursue Pompey.

48 B.C.

Consuls: C. Julius Caesar (II), P. Servilius Vatia Isauricus

4 January	Caesar sets out from Brundisium, arrives at Oricum the next day, and continues on to Apollonia when Oricum opens its gates to him.
11 January	Caesar makes camp at the river Apsus.
	Antony successfully crosses from Italy to join Caesar.
April	The circumvallation at Dyrrachium begins.
8 July	Pompey forces Caesar to extend the circuit of his fortifications.
17 July	Pompey breaks out and nearly overruns Caesar's army.
	Caesar and Pompey maneuver for advantage in Thessaly.
	Caesar reduces Gomphi but spares Metropolis.
9 August	The battle at Pharsalus.

	Pompey flees eastward, joins his son Sextus and his wife, Cornelia.
	Pompey decides to go to Egypt.
28 September	Pompey is murdered in Egypt.
2 October	Caesar learns of Pompey's death.
	Caesar occupies Alexandria, meets Cleopatra.

Appendix 2

A Note on Roman Names

Roman *praenomina* are regularly abbreviated. Although there are many such names, the following are the most common:

A.	Aulus	M'.	Manlius
App.	Appius	P.	Publius
C.	Gaius	Q.	Quintus
Cn.	Gnaeus	Sex.	Sextus
D.	Decimus	Sp.	Spurius
L.	Lucius	T.	Titus
M.	Marcus	Ti.	Tiberius

The names Gaius and Gnaeus should be noted: the "G" in those names is always abbreviated "C," hence C. Caesar = Gaius Caesar, Cn. Pompeius = Gnaeus Pompeius.

A Roman male's name consisted of the *praenomen* (usually one of the names listed above), the *nomen* proper (the *gens* name that corresponds to our surname), and any official or unofficial *cognomen* or *agnomina* that are either traditional to that branch of the family or that have become a regular part of that individual's official identity. The *nomen* was of course hereditary; it identifies the person as a member of his *gens*. Most friends and associates, however, would call a man by his *cognomen*, if he had one. Hence, Romans who had three names are usually known by a version of their third name: Cicero, Crassus, Cato, Gracchus, and so on. If a Roman did not have a *cognomen*, he would be known by his *nomen*, such as Pompey (Pompeius), Livy (Livius), Sertorius, and the like. To refer to any of these individuals in writing, however, Romans would nearly always include the abbreviated *praenomen*: C. Caesar,

L. Crassus, M. Cato, Ti. Gracchus, Cn. Pompeius, T. Livius, and so on.

In this book, all personal names mentioned are listed in the Index Nominum by the *nomen*, if the name is Roman. Persons and places are usually referred to in the discussion and notes, and are labeled on the maps, by their original Latin names (e.g., Ariminum, not Rimini) unless an anglicized version of the name is very familiar (Rome, Mark Antony, Pompey).

Appendix 3

The Roman Legion

In the Late Republic, Roman legions were numbered according to the sequence in which they had been enrolled through the levy (*dilectus*). During the Civil War, for example, Caesar commanded the Thirteenth Legion at the outset, and later acquired the Eighth, Ninth, Tenth, Eleventh, Twelfth, and Fourteenth. Legions sometimes also had names.

A full legion (*legio*) consisted of ten smaller divisions, known as cohorts (*cohortes*), each of which was numbered in order of stature. While each cohort was thus a part of a specific legion, Caesar rarely tells us to which legion any group of cohorts belonged. He will often mention that so-and-so marched off with (say) three cohorts, but he does not ordinarily specify from which legions these cohorts were drawn. Cohorts were in turn composed of three smaller units, called maniples (*manipula*), which in turn were divided into two centuries (*centuriae*) each. Caesar does not mention maniples in *De bello civili*.

A century theoretically should have contained a hundred men, so that each cohort would then have six hundred, and each legion six thousand. In practice, the legion often fell short of this number. Sallust, for example, notes that in his final battle Catiline "filled out" his undermanned forces with poorly armed volunteers so that he could claim two legions in the field, even though he had only 2000 trained soldiers (*Cat.* 56). It was tactically important, however, to be able to match up the battle line against the opponent, so even an undermanned cohort in the proper position was better than no cohort at all or soldiers arranged haphazardly. Caesar also fought shorthanded, most notably at Pharsalus, where

he averaged only 275 men per cohort and had to shuffle the Ninth
Legion badly in order to field ten cohorts.

The basic organizing unit was the century, which was
commanded by a centurion (*centurio*), who was always a veteran,
professional soldier risen from the ranks. The centurions had
substantial authority, including the right to flog a soldier if
necessary. The centurions themselves were appointed and promoted
in regular ranks. Promotion might take place in the first instance
within the individual cohort, in which each of the six centurions
was ranked in relation to the others within that cohort. The sixth
century was the lowest ranking century within each cohort. A
centurion would be promoted from the sixth up to the first
century within his cohort. In turn, the tenth cohort was the lowest
ranking cohort in a legion: a centurion promoted from the tenth
cohort would move to the ninth cohort, then to the eighth, in
regular steps to the first. The senior centurion, the centurion of the
first century of the first cohort, was called the *primipilus*, or *centurio
primi pili*, and was a man of great stature. Caesar often tells of the
brave exploits of individual centurions in his campaigns.

A legion or group of legions was normally commanded by a
proconsul or propraetor, who could then delegate command of one
or more cohorts or legions to a legate (*legatus*). Labienus, for
example, had served Caesar as *legatus* in Gaul, while Afranius and
Petreius were *legati* who virtually ran Pompey's Spanish provinces
on his behalf.

The legion was normally drawn up for battle (*instructa
< instruere*) in lines (*acies*) arranged in a triple (*triplex*) formation:
that is, four cohorts in the front line, and three in each of the
other two, though single and double lines of battle were not
unusual. Caesar won the day at Pharsalus by unexpectedly
employing a fourfold battle line, holding back the cohorts of the
fourth line until he could use them to attack the cavalry with
which Pompey had hoped to flank Caesar's right wing (*cornu*).

Appendix 4

Roman Dates

The calendar of our period had not yet been revised and reconciled to the solar year by Julius Caesar, which he was to do as dictator after the war. It is therefore called the "pre-Julian" calendar and differs from the Julian (and the much later, closely related, Gregorian) calendar in several ways.

First, almost all the months had twenty-nine days. The exceptions were February, which had twenty-eight days, and the "long" months, March, May, Quintilis (July), and October, which had thirty-one. Calculations of dates within a month must be adjusted to this pre-Julian system in order to be accurate. (I have translated in the notes all dates that appear in the text.) Thus, the year officially had only 355 days.

Various measures were taken sporadically to try to keep the seasons and the calendar in harmony. The most common was intercalation, by which a twenty-two-day month called Interkalarius was added between 23 or 24 February and 1 March. But intercalation, supposedly done at the discretion of the Pontifical College, was irregular, subject to political maneuvering, and hence largely ineffective. By the time of the Civil War, the solar year and the calendar year differed from one another by about two months. In the translated dates provided, I have used the "Roman" dates provided in the actual texts: I have not tried to reconcile the date in the text with the solar date of the later calendar.[1] As dictator, Caesar brought the seasons into synchronization with the calendar

---

1. Students who wish to pursue that correction can find nearly all such conversions in Gelzer's biography. On the calendar itself, see A. K. Michels, *Calendar of the Roman Republic* (Princeton, N.J.: Princeton University Press, 1967).

after the year 46 not only by intercalating after 23 February but also by intercalating another sixty-seven days between November and December, so that the official year 46 lasted for 445 days!

A second difference is that July and August were still called by their original names, Quintilis and Sextilis, respectively. Quintilis was later renamed Julius in honor of Caesar, and still later Sextilis (which Caesar had lengthened to thirty-one days) was also renamed in honor of Augustus, hence the modern names of those months.

The "named" days in a Roman month were the Kalends, the Nones, and the Ides.[2] The Nones were always twenty-four days before the Kalends of the following month, therefore usually on the 5th: they were on the 7th for this reason in the "long" months of March, May, Quintilis, and October; the Nones of February were on the 5th as well, an exception to the twenty-four-day rule. The Ides were always eight days after the Nones (sixteen days before the new Kalends), and therefore usually on the 13th. Once again, the extra two days in the long months caused the Ides to move to 15 March, May, Quintilis, and October; and February's Ides were on the 13th, like those of other short months. All other dates within a month were expressed in terms of distance to the next named day: hence, a.d. V Id. Ian. (*ante diem quintum Idus Ianuarias*) meant "five days before the Ides (13th) of January" and would calculate to 9 January (since the Romans reckoned inclusively, counting the 9th itself as the first day and the 13th as the fifth). The "day before" any of these named days was always called *pridie*, "the day before."

Finally, the years were not numbered from some specific date but labeled by the names of the two consuls for that year. Thus, our year 49 was called by the Romans the year "when the consuls were L. Lentulus and C. Marcellus" (expressed in an ablative absolute, *consulibus L. Lentulo et C. Marcello*). In this book, all three- or two-figure numerical dates are B.C., all four-figure dates are A.D.

---

2. There were other days in the year that were named; the Kalends, Nones, and Ides, however, are the only ones that have the same name in every month.

Suggestions for Further Reading

Below is a list of works, primarily in English (with a few notable exceptions), that deal directly with the problem of interpreting the actions of Caesar, his opponents, and the rest of the Roman aristocracy in the period between 51 and 48. It is not intended as a complete bibliography on Caesar or on the period. While the books and articles in languages other than English may prove inaccessible to undergraduates, those in English can all be read with profit by students at that level.

Adcock, Frank E. *Caesar as Man of Letters*. Cambridge: Cambridge University Press, 1956.

Blits, Jan H. *The End of the Ancient Republic: Essays on Julius Caesar*. Durham, N.C.: Carolina Academic Press, 1982.

Boatwright, Mary T. "Caesar's Second Consulship and the Completion Date of the *Bellum Civile*." *Classical Journal* 84.1 (October/November 1988): 31–40.

Bradford, E. D. S. *Julius Caesar: The Pursuit of Power*. London: Hamish Hamil, 1984.

Brunt, P. A. "Cicero's *officium* in the Civil War." *Journal of Roman Studies* 76 (1986): 12–32.

———. *The Fall of the Roman Republic and Related Essays*. Oxford: Oxford University Press, 1988.

Collins, John H. "Caesar as Political Propagandist." *Aufstieg und Niedergang der römischen Welt* 1.1 (1972): 922–66.

Cuff, P. J. "The Terminal Date of Caesar's Gallic Command." *Historia* 7 (1958): 445–71.

Gelzer, Matthias. *Caesar: Politician and Statesman*. Cambridge, Mass.: Harvard University Press, 1968.

Gotoff, Harry C. "Towards a Practical Criticism of Caesar's Prose Style." *Illinois Classical Studies* 9.1 (1984): 1–18.

Gruen, Erich. *The Last Generation of the Roman Republic*. Berkeley: University of California Press, 1974.

Jal, Paul. *La guerre civile à Rome*. Paris: Presses Universitaires de France, 1963.

Mitchell, T. N. *Cicero: The Senior Statesman*, esp. 232–63. New Haven and London: Yale University Press, 1991.

Raditsa, L. "Julius Caesar and His Writings." *Aufstieg und Niedergang der römischen Welt* 1.3 (1973): 417–56.

Rambaud, M. *L'Art de la déformation historique dans les commentaires de César*. Paris: "Belles Lettres," 1953.

Rasmussen, D., ed. *Caesar*. Wege der Forschung, 43. Darmstadt: Wissenschaftliche Buchgesellschaft, 1980.

Richter, W. *Caesar als Darsteller seiner Taten*. Heidelberg: Winter, 1977.

Sabben-Clare, James. *Caesar and Roman Politics: 60–50 BC: Source Material in Translation*. Oxford: Oxford University Press, 1971.

Seager, Robin. *Pompey: A Political Biography*. Oxford: Blackwell, 1979.

Shackleton Bailey, D. R., ed. *Cicero: Epistulae ad Familiares*. 2 vols. Cambridge: Cambridge University Press, 1977.

_____, ed. *Cicero: Epistulae ad Quintum Fratrem et M. Brutum*. Cambridge: Cambridge University Press, 1980.

_____, ed. *Cicero's Letters to Atticus*. 7 vols. Cambridge: Cambridge University Press, 1965–70.

_____. "The Roman Nobility in the Second Civil War." *Classical Quarterly* 10 (1960): 253–67.

Smith, R. E. "Conspiracy and the Conspirators." *Greece and Rome* 4 (1957): 58–70.

Stadter, Philip A. "Caesarian Tactics and Caesarian Style: *Bell. Civ.* 1.66–70." *Classical Journal* 88.3 (1993): 217–21.

Strassburger, H. "Caesar im Urteil der Zeitgenossen." *Historische Zeitschrift* 175 (1953): 225–64.

Syme, R. "The Allegiance of Labienus." *Journal of Roman Studies* 28 (1938): 113–25.

Taylor, Lily Ross. "The Rise of Julius Caesar." *Greece and Rome* 4 (1957): 10–18.

Yavetz, Zwi. *Julius Caesar and His Public Image*. London: Thames & Hudson, 1983.

Listed below are selected school editions and English translations of Caesar which are referred to in the notes.

Carter, J. M. *Julius Caesar: The Civil War, Books I & II.* Text, translation, and notes. Warminster: Aris and Phillips, 1991.

Gardner, J. F. *Caesar: The Civil War.* Translation. Middlesex and Baltimore: Penguin Classics, 1967.

Hadas, Moses. *The Gallic War and Other Writings by Julius Caesar.* Translation. New York: Modern Library, 1957.

Moberley, C. E., and H. Last. *C. Iuli Caesaris De Bello Civili Commentarii.* Text with notes. Oxford: Oxford University Press, 1925.

Perrin, B. *Caesar's Civil War.* Text with notes. Boston, New York, and Chicago: D. C. Heath, 1882.

Peskett, A. G. *Caesar: De Bello Civili III.* Text with notes. Cambridge: Cambridge University Press, (1900) 1933.

_____. *Caesar: Civil Wars.* Text with translation. Loeb Classical Library, 1907.

The works below are not strictly related to Caesar's Civil War *but are mentioned in the section of the Introduction devoted to Roman values.*

Adcock, Frank E. *Roman Political Ideas and Practice.* Ann Arbor: University of Michigan Press, 1959.

Earl, D. C. *The Moral and Political Tradition of Rome.* Ithaca, N.Y.: Cornell University Press, 1967.

_____. *Sallust.* Amsterdam: Adolph Hakkert, 1966.

Lind, L. R. "Toward a History of Roman Ideas." *Res Publica Litterarum* 2 (1979): 167–86.

Saller, R. P. *Personal Patronage under the Early Empire.* Cambridge: Cambridge University Press, 1982.

Thompson, L. *Romans and Blacks.* Norman: University of Oklahoma Press, 1989.

Wallace-Hadrill, A., ed. *Patronage in Ancient Society.* New York: Routlege, 1989.

Wirszubski, Ch. *Libertas as a Political Idea at Rome*. Cambridge: Cambridge University Press, 1950.

Wiseman, T. P. "Competition and Cooperation." In *Roman Political Ideas and Practice*, 3–19. Exeter: Exeter University Press, 1985.

Index Nominum